Graduate Attributes in Higher Education

Graduate Attributes in Higher Education illuminates the value of graduate attributes for students, graduates and lecturers in higher education. A coherent, intelligent, subtle and important enhancement to the field, this text guides readers through a theoretical and historical analysis of graduate attributes, using interdisciplinary and interprofessional lenses.

This unique approach offers pertinent coverage of a wider range of graduate attributes than one usually sees, generating multiple perspectives and discourses that have implications for both theory and practice. Through an open and exploratory analysis, this text asks questions such as the following:

- Are programmes of study which claim 'postgraduate' attributes providing something further, deeper or enhanced in comparison, or just more of the same?
- Should we be developing continuing professional development attributes for our professional learning programmes of study, or are attributes of this nature established at the undergraduate level?
- How can we embed graduate attributes in curricula in a wide range of subject discipline-specific and interdisciplinary ways?
- In a culture of lifelong learning and a cross-disciplinary changing global market, are attributes simply a starting point – a launch pad for future and ongoing development required for a world of increasing complexity?

Clearly structured and offering a mix of case study and theoretical frameworks to explore each GA, practical guidance is offered at the end of each chapter on how to embed the relevant graduate attribute whilst providing well-researched theoretical underpinning.

The varied methods applied and methodological attitudes espoused will prove inclusive to a wide range of readers. Bringing together analysis of specific case studies from a wide range of professional and discipline-specific contexts, *Graduate Attributes in Higher Education* will be a valuable text for educators and professionals focused on curriculum development and professional learning.

Carey Normand is an independent educational consultant for further (FE) and higher education (HE). Formerly (2004–2014), Carey was Senior Lecturer in Education and Head of Learning and Teaching for the College of Arts and Social Sciences at the University of Dundee.

Lorraine Anderson is Assistant Director of Student Services and Head of the Centre for the enhancement of Academic Skills, Teaching, Learning and Employability (CASTLE) at the University of Dundee.

Graduate Attributes in Higher Education

Attitudes on Attributes from Across the Disciplines

Edited by Carey Normand and Lorraine Anderson

Routledge
Taylor & Francis Group

LONDON AND NEW YORK

First published 2017
by Routledge
2 Park Square, Milton Park, Abingdon, Oxon OX14 4RN

and by Routledge
711 Third Avenue, New York, NY 10017

Routledge is an imprint of the Taylor & Francis Group, an informa business

British Library Cataloguing in Publication Data
A catalogue record for this book is available from the British Library

Library of Congress Cataloging in Publication Data
A catalog record for this book has been requested

ISBN: 978-1-138-67801-9 (hbk)
ISBN: 978-1-138-67802-6 (pbk)
ISBN: 978-1-315-55918-6 (ebk)

Typeset in Bembo
by diacriTech, Chennai

For our families, friends, peers and students

Contents

Notes on contributors

Dr Lorraine Anderson is an Assistant Director of Student Services, and Head of the Centre for the enhancement of Academic Skills, Teaching. Learning & Employability (CASTLE) at the University of Dundee. Dr Anderson has been involved with the Quality Assurance Agency Scotland's Enhancement Themes since their inception in 2003–4 and has actively engaged on behalf of the institution with the concept of 'graduate attributes' as part of these activities. Her publications include *Developing your Teaching: Ideas, Insight and Action* (Routledge, 2006) and *Collaborative Working in Higher Education: The Social Academy* (Routledge, 2009), both with Dr Peter Kahn. Dr Anderson is a Fellow of both the Higher Education Academy and the RSA (Royal Society of Arts, Manufacture & Commerce).

Glynis Gibbs began her teaching career initially at Fife College, then at Dundee College where she currently teaches HND advertising, PR and Events students, and mentors staff undertaking their teaching qualifications. During this time she has also gained her professional qualification in Marketing and is currently a member of the Chartered Institute of Marketing. In 2008 she joined the Teaching Qualification in Further Education (TQFE) team at the University of Dundee as a part time teaching fellow, combining this with teaching in the FE sector. Working between sectors has led to an interest in examining the differences between educational sectors and the qualities needed for learners to make a successful transition.

Andy Jackson is Learning & Teaching Librarian at the University of Dundee, and is also the University's Medical Librarian. He is a regular teacher on programmes in Medicine, Dentistry and Nursing, at both undergraduate and postgraduate level and he coordinates a programme of academic professional development training at the university. He has presented papers and facilitated workshops at several international conferences on topics including information literacy, innovative teaching for librarians and the incorporation of graduate attributes in digital literacy training. His professional interests include the role of information in evidence-based practice, teaching skills for Library staff and digital literacy as a tool for employability. Andy has also written and edited several books of poetry.

Christine Kingsley is a design educator and researcher in Design Pedagogy at Duncan of Jordanstone College of Art and Design (DJCAD), at the University of Dundee. The role of narrative research methods and story are key to her work in connecting teaching, scholarship, research and practice and in 2012 Kingsley received the University Senate award for teaching excellence. In a professional practice capacity, she is employed in service design consultation to facilitate change, map conversations, present insights and evidence user experience through graphic recording; a champion of co-design philosophy. Christine is a Fellow of the RSA (Royal Society of Arts, Manufacture & Commerce).

Jackie Malcolm has over 28 years professional experience working as a Graphic Designer within the Creative Industries and established the successful Graphic Design consultancy ARC Visual Communications Ltd in 1999. Malcolm has been lecturing, within Duncan of Jordanstone College of Art and Design (DJCAD) since 1998, and for the last ten years her interest in sustainability and environmental issues for design practitioners has led to her delivering projects to students which facilitate the investigation of such issues for design practice. Through the progressive development of her teaching she has created a new design process model REASON: Research / Environmental Evaluation / Analysis / Selection / Outcome / Nexus, which is used as a framework for embedding environmental issues within the research stage of any design response. Key to this model is Nexus, the link between one learning experience and another, through a reflective process.

Dr Gaye Manwaring MBE is a Senior Lecturer in Education at the University of Dundee. She has many years of experience in running programmes by distance learning methods at undergraduate and postgraduate level. She currently teaches on the Postgraduate Certificate in in Academic Practice in Higher Education programme, a professional development course for new lecturers. Her professional and scholarly interests include the reflexive and student-centred topics of formative assessment, mentoring and qualitative evaluation.

Dr Kate Martin has worked in higher education in Scotland for over twenty years, first as a Lecturer in Community Education and subsequently as Programme Director of an undergraduate degree in Professional Development. Since retiring, she now works part-time with the Centre for Medical Education at the University of Dundee.

Dr Elizabeth Monk is a Senior Lecturer of Management in the School of Business, at the University of Dundee. Her PhD thesis was in Adult Education, and since then she has continued to research and publish in the area of accounting education; including guest editing two themed issue journals on Audit Education and

Case studies in Audit Education. Her research interests include transformational methods of teaching; embedding transferrable, employable skills in the curriculum; and educational transitions. She is currently investigating the implications of the Curriculum for Excellence on the university first year experience.

Sophie Morrison is now in her 10th year of working at the University of Dundee Careers Service as a Senior Careers Adviser with responsibility for credit-bearing careers education in internships. Morrison has a particular interest in work-based learning, embedding careers education in the curriculum and assessing careers education. In addition to her careers education work, She is also a specialist Careers Adviser which involves her in a range of one-to-one guidance interventions and groupwork with current students, graduates and prospective students.

Dr Carey Normand is an independent educational consultant for further education (FE) and higher education (HE). Formerly, (2004–2014) Carey was Senior Lecturer in Education and Head of Learning and Teaching for the College of Arts and Social Sciences, University of Dundee. Her research interests and publications are in the spheres of professional learning and teaching, leadership and the policy-practice nexus in FE and HE; with a particular focus on the Scottish educational context. Her doctoral thesis examined conceptualisations of professionalism, professional identity and professional status for lecturers working in the College sector in Scotland. In 2013 Dr Normand received £100,000 to support student transitions between FE and HE. She recently co-authored a chapter 'Techniques and strategies for the development of professional identity' in Fehring, H. and Rodrigues, S. (2017) *Teaching, Coaching and Mentoring Adult Learners: Lessons for Professionalism and Partnership*. Taylor Francis, Routledge.

Dr Patrick O'Donnell has taught in the further and higher education sectors for more than two decades. Dr O'Donnell has published on a range of issues including cultural and structural changes within further and higher education, learner transitions and professionalism. He teaches engineering at the Perth campus, University of the Highlands and Islands. His latest publication: O'Donnell, Patrick, Murphy, M. and Normand, Carey (2015) The Reinvigoration of Scottish Further Education Sector: an exploration and analysis of the recent reforms, *Scottish Educational Review*, 47(2): 59-77.

Ruth O'Riordan is a Senior Careers Adviser and has worked in the Careers Service at the University of Dundee for 10 years. Prior to this she worked within the recruitment industry for a range of organisations in the public and private sector. Ruth has a particular interest in supporting undergraduate students to realise and achieve their potential careers through interactive, innovative and inclusive methods and she leads the Careers Service in the delivery of credit-bearing careers education across a range of modules. She is also a specialist careers adviser and supports students through one-to-one guidance and in large group settings with tailored practical advice. O'Riordan was the recipient of the University of Dundee Honorary Graduates' Award for Inclusive Practice in 2013.

Professor Andrew Rae has held a variety of technical and leadership roles in both industry and academia. Having been involved in the recruitment of graduates into science, engineering and project management functions and in the development of undergraduate and postgraduate qualifications he has a keen interest in producing graduates with the prerequisites to function in modern industry. These skills range from the traditional knowledge-based abilities to functioning effectively within multi-disciplinary, geographically-dispersed teams. He is a professor of engineering at the University of the Highlands and Islands.

Dr Bassam Rakhshani has a PhD in Aerospace Engineering from the University of Manchester. He has experience in aircraft technical system assessment, numerical/experimental aerodynamics, noise prediction, and system testing (data acquisition, data processing, verification and validation). His research interests include aerodynamics and aeroacoustics, aerostructures, aircraft design and performance, aircraft maintenance, and aircraft certification. He has extensive experience of a vast array of test and evaluation techniques and instrumentation, including the measurement of forces, pressure, vibration, temperature and acoustics extensive experience of a vast array of test and evaluation techniques and instrumentation, including the measurement of forces, pressure, vibration, temperature and acoustics. Dr Rakhshani formally taught at the Perth campus Highlands and Islands and now teaches engineering at University of the West of Scotland.

Mike Ramsay is a lecturer in mental health nursing at the University of Dundee, contributing widely to undergraduate and postgraduate teaching in the field. He has published widely on mental health topics and chairs the editorial board of the journal Mental Health Nursing. As a student undertaking a professional doctorate in education in his home university, he is interested in nurse education and his thesis is centring upon graduateness in nursing, supplementing his clinical research interests in dementia and carer support. The latter is reflective of his previous 20-year clinical career prior to entering academia.

Jill Shimi has had experience of teaching at all stages P1 to P7 in primary schools in Scotland. She is currently a lecturer in Education at the University of Dundee. Jill has participated in research regarding games based learning in education and collaborative working. Her main research interest is mentoring. Shimi delivers programmes to Childhood Practice students and those studying Education at postgraduate and Masters' level. She particularly enjoys working with students who implement their ambitious research projects within their professional settings.

Robert Smith is a Subject Network Leader for Energy and Technology at the University of the Highlands and Islands and has lead a number of curriculum enhancements, including the new 5-year MEng in Engineering Design, incorporating novel pedagogical ideas such as the 'Flipped Classroom'. He has taught a variety of technical and management subjects on a variety of engineering courses and has first-hand experience of the needs of cross-disciplinary industry and education.

Introduction

The discourse on graduate attributes in the late twentieth century emphasised knowledge and skills acquisition, demonstrable through specified outcomes, for example, employability. This way of conceptualising graduate attributes has perpetuated into the twenty-first century and has resulted in most Higher Education Institutions (HEIs) having a set of clearly defined graduate attributes that are used as an adjunct to the degree and categorised as 'added value'. The graduate attributes (GAs) identified usually make an explicit statement about the transferable knowledge and skills that the graduate has and, pertinently, how these can be used to secure employment. This shift from the implicit to the explicit is, arguably, 'job done', and yet the question emerges as to the capital of GAs: What is the added value if every graduate has acquired this knowledge and skill set? This question is apposite for contemporary higher education, as it grapples with the demands created by the massification of Higher Education (HE) over the preceding decades. Interestingly, for the authors of this book, our home university is one of the very few in the country not to have a set of GAs, having previously decided on the development of a Student Graduate Skills Award that is voluntary and absolutely tied to employment. The authors in this book suggest that the time is right to re-examine GAs and illuminate what they are, their purpose and their current value.

In the twenty-first century there is less certainty about the landscape that the student will graduate into, consequently, educators in higher education are acutely aware that they are educating a generation for a world that is unknown and, indeed, will be shaped by those very learners. This has led to a way of conceptualising teaching and learning that is cognisant of both subject discipline imperatives and wider educational gains and experiences. This sits comfortably within the Scottish educational tradition that has always eschewed narrow specialism in favour of the breadth of interdisciplinary study (Davie, 1961). In this approach, the learning gained in studying a wide range of different subject disciplines, enables illumination of each subject through the lens of another discipline (Macdonald, 2009) and, often, paradigm. These educational values exemplify Enlightenment ideals but are also consonant in a Conceptual age (Pink, 2008). This book seeks to provide depth through discipline-specific knowledge and breadth through the application of interdisciplinary understandings. The authors analyse ten discrete attributes, through multidisciplinary lenses, and provide compelling evidence to illuminate graduate attributes as ways of being, thinking and acting.

A recent study identifying the impact of graduate attributes on employability found that employers placed the highest importance on "soft-skills" and the lowest importance on "academic reputation" (Osmani et al., 2015: 373). Subject and technical discipline specific knowledge and skills are highly valued by students and employers but these alone do not enhance employability unless accompanied by interpersonal skills and attributes. It is argued that universities need to narrow the gap between curricula and industry needs (ibid: 376).

This book will help to do this as most authors have provided practical examples of how curricula can be aligned to embed graduate attributes. You will find this Practice Guide at the end of each chapter.

Chapter Synopses

In Chapter 1 the author explores the extent to which a set of attributes can be generated coherently and authentically within undergraduate, postgraduate and professional learning, through an analysis of the contextual factors pertinent in the development of the *Learning Graduate*. Chapter 2 sees the authors question the sort of transferable skills and attributes that are needed for adaptability. Drawing on a two-year-long case study in aeronautical engineering, the authors explore learning experiences that offer both 'vertical progression' (within discipline) and 'horizontal progression' (across disciplines) and argue that the coalescence of the two generates the *Adaptable Graduate*. In Chapter 3 the authors explore the idea that self-awareness is the key to the development of many graduate attributes and that this essential foundation can be successfully enhanced through Careers Education in order to ensure that the *Self-Aware Graduate* is prepared for the future. Chapter 4 examines the skills, attitudes and support involved in enabling students to respond positively to personal and academic problems and to developing a transformative approach to challenges. The authors draw on four strands of resilience: confidence, adaptability, purposefulness and social support (Robertson and Cooper, 2013) and interrogate these through evidence from first-hand interviews with university support and academic staff, from divergent disciplines, to elicit the factors pertinent to the *Resilient Graduate*. The authors of Chapter 5 observe the progress of graphic design students as they make the transition from further education to higher education and examine the key attributes that are understood to have enhanced the students' academic journey. The authors analyse this through the lens of reflexivity, and discuss the individual intent to 'change' and be 'different' through a transformation of the 'self' across space and time exemplifying the *Agile Graduate*. In Chapter 6 the authors use Narrative inquiry methods that draw on graduate case studies and autobiographical self-reflection to explore conceptualisations of empathy, its formation and the construction of the *Empathic Graduate* in twenty-first century learning. In Chapter 7 the author contends that the transferable ethical values embedded in graduate attributes may be enhanced by the interdisciplinary, investigative and participative experiences of higher education. The *Ethical Graduate* can be developed through subject disciplinary study but, equally, through active participation in wider forms of engagement, including practice-based and online learning. Vignettes from the professional disciplines of Accountancy and Nursing are used in Chapter 8 to illustrate the differences and similarities in the graduate attributes required to enter these professions and the extent to which the requirements of professionalism and 'graduateness' shape perceptions of 'desirable' skills and attributes for the *Professional Graduate*. In Chapter 9 the author explores the range of behaviours that the digitally-literate graduate exhibits in a professional or vocational role, within the context of a rapidly changing landscape of resources and technologies. Data generated from case studies and examples from the UK and beyond is examined and the author proffers a suggestion of how digital literacies can be explicitly incorporated into the undergraduate curriculum to effect real changes in student behaviour, attitudes and skills developing the *Digitally-Literate Graduate*. In Chapter 10 the focus is on the lecturers as well as their students and examines the concept of reflexivity as an attribute beyond reflection. The author explores how lecturers can address and teach reflexively through aspects of aligned curriculum design and delivery, facilitating the *Reflexive Graduate*.

References

Davie, G. E. (1961) *The Democratic Intellect*. Edinburgh: Edinburgh University Press.

Macdonald, M. (2009) *Patrick Geddes and the Generalist Tradition*. The Royal Town Planning Institute in Scotland's 2009 Sir Patrick Geddes Commemorative Lecture at The Royal Society of Edinburgh.

Osmani, M., Weerakkody, V., Hindi, N.M., Al-Esmail, R., Eldabi, T., Kapoor, K. and Irani, Z. (2015) 'Identifying the trends and impact of graduate attributes on employability: a literature review'. *Tertiary Education and Management*, 21(4): 367–379.

Pink, D. (2008) *A Whole New Mind – Why right brainers will rule the world*. Croydon, UK: Marshall Cavendish Business.

Robertson, I. T., and Cooper, C. L. (2013) *Resilient graduate series – 3. Recruitment, development and resilience*. http://www.robertsoncooper.com/blog/entry/resilient-graduate-series-3-recruitment-development-and-resilience. Accessed 20/09/2016.

Chapter 1

The Learning Graduate

Lorraine Anderson

[signature: Lorraine Anderson]

Introduction: A Skilful Start

The 'ivory tower' image of higher education has become an increasingly inaccurate one over the years. What was once unattainable and perhaps incomprehensible to many has now become a mainstream path for growing numbers of school leavers and for significant numbers of 'mature' students, aiming to either engage with an opportunity which may have been unavailable to them when younger, to expand or further develop their skills or to gain a qualification now anticipated by their employer in an increasingly professionalised workplace. In some cases, it may simply be an opportunity to learn and to grow personally, although the financial implications of a university education mean that this may now account for a relatively small number of individuals. It is to be hoped, nonetheless, that every student who engages with a university education has learning as a key ambition.

The reasons behind individual engagement with higher education are doubtless complex, multifarious and perhaps indistinct and quite muddled for some. A blend of personal interest, societal expectation, career ambition, peer or parental pressure, limited alternative options; all will doubtless contribute to some extent. Increasingly, however, sociopolitical drivers play a role in this process. Some aspects of this will be overt and others covert. Much of the destruction of the ivory tower in the UK, however, has been the result of government intervention into the processes of higher education. In 1997, Dearing's report of the National Committee of Inquiry into Higher Education (NCIHE) in the UK made a number of recommendations for the direction of higher education over the next 20 years, including an emphasis on widening participation and an increased focus on student learning. The report noted that "[w]hile traditional but still-relevant values must be safeguarded, higher education will need to continue to adapt to the needs of a rapidly changing world and to new challenges" (Dearing, 1997: 11). This blend of social and economic drivers has continued to be reflected in subsequent UK governmental investigations, including the Leitch Review of Skills, which was published in 2006 (Leitch, 2006). The focus of this sector-wide report was on the skills that would be required to enhance the global competitiveness of the UK, looking to 2020. The outcome of Leitch was that if the country was to remain competitive there needed to be a significant increase in skills of all levels across the working age population.

Unsurprisingly, perhaps, this driver has not gone away. As more and more learners swell the ranks in universities across the globe, a means to develop, capture and harness those skills in a way that is distinctive from vocational courses of further education and palatable to the sensibilities of higher education, has been developed under the umbrella concept of 'graduate attributes'. The skills agenda continues its close association with graduate attributes, as seen in the report of the UK Commission for Employment and Skills, *The Future of Work: Jobs and Skills in 2030* (UKCES, 2014), which identifies a future focus on the development of

> key skills and attributes that will be at a premium ... including resilience, adaptability, resourcefulness, enterprise, cognitive skills (such as problem solving), and the core business skills for project based employment.

A further example is provided by the requirements of the developing Teaching Excellence Framework in the UK, with its focus on 'institutional accountability in ensuring graduates leave university with the necessary skills' (*Phoenix* Editorial, 2016). The years roll on into the future but the story remains the same, with the concept of 'graduate attributes' viewed as a key vehicle to enable the effective translation of academic study into skills and employability.

Institutional Influences on Graduate Attributes

The continuing link between graduate attributes and employability can therefore be seen to have been the result of the skills agenda and continuing governmental initiatives and drivers. Yet, despite this sector-wide approach, close links with employers and the current or anticipated demands of the workplace, no accepted set of core graduate attributes has emerged; although several skills make a regular appearance in discussions about graduate attributes, such as teamwork or proficiency with communication and & information technologies (C&IT). It could be argued that the rapidly changing environment of the twenty-first-century global workplace makes it too challenging to identify a 'core set' of attributes as such an exercise inevitably comes with an element of inbuilt redundancy. Nonetheless, efforts continue to try to capture and develop a definitive list, at both the macro and the micro level. Looking first at a macro, or global, perspective, Salazar-Xirinachs (2015) highlights two such approaches in his discussion on the perceived skills gap: the Assessment & Teaching of 21st Century Skills (ATC21S) project and the work in this area of the World Economic Forum (WEF). Based at the University of Melbourne, the ATC21S project identified ten skills, set within the following four categories: ways of thinking, ways of working, tools for working and ways of living in the world. The WEF, meanwhile, took a more expansive view, identifying 16 skills in three categories: foundational literacies, competences and character qualities (Soffel, 2016). At the micro-level, universities pursue the identification of institutionally-linked graduate attributes with alacrity. Indeed, the direction that the development of graduate attributes has taken as the concept has continued to evolve, has increasingly been one that reflects an individual university's philosophy, ethos and ultimately institutional ownership, as opposed to the development of an agreed set of universal attributes that any graduate, from any university, might be expected to possess.

This development was acknowledged by the Australian National Graduate Attributes Project (National GAP, 2007–08) which identified graduate attributes as "the set of core outcomes *a university community agrees* all its graduates will develop during their studies [our emphasis]"; and this is a trend that has continued over the last ten years. A consideration of a range of current examples can help illuminate this development. At the time of writing, the Hong Kong Baptist University (HKBU) has seven institutional graduate attributes:

- Citizenship
- Knowledge
- Learning
- Skills
- Creativity
- Communication
- Teamwork

(HKBU, 2016a)

These headline categories are expanded upon at undergraduate, taught postgraduate and research postgraduate/professional doctoral levels. HKBU took deliberate steps to establish institutional ownership of their graduate attributes, generating community engagement with the concept through a variety of means, including an institution-wide competition for staff and students to develop ideas for creative ways to help the university community remember the attributes. They now have a Graduate Attributes Ambassadors' Scheme to recruit students "to support and organize a wide range of events and activities to promote the 7 Graduate Attributes within and outside the HKBU community" (HKBU, 2016b).

A sense of institutional ownership that is more often than not community-generated is evident in many sets of institutional graduate attributes but their content across the sector can be quite diverse, despite the fact that they have employability as a unifying driver behind their generation. An in-built tension between government agendas and institutional objectives may lie at the root of this discrepancy. While governments aim to raise the skills of students and graduates across the sector in order to drive optimum employability, the need to recruit increasing numbers of students in a burgeoning marketplace of higher education 'products' means that universities are driven by the need to develop an identifiable and valuable academic 'brand' in order to top the league tables and to attract students. We can see this approach in action in the close association of institutional graduate attributes with the university itself, as opposed to generic benefits of graduate status for employability or wider society. One Scottish institution, the University of Glasgow, has developed a set of graduate attributes which for them defines 'the Glasgow graduate' (University of Glasgow, 2016a). The development of the Glasgow attributes was informed by consultation with a range of stakeholders, including students, staff and employers. These ten attributes form a matrix within three dimensions: academic, personal and transferable, and the operationalisation of these attributes within each dimension is clearly spelled out for students. Despite the inclusion of the three dimensions, only one of which pertains to the academic domain, Glasgow's philosophy on, and orientation to, their set of graduate attributes is directly connected to the idea of developing the academic role as opposed to a generic skill set. Guidance to students on graduate attributes points out that subject specialism is "a particularly important attribute because it underlies all of [the] other generic graduate abilities" and that "the more you develop your academic identity, the less generic your other attributes will be" (University of Glasgow, 2016b).

While governments attempt to impose unifying stamps on universities across the sector as part of higher education's role as a significant economic player, institutions strive for differentiation. This is an understandable response, as although there has been a global acceptance of both the existence of a 'skills gap' and the concept across the higher education sector of graduate attributes as an approach to address this gap, the result could be the homogenisation of the global graduate. If all students develop the same skills and attributes, regardless of the institution of learning that they attend, then what is it that differentiates one institution from another in terms of its graduates? Why attend one university in preference over another? The creation of a core set of skills resulting in an institutional set of graduate attributes, can be seen to be driven as much by the need of institutions to stamp their ownership on their graduates as products of their own institutional philosophy, as it is by any employer-driven or governmental agenda. The institution's market niche is therefore also simultaneously assured. What impact is this having on learners at all levels: in their studies, preparation for the workplace, and identities as global citizens?

The Learning Graduate: Demonstrating Graduate Attributes at Undergraduate Level and Beyond

Our understanding, therefore, of the concept of graduate attributes is as much driven by institutional ownership and the need for differentiation in a crowded higher education marketplace as by employability demands. This has implications not only for the role of graduate attributes at undergraduate level but also for the continuing learner journey in postgraduate study or continuing professional development (CPD) courses. Where is the learner in this developing story? What does the demonstration of those attributes look like at an individual level and what are the most effective vehicles for their development, both at undergraduate and in higher or further study? In order to be meaningful and achievable, graduate attributes need to be addressed appropriately within a student's learning journey. Increasingly, as with a good deal of skills-based development opportunities, the most appropriate approach is often viewed as being embedded within the curriculum; however, this does not come without its own challenges.

Work on developing a curriculum-based approach has taken place across the sector at strategic, operational and student-facing levels. An influential example at the sector level is provided by the Quality Assurance Agency Scotland (QAAS) Enhancement Themes, notably 'Research-Teaching Linkages—Graduate Attributes' (QAAS, 2006–08) and 'Graduates for the 21st Century' (QAAS, 2008–11), part of the enhancement-led approach to developing quality teaching and learning across the Scottish sector, was instrumental in almost every Scottish higher education institution (HEI) developing its own set of graduate attributes. At an institutional level the University of the Western Cape in South Africa provides an example where it saw its "own understanding of the nature and purposes of higher education" play a central role in the development of their graduate attributes, which subsequently translated into a Graduate Attributes Charter "that guides the University in developing the knowledge, skills and competencies of graduates" (University of the Western Cape). A student-facing approach is demonstrated by the University of Greenwich, in England, which has developed a guide "for students, by students", to engage their learners in what it means to be a 'Greenwich Graduate". The Greenwich Graduate Student Network also "works with students and staff running workshops on request and developing resources" (University of Greenwich).

The development of graduate attributes using disciplinary learning as a vehicle can take either an embedded or integrated approach within the curriculum, or a 'bolt-on' approach to the core content where generic courses or modules are taken by students to supplement and complement their subject-based studies. The jury remains out as to which of these two methods is the more efficacious. An embedded approach should see graduate attributes aligned with intended learning outcomes which *should* mean that the student is unable to avoid the learning. However, it can also mean that learners do not 'see' the graduate attributes or fully comprehend their value; and this can have implications for learner engagement with the concept. Highlighting skills and attributes through the bolt-on approach means that they are visible; however, it also means that they can be viewed as additional to the 'real' course and therefore optional.

As a result, the extent to which this curriculum-based approach, whether embedded or bolt-on, has been successful in supporting the development of graduate attributes remains questionable. As part of the work undertaken in Scotland under the auspices of the Enhancement Themes, David Nicol (2010) noted:

> Considerable effort has been expended in Scotland and internationally to
> describe graduate attributes, the skills, personal qualities and understanding

to be developed through the higher education experience so as to prepare graduates for life and work in the 21st century. However, much less attention has been paid to how these attributes will be developed.

Rust and Froud (2016: 9) argue that there is "often a false dichotomy in the minds of academics between employability (and the so-called 'skills agenda') and the teaching of academic disciplines" and this is perhaps a further reason why delivery of graduate attributes via the curriculum remains challenging. When Barrie looked at this approach in Australian HEIs he found that in many instances, "graduate attributes have not developed beyond a specification of learning outcomes, which should be, though rarely are, 'measured' or 'assured'." Subsequently, Barrie's view on the role of graduate attributes has been to position them as "orienting statement [s] of education outcomes used to inform curriculum design and the provision of learning experiences at a university" (Barrie, 2009 cited in Barrie et al., 2009: 1), therefore shifting the focus of graduate attributes from an *embedded* to an *informing* principle.

Graduate attributes have therefore been in danger of remaining 'hidden' within or rarely accounted for as part of the curriculum, or of spending their existence languishing on an institution's professional services' web pages in splendid isolation from other learning opportunities, awaiting the next 're-fresh'; so what other approach can extend their reach into the consciousness of our learners? A different view on the most appropriate vehicle to carry graduate attributes may be necessary, which places the focus more on the individual learners themselves than the curriculum content. If we accept the premise (Barrie, 2007) that it is students' engagement in their *learning* that is of central importance to the development of graduate attributes, as opposed to the idea of graduate attributes as something that is *taught*, then it is learning itself that becomes the most appropriate vehicle for their development.

Providing an environment that can facilitate authentic learning opportunities plays a key role in enabling students to begin to fully appreciate and put into practice the skills and attributes that they are developing through their academic studies. Interaction with academics who continue to practise in their subject area and academic modules that allow students to explore career planning, enterprise or entrepreneurship all introduce authenticity from the workplace into the classroom. An approach with even greater success sees learning situated within the workplace itself through student placements and internships. The affordances of work-based learning are captured anecdotally in the feedback from students who have undertaken placements and increasingly reported in studies in this area (Anderson et al., 2016). Work placements or internships can be self-sourced or embedded as part of curricula. The more commonly known placement learning opportunities can be identified in degree study paths in healthcare, social work and teaching, however, increasing numbers of less vocationally oriented degree subjects are also looking to include optional placement opportunities as a value-added opportunity for students. Some institutions, such as the University of Dundee, also provide stand-alone modules in career management or internships (see Chapter 3). At post-graduate level, an award-winning Scottish sector-wide initiative 'Making the Most of Masters' (MMM) is also providing an opportunity for postgraduate students to embed authentic learning opportunities by replacing their traditional dissertation with a work placement (MMM, 2016a). MMM (THE Award winner 2013 for outstanding employer engagement initiative) outlines the benefits of this approach as follows:

- **Engag[ing] with the employability agenda** – The 2010 Scottish Employers Skill Survey found that 1 in 5 HE graduates were not well prepared for work, particularly lacking the "softer workplace skills" such as planning and organis-ing, oral communication and problem solving skills. Work based projects aim to bridge this gap;
- **Support[ing] University strategy** – University strategies are increasingly prioritising student employability through workplace-based schemes.
- **Improv[ing] employer links** – develop a network of employer contacts in sectors and industries which look to recruit from your programme.
- **Respond[ing] to student demand** – by offering them the opportunity to meet and collaborate with potential employers during their programme.
- **Rais[ing] programme profile** – building ongoing relationships with employers in key sectors and industries can improve programme marketing through testimony and case studies, thus aiding recruitment (MMM, 2016b).

A related discussion here is the definition of what it means to be a learner in a higher education context and an understanding of individual learner journeys. John Biggs and subsequently Biggs and Tang (2011), building on the earlier empirical research of Marton and Säljö (1976) and Ramsden (1988), amongst others, consid-ered the approaches that learners may take to their studies: namely 'deep', 'surface' and 'strategic'. A student who adopts a 'deep' approach to their learning is more intrinsically motivated and is more likely to engage with, understand and value the concept of graduate attributes. An extrinsically, or assessment-driven student is more likely to adopt a 'surface' approach in their learning and to potentially 'miss' the meaning of a graduate attributes approach. Individual self-awareness of, and reflection on, their learning is therefore key to a deeper engagement with the concept of graduate attributes. Strong identification with practice can also be seen to support students in taking a deeper approach to their learning and can provide a more authentic vehicle for graduate attributes.

While it is important to remember that 'deep', 'surface' and 'strategic' are *approaches* to learning, which individuals may adopt or reject at different stages during their period of study, is any one group of learners more likely to demonstrate the traits of deep learning? Are postgraduate students, for example, more likely to be deep learners? The assumption could be made that as postgraduates have demonstrated themselves to be successful learners by virtue of their postgraduate status, that this could be the case. Thomson (2015: 2) notes, however, the challenges reported by students entering postgraduate study, commenting on the large numbers of post-graduate programmes that comprise students who have not transitioned directly from being an undergraduate but may be returning to study after time spent in the workplace or entering postgraduate study as an international student, unfamiliar with the context and culture of the new environment.

> Postgraduate students can no longer be seen as a homogeneous group of high achieving students who have decided to continue studying their undergradu-ate subject, rather they are a heterogeneous group with their own motivations, previous educational experiences, expectations and differing support needs.
>
> (Alsford & Smith, 2013: 2)

It cannot be concluded therefore that individuals entering postgraduate studies are necessarily deeper, or more effective, learners within any given higher educa-tion context. Indeed, the more time intensive nature of many Master's level pro-grammes or CPD courses of study could mean that these postgraduate students adopt more strategic learning approaches, in order to cope with the demands of study. Engagement with graduate attributes at postgraduate level is therefore not a given: but to what extent is it an important part of study at this level?

Graduate Attributes and the Postgraduate-Level Learner

The approach taken by some universities to the development of their institutional graduate attributes is to create a framework that spans both undergraduate and postgraduate experiences. This approach is based on the model of graduate attrib-utes as a reflection of institutional aspirations and philosophy, and can take the form of a blanket approach to attributes at all levels; or a graduate attributes core with dif-ferentiation at undergraduate and postgraduate levels. Oxford Brookes University in the UK currently identifies the following five attributes that are deemed core to all programmes of study, at foundation undergraduate and postgraduate level:

- Academic literacy
- Research literacy
- Critical self-awareness and personal literacy
- Digital and information literacy
- Active citizenship.

The University's vision for its Graduate Attributes is the enabling of:

> abilities, dispositions or qualities that... graduates will need in order to translate and apply their discipline knowledge to new contexts.
> Employability is enhanced by applying Brookes Attributes within the work context... (Strategy for Enhancing the Student Experience, 2015–2020)

HKBU's core of seven graduate attributes, meanwhile, differentiates between taught postgraduate and research postgraduates in the interpretation of the level, akin to intended learning outcomes. It has been argued that postgraduate attributes could help students to prepare for and engage with the requirements of Doctoral level study (Jones, 2016: 24) as the demands at this level, as distinct from Master's study or professional learning in the workplace, can be more challenging for students. The extent to which PhD students are aware of the intended learning outcomes for their programme of study, or any associated postgraduate attributes, is, however, debatable. It is also worth considering to what extent these attributes and skills might be different at Doctoral level than at undergraduate or Master's level? Is it the context and level that are most relevant here or is there distinctiveness in terms of anticipated depth of engagement?

When considering the ways in which graduate attributes can effectively inform postgraduate study at Master's level, the approach taken needs to be more intensive than extensive, reflecting the nature of Master's programmes which are by design relatively 'short and fat' rather than 'long and thin'. The three or four years of study which undergraduate or Doctoral level learners have available to complete their studies provides a different vehicle for engagement with graduate attributes than that available to Master's students. Consequently, the approach needs to be different in order to be effective. As a starting point, what should graduate attributes look like at Master's level? Work undertaken for the QAAS by Bamber and colleagues as part of the Learning from International Practice (LFIP) project on 'Mastersness' identified a number of facets of being a Master's level student, namely: abstraction, depth of learning, research and enquiry, complexity, autonomy, unpredictability and professionalism. These facets are discussed in greater detail within the QAAS *Mastersness Toolkit* (2014) and are outlined below in Figure 1.1.

Figure 1.1 QAAS Mastersness Toolkit (2014).

Bamber et al. (ibid.) consider each facet as being "an aspect or characteristic of the learning processes that...underpin the concept of 'Mastersness'"; however, they could also be identified as being allied to postgraduate attributes at Master's level. These facets were developed by a working group under the auspices of the QAAS Enhancement Themes and are therefore not aligned to a specific institution, which as we have seen is a common factor with undergraduate attributes, but rather reflect the Scottish sector's evidence-informed view of the traits required of a Master's level student. There is also some justification in claiming status for them as a reflection of international Masters' students' 'ways of being' as the development of the 'Mastersness' framework within the LFIP project drew on international practice, and built specifically on the work of Susan Warring's (2011) analysis of learning levels between qualifications in New Zealand.

In a world of shrinking resource and growing competition for scarce university positions increasing numbers of postgraduates studying at Doctoral level will look to pursue careers outwith academia, either through choice or necessity. With that in mind, it could be anticipated that the skills agenda is of as much, if not more, relevance to postgraduates as it is to undergraduates. This has been acknowledged by Vitae, amongst others, which describes itself as "the global leader in supporting the professional development of researchers" (Vitae). Vitae's perspective on supporting professional development takes an approach that resonates with the concept of graduate attributes. Centred on their Researcher Development Framework (RDF), Vitae has identified a number of attributes which sit within the four domains of knowledge and intellectual abilities; personal effectiveness; research governance and organisation; and engagement, influence and impact. These domains are then further subdivided into specific attributes and skills and a sample of these subdivisions taken at random: creativity, self-management, professional conduct and working with others, indicates that they reflect those that are prevalent in many institutional sets of graduate attributes.

CPD students as postgraduate learners

Postgraduate learning delivered through continuing professional development courses, whether accredited or unaccredited, plays an increasing role in the upskilling of the workforce to cope with the demands of the changing professional environment. Life-long learning is a concept with an established history and one that was adopted as a key idea by UNESCO in the 1970s (Smith, 1996, 2001) although as Smith (ibid.) notes it is a "problematic notion" in the ways in which it has been used. A twenty-first-century take on life-long learning is put forward by Jackson (in Jackson and Willis, n.d.) who refers to both life-long, life-wide and life-deep learning, characterised by Banks et al. (2007: 13) as follows:

Life-long Learning: Language and interactional strategies that determine orientations toward engaging one's body and mind in learning.

> Life-wide Learning: Experience in management of ourselves and others, of time and space, and of unexpected circumstances, turns of events, and crises. This learning brings skill and attitudinal frames for adaptation.
>
> Life-deep Learning: Beliefs, values, ideologies, and orientations to life. Life-deep learning scaffolds all our ways of approaching challenges and undergoing change.
>
> (Jackson, n.d.: 7)

Jackson dates the first "explicit use and elaboration of the term 'lifewide learning'" to Jost Reischmann in 1986, in reference to "the full scope of adult learning and development" and in UK HE by Jackson in 2008 (Jackson, n.d.: 6; 9). Three domains are articulated within a life-wide learning approach: academic curriculum (credit-bearing), co-curriculum (which may or may not be credit-bearing) and extra-curriculum (self-determined by learners) (ibid: 10).

> The important characteristic of lifewide learning is that it embraces a comprehensive understanding and practice of learning, development, knowledge and knowing and achievement ... To be a competent lifewide learner requires not only the ability to recognise and take advantage of opportunities and the will and capability to get involved, it also requires self-awareness derived from consciously thinking about and extracting meaning and significance from the experiences that populate our lives. (ibid: 3)

The aims and aspirations of attribute development sits comfortably with postgraduate study and continuing professional development and learning.

Conclusion

In 2007, Simon Barrie and colleagues noted:

> The complexity of what is being referred to in shorthand as 'graduate attributes' is often masked by simplistic formulations of graduate skills lists and as a consequence the authenticity and utility of graduate attributes has been disputed by some (Hyland and Johnson, 1998; Washer 2007).
>
> (Barrie et al., 2007: 6)

To what extent has this changed over the last ten years in relation to the ongoing development of graduate attributes as a concept that can be a useful vehicle for undergraduate, and potentially postgraduate and CPD, learning? The twenty-first-century world is one of flux and challenge that places increasing demands on us as learners, workers and useful members of society – and indeed as global citizens. We are constantly bombarded with information, statistics, facts and figures and can often feel that in a world where knowledge is increasingly provisional and subject to change, we are being either swamped by a deluge of reports and opinion pieces or overtaken by the speed at which information on any given topic emerges, develops and changes.

In many ways this situation is not helped for our learners, whether they are entering the workplace for the first time as a new graduate or developing and enhancing their career through postgraduate study, by the proliferation of 'graduate attributes' to which they are exposed.

The generation of endless lists of attributes and employability skill-sets mean it is inconceivable that anyone could ever attain and encompass all of these attributes at any given time; let alone the fact that they keep changing! Furthermore, despite the ongoing skills agenda, graduate attributes are also now very much more than what has traditionally been thought of as 'skills' or 'competences'. Their development involves a more insightful and informed approach to the nurturing of a range of attributes, attitudes and characteristics that may more accurately be described as personal traits. Working *with* students to take ownership of and to develop their attributes is the way to underpin an effective learning experience that travels beyond simple acknowledgment of a listed attribute to its incorporation within a learner's worldview. Working with learners to help them identify the attributes they already have, and those that they would like to work to develop, or further enhance, through their studies is the starting point for their learning in this area.

The key to meaningful graduate attributes in the twenty-first century is to place the learning in the hands of the learner and to move away from previous conceptions of attributes as an idea or an entity that is *delivered* through the curriculum, or *taught* to learners. The graduate attributes that are discussed throughout this book, such as reflexive, adaptable, resilient and agile, outline a way of being in the world that we would like our learners at all stages to attain and to continue to develop and enhance.

Practice Guide

Engaging with our learners, whether they are undergraduate or postgraduate students, or professionals in practice undertaking continuing professional development, provides us with an opportunity to support and work with individuals to identify the kinds of attributes that they need to develop. The identification stage of this process is a vital step in encouraging individuals to engage with the concept of graduate attributes and to view them as not just a useful, but a key part of their learning.

Validation of their current attributes, at any level, can provide confidence for individuals that what they have learned or developed through their practice has proved an important aspect of their studies or work-based learning to date. In turn, this can encourage your students to take a proactive stance towards developing new attributes in their current studies. Identification of attributes is only the initial stage.

1 Reflect on ways in which you can support your learners in identifying the attributes that they already have.

2   Support your learners in validating this learning by providing ways for them to demonstrate and evidence their current attributes.

3   Engage your learners in exercises and activities that promote their individual agency and self-authorship, identified by Baxter-Magolda (2004) as an educational common goal of the twenty-first century, in order to take control of the identification of the attributes they need and want to develop for their future place in the world.

References

Alsford, S. and Smith, K. (2013) Postgraduate student transition: how different is it from undergraduate transition? http://www.enhancementthemes.ac.uk/pages/searchresultdetails/docs/paper/postgraduate-student-transition—how-different-is-it-from-undergraduate-transition. Accessed 30/06/16.

Anderson, L., Monaghan, E.D., del Rio, E., and Matthews, M. (2016) 'Capturing learning gain from work placements', Report for the Higher Education Academy, Vice-Chancellor's Strategic Excellence Initiative. www.heacademy.ac.uk/about/our-role-institutions/strategic-excellence-initiative-vice-chancellors-or-principals-6. Accessed 22/09/16.

ATCS21 project. http://www.atc21s.org/. Accessed 07/02/17.

Australian National Graduate Attributes Project (The National GAP, 2007–08) www.sydney.edu.au/education-portfolio/ei/projects/nationalgap/introduction.htm. Accessed 22/09/16.

Banks, J.A., Au, K. H., Ball, A.F, Bell, P., Gordon, E.W, Gutiérrez, K.D., Heath, S B., Lee, C.D., Lee, Y., Mahiri, J., Suad Nasir, N., Valdés, G., Zhou, M. (2007) 'Learning in and out of school in diverse environments: Lifelong, lifewide, lifedeep', The LIFE Center (The Learning in Informal and Formal Environments Centre), University of Washington, in N. Jackson and J. Willis (Eds.) (n.d.) *Lifewide Learning & Education in Universities and Colleges.* http://www.learninglives.co.uk/e-book.html. Accessed 25/06/16.

Barrie, S. (2007) 'A conceptual framework for the teaching and learning of generic graduate attributes'. *Studies in Higher Education,* 32 (4), 439–458.

Barrie, S. (2009) 'Today's learners; tomorrow's graduates; yesterday's universities', Keynote address at the Improving Student Learning for the 21st Century Learner conference, London, 7 September 2009, in Barrie, S., Hughes, C. and Smith., C. (2009) Final Report of *The National Graduate Attributes Project: Integration and assessment of graduate attributes in curriculum.* The National Graduate Attributes Project (National GAP). Australian Learning & Teaching Council: NSW. http://sydney.edu.au/education-portfolio/ei/projects/nationalgap/resources/GAPpdfs/National%20Graduate%20Attributes%20Project%20Final%20Report%202009.pdf. Accessed 22/09/16.

Barrie, S., Hughes, C. and Smith., C. (2009) Final report of *The National Graduate Attributes Project: Integration and assessment of graduate attributes in curriculum.* The National Graduate Attributes Project (National GAP). Australian Learning & Teaching Council: NSW. http://sydney.edu.au/education-portfolio/ei/projects/nationalgap/resources/GAPpdfs/National%20Graduate%20Attributes%20Project%20Final%20Report%202009.pdf. Accessed 22/09/16.

Baxter Magolda, M. (2004) 'Self-authorship as the common goal of 21st-century education' in Baxter Magolda, M. and King, P. M. (Eds.), *Learning Partnerships: Theory and models of practice to educate for self-authorship.* Sterling, Virginia: Stylus Publishing.

Biggs, J. and Tang, C. (2011) *Teaching for Quality Learning at University* (4th edition). Maidenhead, Berks: OUP.

Dearing, R. (1997) *Higher Education in the Learning Society*. The National Committee of Inquiry into Higher Education. HMSO.

Hong Kong Baptist University. (2016a) *Seven Institutional Graduate Attributes*. http://chtl .hkbu.edu.hk/main/hkbu-ga/. Accessed 21/06/16.

Hong Kong Baptist University. (2016b) *Graduate Attributes for Postgraduates*. http://gs.hkbu .edu.hk/en/current/rpg/grad_attributes/. Accessed 21/06/16.

Hyland, T. and Johnson, S. (1998) Of cabbages and key skills: exploding the mythology of core transferable skills in post-school education, *Journal of Further and Higher Education*, 22 (2), 163–172 in Barrie, S., Hughes, C. and Smith., C. (2009) Final Report of *The National Graduate Attributes Project: Integration and assessment of graduate attributes in curriculum*. The National Graduate Attributes Project (National GAP). Australian Learning & Teaching Council: NSW. http://sydney.edu.au/education-portfolio/ei/projects/nationalgap/ resources/GAPpdfs/National%20Graduate%20Attributes%20Project%20Final%20 Report%202009.pdf. Accessed 22/09/16.

Jackson, N. (n.d.) 'Lifewide learning and education in universities and colleges: concepts and conceptual aids' in N. Jackson and J. Willis (Eds.) (n.d.) *Lifewide Learning & Education in Universities and Colleges*. http://www.learninglives.co.uk/e-book.html. Accessed 25/06/16.

Jones, C (2016) 'Are graduate attributes for postgraduate students too?'. *Phoenix* (148: 24). Association of Graduate Careers Advisory Services http://www.agcas.org.uk/agcas_ resources/25-Phoenix. Accessed 11/07/16.

Leitch, A. (2006) *Prosperity for All in the Global Economy – World Class Skills*. HMSO. http:// webarchive.nationalarchives.gov.uk/20070701082906/http://www.hm-treasury.gov.uk/ media/6/4/leitch_finalreport051206.pdf. Accessed 30/06/16.

Marton, F. and Säljö, R. (1976) 'On qualitative differences in learning – 1: outcome and process.' *British Journal of Educational Psychology*, 46, 4–11.

MMM (Making the Most of Masters) (2016a) http://www.mastersprojects.ac.uk/. Accessed 22/09/16.

MMM (Making the Most of Masters) (2016b) http://www.mastersprojects.ac.uk/index .cfm/employers/. Accessed 22/09/16

Nicol, D. (2010) 'The foundation for graduate attributes: developing self-regulation through self and peer-assessment'. *Graduates for the 21st Century: Integrating the enhancement themes* http://www.enhancementthemes.ac.uk/docs/publications/the-foundation-for- graduate-attributes-developing-self-regulation-through-self-and-peer-assessment.pdf. Accessed 22/09/16.

Oxford Brookes University Strategy for Enhancing the Student Experience (2015–2020) https://www.brookes.ac.uk/about-brookes/strategy-2020/strategy-for-enhancing-the- student-experience/. Accessed 07/02/17.

Phoenix Editorial (2016), 148, Association of Graduate Careers Advisory Services http:// www.agcas.org.uk/agcas_resources/25-Phoenix. Accessed 11/07/16.

QAAS (2014) *Mastersness Toolkit* http://www.enhancementthemes.ac.uk/docs/publications/ mastersness-toolkit.pdf?sfvrsn=4. Accessed 22/09/16.

QAAS *Research-Teaching Linkages – Graduate Attributes* (2006–08) (/www.enhancementthemes. ac.uk/enhancement-themes/completed-enhancement-themes/research-teaching-linkages) and Graduates for the 21st Century (2008–11) (http://www.enhancementthemes.ac.uk/ enhancement-themes/completed-enhancement-themes/graduates-for-the-21st-century).

Ramsden, P. (1988) *Improving Learning: New Perspectives*. London: Kogan Page.

Rust, C. and Froud, L. (2016) 'Shifting the focus from skills to "graduateness"'. *Phoenix* (148: 8–9). Association of Graduate Careers Advisory Services http://www.agcas.org.uk/ agcas_resources/25-Phoenix. Accessed 11/07/16.

Salazar-Xirinachs, J. (2015) '6 ways Latin America can close its skills gap.' *World Economic Forum.* www.weforum.org/agenda/2015/05/6-ways-latin-america-can-close-its-skills-gap/. Accessed 25/08/16.

Smith, M. K. (1996, 2001) 'Lifelong learning', *The encyclopedia of informal education* www.infed.org/lifelonglearning/b-life.htm. Accessed 22/09/16.

Soffel, J. (2016) 'What are the 21st-century skills every student needs?' World Economic Forum https://www.weforum.org/agenda/2016/03/21st-century-skills-future-jobs-students. Accessed 07/02/17.

Thomson, K. (2015) *Managing transitions by understanding conceptions of learning in post-graduate students.* Enhancement and Innovation in Higher Education conference, Glasgow, 9–11 June 2015. http://www.enhancementthemes.ac.uk/docs/paper/managing-transitions-by-understanding-conceptions-of-learning-in-post-graduate-students.pdf?sfvrsn=6. Accessed 30/06/16.

UKCES. (2014) *The Future of Work: Jobs and Skills in 2030.* https://www.gov.uk/government/publications/jobs-and-skills-in-2030.

University of Glasgow (2016a) http://www.gla.ac.uk/students/attributes/yourattributes/. Accessed 22/09/16.

University of Glasgow (2016b) http://www.gla.ac.uk/students/attributes/yourattributes/subjectspecialists/#tabs=1. Accessed 22/09/16.

University of Greenwich http://www2.gre.ac.uk/__data/assets/pdf_file/0020/832043/BecomingAGreenwichGraduate.pdf. Accessed 22/09/16

University of the Western Cape, Republic of South Africa www.uwc.ac.za/TandL/Pages/Graduate-Attributes.aspx. Accessed 22/09/16.

Vitae www.vitae.ac.uk/about-us. Accessed 22/09/16.

Warring, S. (2011) 'An analysis of learning levels within and between a degree and a diploma: New Zealand case study', *Quality Assurance in Education*, 19 (4), 441–450 in QAAS (2014) *Mastersness Toolkit* http://www.enhancementthemes.ac.uk/docs/publications/mastersness-toolkit.pdf?sfvrsn=4. Accessed 22/09/16.

Washer, P. (2007) 'Revisiting key skills: a practical framework for higher education'. *Quality in Higher Education*, 13 (1), 57–67 in Barrie, S., Hughes, C. and Smith., C. (2009) Final Report of *The National Graduate Attributes Project: Integration and assessment of graduate attributes in curriculum.* The National Graduate Attributes Project (National GAP). Australian Learning & Teaching Council: NSW. http://sydney.edu.au/education-portfolio/ei/projects/nationalgap/resources/GAPpdfs/National%20Graduate%20Attributes%20Project%20Final%20Report%202009.pdf. Accessed 22/09/16.

Chapter 2

The Adaptable Graduate

Patrick O'Donnell, Bassam Rakhshani, Andrew Rae and Robert Smith

Introduction

The transformation in the nature and structure of universities as a sector accelerated rapidly in the UK towards the end of the twentieth century. These developments must be viewed as part of a wide range of intersecting factors including global networks and communications as well as economic and political pressures (Land, 2004: 1–3). The university landscape has expanded and evolved in new and novel ways, creating in some instances a sharp departure from the once traditional defining features of the sector, both structurally and culturally. For many commentators it has been a period marked by teaching an increasingly large and diverse student body with constrained resources. Added to this is the potential threat of institutional decline, unless there is a continual drive for efficiency gains, innovation and flexibility in terms of delivery and the pursuit of new markets (ibid.: 2).

The advancement of global economic forces has ushered in a new era of heightened awareness of the economic importance of universities (Mayhew et al., 2004: 69 and Halsey et al., 2003: 1–33). One result of which has meant that the sector has been under increasing pressure to justify its contribution to human capital development and economic growth. The last two decades have witnessed a protracted policy drive to open up the university sector to more levels of accountability and harness it more directly to serve economic interests. The drive to realign the university curriculum – its aims, processes and outcomes – to be more closely allied to the global economy and emerging employability imperatives has intensified and within this overarching policy drive the concept of transferable skills and attributes (TSA) (O'Donnell et al., 2016) for graduates has surfaced to occupy an increasingly important place. As Barrie (2012: 81) suggests: 'graduate attributes sit at a vital intersection of many of the forces shaping higher education today.'

TSA are, so the argument follows, crucial in ensuring that new graduates are equipped to compete in a rapidly changing technological, social and economic environment. This argument is constructed on the perceived need for greater mobility and for individuals to move within and across different sectors of employment. Flexible career paths loom large here. Such ideas explicitly resonate with post-Taylorist and post-Fordist thinking where adaptability and flexibility are perceived as an essential component in the drive to increase a nation's competitive edge on the global market (Blackmore, 2003: 224; Brehony and Deem, 2005: 356). This chapter considers the nature and practical reality of introducing initiatives that develop and nurture TSA within the university setting to produce adaptable capacities within graduates. It engages with the following question: What potential do research-based case studies have in fostering adaptable capacities within graduates? However, in order to explore this question the scope and nature of TSA must be considered. As such, the chapter will also consider the following question: What sort of transferable skills and attributes are needed for adaptability?

The first part of the discussion will map the main contours of TSA, looking at the assortment of approaches presented in the literature and how they contribute towards notions of adaptability. The second part will take a more focused and practical approach, offering a description and analysis of recent attempts to integrate TSA within degree level aeronautical and aircraft engineering programmes delivered at Scotland's newest university – the University of the Highlands and Islands (UHI), modelled on the idea of a federal, collegiate university based on a number of existing and geographically dispersed further education (FE) colleges and research institutions. This work is drawn from a two year study covering a series of investigations and observations, including data gathering on student and employer perceptions, in relation to the application of research-based modelling to nurture graduate adaptability through TSA (Rakhshani, 2012).

Transferable Skills and Attributes: Reflecting Economic Imperatives

Taking stock of the last two decades one can detect powerful drivers and levers creating substantial change; much of which has often been perceived as unsympathetic and perhaps antagonistic to certain key elements of the Humboldtian model that once underscored the European university tradition (Pritchard, 2004: 511; Delanty, 2001: 8). The Dearing Report (Dearing, 1997) can be seen as an important milestone in the drive to shape the sensibilities of UK higher education and its university sector to become more attuned to economic needs. The introduction of the report (ibid.: 3) sets out its objectives as making "recommendations on how the purpose, shape, structure, size and funding of Higher Education including support for students, should develop to meet the needs of the UK over the next 20 years". The post-Dearing years have witnessed an increasing stress on universities to meet economic imperatives and employment-relevant competencies (Mayhew et al., 2004: 69) resulting in much discussion and debate on the changing nature and role of universities.

Hesketh (2010: 246) notes how the rapid and far reaching changes to modern economies stemming from information communication technologies (ICT) resulted in corresponding changes in the demand for highly qualified and flexible workers as the nature, scope and skill requirements of the labour markets simultaneously became more wide-reaching and more demanding. Within this overall policy drive to secure economic sustainability and competitive advancement the proposal that TSA should be developed as an explicit aim within the university curriculum has found increasing currency. Much of the rhetoric framing the need for TSA concentrates on the desire to make graduates more adaptable, allowing for better mobility between and across subject disciplines. The suggestion here is that the 'world of work' will become more and more interconnected, with disciplinary boundaries softening and becoming more porous.

Against this backdrop the goal for university departments may be seen as twofold. Firstly, to provide learning experiences that enable students to develop a repertoire of skills, attributes, capabilities and learning strategies that ensure they can operate effectively and efficiently within their elected academic field of study – described here as 'vertical progression' within a bounded discipline. The second goal aims at fostering certain skills and abilities that enable students to operate successfully within a variety of employment settings – referred to here as 'horizontal progression', moving across traditional disciplinary boundaries. Together, these two aims coalesce, producing the idea of the adaptable graduate; defined here as having the capacity to adapt to changing workplace conditions and different employment settings (O'Donnell et al., 2016).

Tladinyane and Van der Merwe (2016: 2) describe career adaptability as an adaptive and resiliency resource that facilitates individuals to cope with career transitions. The linkages to TSA are clear here. Essentially, programmes aimed at fostering TSA are a deliberate and systematic attempt to share perceptions and values, manipulate cognitions and direct behaviour to achieve certain outcomes. The literature reveals that TSA is framed by a rather seductive discourse of flexibility, adaptability and mobility, offering benefits for a range of stakeholders. For governments, it promotes new pathways for mobility between different employment realms, thus, creating new levels of economic sustainability. For employers and industry, TSA has been explicitly linked to the overarching concept of 'employability', defined as 'work readiness' or 'oven ready', that is, the possession of certain skills, knowledge and abilities that will enable new graduates to make positive contributions to organisational objectives as soon as they commence employment (Mason et al., 2009: 1). In other words, if programmes aim to foster TSA then the time scales for newly qualified graduates to be fully productive employees will be much shorter, as employers require newly qualified graduates to be resourceful and flexible, adapting their skills and knowledge to succeed in unfamiliar and challenging situations. For the newly qualified graduate, TSA offers the promise to open up opportunities for graduates to acquire and gain recognition for certain skills which are deemed to have transferable currency between a range of work situations and career paths. As such, there is a sense of future economic security, where newly qualified graduates have greater career choice. Here TSA enable the individual to proactively adapt to changing career circumstances.

Engaging with Transferable Skills and Attributes: Finding Common Ground and Core Elements

So how do university departments nurture desirable attributes and skills in their graduates that are, in some way, transferable to contexts outside their academic field of study? This is a legitimate but also a rather thorny question for anyone teaching within higher education. Legitimate in the sense that it is the most glaring question to pose for anyone dealing with and seeking to promote TSA within the university setting. It is also a rather thorny question, however, in the sense that it is likely to expose a range of epistemological and practical issues while yielding no clear-cut answers that will gain universal consensus. Unpacking this question will inevitability call attention to a range of fundamental sub-questions such as, what constitutes TSA? How should it be included into the existing curriculum: a bolt-on approach introduced during the final phases of the degree programme or a fully integrated approach? How can TSA be taught? How can programmes designed to nurture desirable TSA be best supported? How will success in desired graduate TSA development be acknowledged, monitored, evaluated and recorded? These are challenging questions to consider, generating different responses from different disciplines, as discussed elsewhere throughout this book.

Clearly there is not a monolithic entity and project called TSA, which originated in, and emanated from, an authoritative centre. TSA is a discursive concept, residing within a complex landscape. Inevitability the nature, scope and complexity of the concept is often overlooked in institutional definitions that invest it with narrow, parochial meaning and headline activities or statements. Confusingly, the various lists referencing TSA activities and dispositions derived from employer surveys; those contained in government reports are shown to be diverse in terminology, size and purpose, reflecting both subtle and substantial disparities in definitions and interpretations of their significance to both human capital and social capital (Bennett et al., 2000: 10). These differing headline lists and approaches also raise the question of whether they indicate separate concepts or are the lists simply different ways of expressing the same concept. There is a case for arguing that TSA engage with a complex interplay of emotional, cognitive, practical and motivational dispositions. As Bennett et al., (2000: 12) note, it is shrouded in "conceptual fuzziness and equivocation".

Setting aside for a moment this claim of conceptual fuzziness and equivocation, most, if not all, universities will offer programmes of study aimed at developing and nurturing a set of TSA in their graduates. In some cases, the embedding of TSA within the curriculum has simply involved closer engagement with employers, such as, student internships and or industrial placements as part of their undergraduate and postgraduate education. Major graduate employers have been active agents here, outlining what they perceive as essential skills developments that would help individuals to be more effective and better prepared to compete in a rapidly changing technological, social and economic environment. The approach can be varied, for example, the integration into existing curricula or alternatively there may be a bolt-on approach with the introduction of discrete and often credit-bearing modules that explicitly focus on the connection between academia and the discursive needs of the workplace. Other national initiatives such as the creation of the Quality Assurance Agency for Higher Education Scotland (QAAS) and the Higher Education Academy (HEA) have also contributed to the debate over the role of universities in preparing graduates for the world of work. Within these discussions the student is more often perceived as an 'active agent' and not simply a passive entity to be processed (see QAAS, 2016; and York, 2006).

However, developing a clear understanding on what 'employers needs' actually are and then translating those needs into a coherent set of educational experiences attached to TSA is not always a simple process. Bennett et al. (2000: 14), drawing from the work of others (including Harvey et al., 1997), highlight the potential difficulties and fault lines:

> ... employers want people who are going to be effective in a future changing world – intelligent, flexible, adaptable employees who are quick to learn and who can deal with change. They want graduates who can fit rapidly into workplace culture, work in teams, and exhibit good interpretational skills, communicate well, take on responsibility for an area of work and perform efficiently and effectively to add value to the organisation – they want adaptive recruits. They want employees who can use their abilities and skills to evolve the organisation, who exhibit an ability to use their abilities and skills in the face of change. They want people with bright ideas, who are able to communicate them to others, develop them in teams and persuade colleagues to attempt new approaches – adaptable people. And they are looking for people who can anticipate and lead change, to help them transform their organisations, who can use high-level skills like analysis, critique, synthesis and multi-layered communication to facilitate innovative teamwork – transformative employees.

Bennett et al. (2000: 15) suggest that some of the demands cited by employers can be excessive, resembling a "wish list" with little empirical anchoring points. The portrayal cited above, for example, contrives certain 'power relations and persuasive powers' in that it presumes newly qualified graduates entering the world of work will enjoy high levels of autonomy from conditions of hierarchical domination, possessing the strength of will and confidence to simply circumscribe, displace or ignore habitual structural arrangements and cultural dynamics within the workplace. Indeed, the introduction of new and radical ideas, processes and approaches in the workplace will always have an element of perceived risk and as such, will meet different levels of resistance and perhaps even forms of passive aggression. This is more likely to happen if the call for change emanates from newly qualified graduates entering into a work setting with very little industrial experience or a proven track record.

Bridgstock (2009: 32), quoting Bowden et al. (2000), posits that graduate attributes are the qualities, skills and understandings a university community agrees its students would desirably develop during their time at the institution and, consequently, shape the contribution they are able to make to their profession and as a citizen.

This characterisation can be seen to embody an obvious dualism. Firstly, it relates to an individual's capacity for citizenship, engaging in democratic processes and contributing towards a well-functioning society, what might be seen to promote 'social capital'. Secondly, it relates to adaptability and employability; developing human capital and meeting the needs of knowledge economy (Bridgstock, 2009: 32). Unsurprisingly perhaps, it is the skills and attributes linked to human capital that receive the most attention in the literature and reports. Nicol (2010: 2), drawing on studies from both Australian and Scottish higher education, identifies what he refers to as "core processes that are a prerequisite for, and that underlie, all attribute development". These include: self-regulation, self-responsibility and the ability to critically evaluate the quality and impact of their own work (ibid.: 11). For Nicol (ibid.: 6) the latter is the most important core process for higher education institutions to focus on.

Underscoring what they see as common themes within the literature, Andrews and Higdon (2008: 413) identify a number of transferable "soft" skills integral to graduate employability:

- Professionalism
- Reliability
- Ability to cope with uncertainty
- Ability to work under pressure
- Ability to plan and think strategically
- Capability to communicate and interact with others, either in teams or through networking
- Good written and verbal communication skills
- Information and communication technology skills
- Creativity and self-confidence
- Good self-management and time-management skills
- A willingness to learn and accept responsibility

Others, such as Atlay and Harris (2000: 77), have identified areas that should underpin all degree courses: 'information retrieval and handling', 'communication and presentation', 'planning and problem solving' and 'social development and interaction'. Bath et al., (2004: 315, drawing from Candy, 2000) suggest that whereas disciplinary knowledge has a transient nature, in that it can quickly become outdated, other generic and transferable skills such as "communication", "problem solving", "team working" and "analytical and critical thinking" share an enduring quality, character and expansive currency and as such, should be the "hallmark" of any undergraduate education irrespective of the subject field of study. Whilst by no means exhaustive, the above is useful in helping to trace some of the more obvious contours and features found within the literature and espoused by universities. They also point to flexible career pathways and adaptability, where graduates build their professional lives in a dynamic manner, exhibiting the ability to handle change both proactively and effectively with regard to the particular socio-economic context within which they live.

However, although such decontextualised renderings at first sight look plausible, they do inevitability disguise certain fundamental complexities. As Harrison (1996: 266) points out, we have to be careful in assuming that general skills learned and developed in one setting can be easily redeployed with equal success in other areas. Making his case he argued that "problem-solving" will inevitability mean different things in different settings. Some writers have ventured to tease out the different requirements, creating useful insights on contextual issues. Discussing the sorts of philosophical perspectives associated with transferable skills, Bridges (1993: 50) signals a dualistic mode of thought, resulting in a dichotomy between two dynamics: "context-independent" and "context-dependent". As the term suggests, 'context-independent' refers to skills that can be deployed within a variety of social or workplace contexts with little or no modification. By way of example, Bridges (ibid.) states: "Word processing might arguably be held to involve the same skills whether you were doing it in a university centre, an office pool or as a professional writer at home". In other words, context-independent skills can be transplanted and applied to different contexts with corresponding realisation – it is generally perceived as an unreflective activity.

In contrast, 'context-dependent' are perceived as specific skills that may require adjustment or mutation dependent on the specific context – discursive values and attitudes come into play here. By way of example, Bridges (ibid.) states that

> negotiating skills might be heavily context dependent, relying on all sorts of sensitivity to, responsiveness to and adaption to relations between you and your partner, your class of students, your employer or your bank. And, indeed, it will be a recipe for disaster if you do not adapt your style and approach to these social relations.

Within this context-dependent dynamic, transferability of particular skills is not a simply unreflective process; its potential applicability and relevance to a situation requires an appreciation of situational understandings, or what Bridges (1993: 50) terms "meta-skills". Meta-skills (sometimes referred to as metacognition) necessitate creative, interactive manoeuvring and reframing, in that our skills and behaviours have to be customised and realigned to suit the new situation. Within this framing, where situational awareness and skills mutability is utmost, there is a complex and fluid process of reflexive learning requiring individuals to adopt a critical perspective on their own skills and behaviours, making appropriate negotiations as when and how to apply them. Of course, situational awareness is dependent upon and actually a knock-on effect from several cognitive processes interacting under complex dynamic conditions. Having the ability to interpret the discursive political, structural and cultural undercurrents of the workplace setting is at the heart of this context-dependent dynamic. According to Bridges (ibid.) the premium must be placed on the sorts of "meta-skills" that enable a person to select, adapt and realign their skills to different situations, across different social contexts and cognitive domains.

The following case study sets out an approach to support the development of the adaptable graduate. For conceptual clarity it is divided into two sections. The first part, using data gathered from industry deals with the construction of lists of TSA for the case studies. The second part, or User Guide, maps the development of the two case studies and its implementation and encourages the reader to reflect on the ways in which this approach could be used in their own practice.

Research-Based Case Studies: A Method for Developing and Nurturing the Adaptable Graduate

It's not difficult to find reports and studies revealing perceptions that there is a misalignment or gap between the knowledge and skills developed at university and those actually needed in the workplace (Nair et al., 2009: 132). Peng et al, (2016: 445–46), for example, highlight a perceived mismatch between educational attainment of Master in Engineering graduates and industry requirements in China, Australia, the United States and Europe. Engineering graduate skills such as "oral and written communications", "decision-making", "problem solving", "leadership" and "emotional intelligence and interpersonal skills with colleagues and clients" have all been cited as either lacking or well below employer expectations (ibid.). Interestingly, global mobility of the engineering profession, an increase in multicultural and multinational workplace environments, the pace and nature of technological changes and the content and design of engineering programmes taught at universities are some of the dynamics claimed to be embroiled in the recent debates on the skills gap within engineering. With respect to curriculum design, Barrie (2012: 81) suggests that not all initiatives aimed at embedding generic attributes have been met with equal enthusiasm:

> In much of the literature there is a suggestion of apathy and even resistance on the part of some colleagues to generic attributes initiatives. Even where such initiatives occur, approaches to the teaching and learning of graduate attributes are highly varied and, despite sometimes extensive support, have not always met with success when considered at an institutional or national university system level.

Not wishing to underplay or deny the conceptual complexities touched upon earlier, we must consider that any lists referencing TSA are, on a fundamental level, both strategic and tactical, offering both an entry point and framework from which to develop. With this in mind, this study collected data on perceptions on TSA from a sample of aircraft and aeronautical engineering employers and research institutions (n=10). A mixed-method approach was adopted and the data gathered through surveys and follow-up interviews. It was administered over a six month period by two teaching staff with extensive research experience within engineering.

Potential survey participants were contacted (initially by telephone or email) to explain the purpose of the study and request organisational participation. Full study details were sent to the organisation (including ethical statements highlighting how all data gathered would be anonymized and the identity of individuals kept confidential) and contact with suitable participants was then initiated and arrangements were made for the most convenient way to administer the survey. Post-survey results were followed by telephone interviews with participants to gather more nuanced and contextual information on individual respondent's perceptions on TSA. An initial list of graduate attributes and skills, derived from research literature, was used in the survey as a starting point. We referred to this list as the 'TSA constellation' and interview participants were asked to rate each attribute in terms of relevance. To capture a full and more nuanced picture, participants were also asked to augment the list if they wished to do so. The survey results identified what was perceived as the most important TSA and the subsequent follow-up interviews provided important contextual narratives on each of the skills and attributes. The final results were collated into what was referred to as the 'designated list' referencing TSA.

- **Knowledge and understanding** – have a good understanding of core knowledge of discipline(s) and awareness of a variety of ideas/contexts frameworks which may apply to this.
- **Ethical and professional understandings** – hold personal values and beliefs consistent with their role as a responsible member of the professional communities.
- **Computer-based skills** – have an extensive understanding of computer technology - proficient at using software modelling.
- **Written and oral communication and presentation** – ability to organise thoughts and ideas and present them clearly and convincingly to a range of audiences, including internal and external experts and external agencies. Communicate quantitative information effectively using appropriate formats, charts and graphs etc. The ability to discuss and argue a case and to win support and co-operation from others and generate enthusiasm for new ideas and methods – especially in terms of building a persuasive argument for carrying out short term research projects/pilot studies to evaluate design ideas/processes.
- **Adaptability and flexibility** – have resilience, resourcefulness and agility in a range of working contexts/environments. To draw on the existing and evolving stock of knowledge to be able to deal with unexpected circumstances, circumventing problematical issues while finding effective solutions.
- **Time management and organisational skills** – ability to create a plan of action (individually or with others) to achieve desired objectives. Setting and

maintaining realistic and achievable plans and short-term/intermediate targets. Showing perseverance and resourcefulness when working to deadlines and having the ability to think ahead and overcome/manage potential obstacles to progress.

- **Management and leadership** – can assume leadership qualities where appropriate, bringing out the best qualities in others. Ability to motivate individuals and teams. Identify the necessary criteria for success and evaluate group/individual performance (including one's own) against preset criteria. Demonstrating self-reflection, recognising limitations as well as opportunities for success.
- **Team working and social interaction/interpersonal skills** – the ability to co-operate and work with others within a variety of contexts. Displays high levels of integrity, empathy and emotional intelligence – respectful of other beliefs.
- **Information retrieval and handling** – ability to seek, describe, interpret and arrange relevant information within the context of engineering disciplines. Identify information needs to assist the problem-solving processes. Use a variety of primary and secondary sources and arrange appropriately, including protecting data against accidental loss or disclosure of information to unauthorised individuals/companies.
- **Problem-solving and analytical skills** – can display critical and analytical thinking when reviewing evidence supporting conclusions/recommendations, including reliability, validity and significance. Apply major theories and analytical tools/methods to help define the nature of engineering problems and draw appropriate conclusions when establishing priorities, allocating resources and implementing solutions. Considering issues from a range of perspectives when deciding on and drawing up action plans or solutions.
- **Research and enquiry** – be able to create new knowledge and understanding through the process of research and enquiry. Be familiar with research methodologies and be able to locate and critically evaluate engineering research publications.
- **Synthesis/creativity** – can consider issues from a range of perspectives, reorient and restructure ideas/concepts/frameworks to create innovative combinations of new ideas and processes.

The interviews suggest that the whole conceptualisation of TSA should be seen as a dynamic and mutating process, and as such, it should be constantly reviewed and updated to suit changing work practises. Furthermore, the study revealed opinions indicating that TSA should and must sit at the very heart of the teaching of aeronautical/aircraft engineering, integrated throughout. With respect to rankings, the survey data gathering found that the following six areas were rated as having high value and currency in the workplace: "knowledge and understanding"; "computer-based skills"; "written and oral communication and presentation"; "adaptability and flexibility"; "team working and social interaction/interpersonal skills" and "problem solving and analytical skills".

The interviews also revealed that skills and attributes were not seen as separate isolated entities but rather, as an interwoven network that intersect, overlap and interact with each other. Unsurprisingly, perhaps, while the study found that there was general agreement among the interview respondents on the value and meaning of TSA in terms of what it should comprise and operational definitions, differences did arise on how TSA should be taught and cultivated in an educational setting.

Practice Guide: Research-Based Case Studies

Modelling your own disciplinary curriculum can be a useful starting point in thinking about the ways in which TSA can be embedded within the teaching and learning processes. The model below (Figure 2.1) is a generic model indicating the three main elements that make up the curriculum for engineering undergraduates and provide the overall contextual backdrop.

In the case of aircraft and aeronautical engineering, the 'science-based engineering education' element generally refers to science theory of engineering and includes areas such as applied mathematics and physics, fluid and structural mechanics, thermodynamics and electronics. The 'technical training' element relates to the practical aspects of engineering and embraces a range of practical applications of engineering systems such as hydraulic, pneumatic or mechanical systems, and electrical and electronic processes and systems. This 'technical training' dynamic may be seen as the tangible expression of the engineering science/principles. The 'research-based engineering modelling' element can be seen to interlink the theory elements and technical/practical dimensions and includes the synthesis of knowledge (theoretical and practical) into 'design'.

It is argued here that research-based engineering modelling has the potential to be a valuable mechanism for nurturing and developing TSA (Rakhshani, 2012). It is the technique of designing the various engineering IT-based platforms to perform

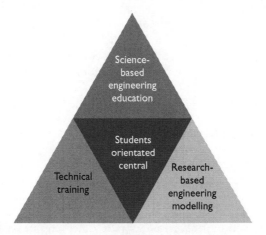

Figure 2.1 Curriculum model for engineering (Rakhshani, 2012).

predictable design tasks which can be evaluated for performance. Such modelling involves engineering process simulation, engineering system performance analysis and engineering problem-solving. Naturally this will draw on and contextualise theoretical approaches, as appropriate. One major benefit was that the various engineering systems can be generated, studied, designed/redesigned, practised and analysed thoroughly (though not necessarily completely) on computer platforms like geometry handling and numerical simulation environments (ibid.).

Two engineering research-based case studies displaying different levels of design complexity and involving prototype modelling (the design, creation, testing and modification of prototypes) were created with the specific aim of nurturing and developing the TSA outlined above. Our aim was to ensure that TSA play a role in creating what Bath et al., (2004: 325) refer to as a "living curriculum":

> A validated curriculum is one in which the planned, enacted and experienced curricula are aligned in the eyes of relevant stakeholders, including students. A process of regular review and renewal ensures that the validation of the curriculum is continuous, producing a living curriculum.

Prototype modelling is often used as part of the product design process to give engineers and designers the ability to explore design alternatives, test theories and confirm performance parameters prior to commencing production of a new product. Thus, prototype modelling offers a rich and vast field for developing TSA. Moreover, the research-based case studies are conceptualised as a form of scaffolding to support the student's evolving understanding of knowledge domains and skills development. Figure 2.2 outlines the cyclical process of the development of the case studies, which can be adapted for use across a range of disciplines.

The research-based case studies deal with tangible and real life practical problems and solutions and as such they are explicitly linked to problem-based learning (PBL). PBL is an alternative to conventional didactic teaching and has its origins in the university setting, first developed in the 1960s to increase and enhance the quality of the practical aspect of medical school education (Takashi and Saito, 2013: 694). It is now widely used in a range of educational institutions and disciplines, adopting a learner-centred approach in which students are encouraged and steered by their teacher to take the initiative to solve problems through interacting with their peers in group settings. Promoting the benefits associated with their research on PBL, Takashi and Saito (2013: 704) note that

> beyond knowledge building and skill acquirement, PBL may have contributed to broadening learner's perspectives and promoting their personal development. In this regard, PBL can defined as learning that generate rich and varied emotions in learners concurrently as they face problems, enabling them to acquire subject matter knowledge and relational skills through dialogue, and eventually guide them to the threshold of personal transformation.

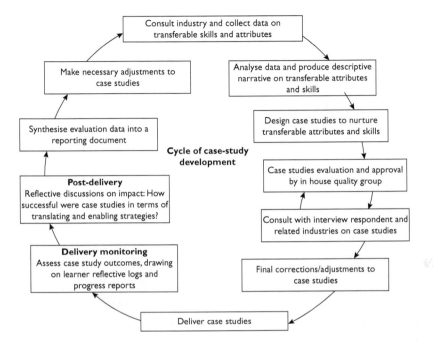

Figure 2.2 Cycle of case study development.

Working with the Case Studies: Orienting the Students

A class group approach was adopted (n=12 students) in dealing with the case studies. Lecturers already held an intimate knowledge of the case study and how the different stages/phases should unfold and progress. This insider knowledge and panoramic perspective helped to provide a well-structured and co-ordinated case study – critical for ensuring students were intellectually challenged but not overwhelmed to such an extent that they became disheartened. A number of short-lived subgroups were formed to deal with the different aspect, stages and dynamics associated with the case studies. During the unfolding phases student were allocated roles within their respective teams. However, these roles changed as group dynamics evolved, a process referred to by Pagal (2012: 364–5) as the "social viscosity of groups" – formation of sub-groups within a group. The case studies were conceptualised as 'translating and enabling' strategies, encouraging students to engage with the designated list of TSA. In other words, the enactments of case studies were seen as a form of 'character building', with the list of TSA being perceived as the profiling elements/characteristics. In many respects the students are going through a transitional journey, where they undergo large and small adjustments as they enter into, and through, the new and unfamiliar educational experience associated with the research-based case studies. Transitional journey within this context is perceived in performative and dialectical terms, involving the academic ability and mental agility of the individual to engage with the research-based case studies on a number of levels. It encapsulates a multidimensional process, some of which will comprise certain linear steps and dynamics, others more fluid and unpredictable processes. The main learning trajectories here are 'TSA awareness', 'TSA engagement' and 'TSA enculturation'. The first two relate to the familiarity of the designated list of TSA, linking it to the nature, scope and practical realities of the research-based case studies. The third is more nuanced and complex, involving the process by which the student acquires the values and behaviours associated with the designated list of TSA. TSA enculturation suggests a form of meta-thinking takes route where students, during the case studies period, attempt to locate themselves within a wider network of significance.

Prior to engaging with the case studies, the students were given the designated list of TSA, and group discussions took place on their significance to the case studies as well as how they help build the identity of the graduate engineer. It was important that students had a clear understanding of what was expected of them. Before engaging with the case studies, students were given a good grounding on the meaning, purpose and practise of self-critical evaluation and peer review. Lecturers took on a dual role and identity, acting as a lead researcher and project manager. The first case study was designed to illustrate the potential interconnection of disciplinary boundaries, allowing important insights into skill transfer across professional disciplines within the field of aircraft and aeronautical engineering. Dealing with the different professional disciplines associated with this field, this case study expressed multidisciplinary collaboration, normally characterised by a consensual approach that rests on respect for and acceptance of disciplinary differences. Those operating within a multidisciplinary team may be in a position to learn something of the work of the other disciplines involved, but their own expertise or methodological approaches are not contested, nor would they challenge the position and approaches of other participating disciplines. The research question/problem tends to be divided up between the disciplines involved. Although this requires co-ordination of the different activities, the integrity of discipline silos are intact: each discipline contributes from its own expertise to a particular aspect of the research question/problem. It was envisaged that this multidisciplinary case study would mobilise discussions and understandings on the emerging trends on potential career mobility within aircraft and aeronautical engineering.

The first case study resonates with the concept of pre-professional identity (PPI). According to Jackson (2016: 1), PPI "relates to an understanding of and connection with the skills, qualities, conduct, culture and ideology of a student's intended profession: Jackson (ibid.: 2), drawing on earlier commentators (Trede et al., 2012), suggests PPI is about work readiness, learning about professional roles and a form of professional socialisation.

The second case study looks at engineering design associated with automotive engineering and formula motor sport. With this second case study the skills and knowledge associated with aircraft and aeronautical engineering transcend the disciplinary context in which they were originally acquired, finding new engineering fields to operate within. As such, this case study reflects transdisciplinary characteristics. Under the 'transdisciplinary' arrangement there is an inclination to cross or transcend disciplinary boundaries, jettisoning familiar structures and conventions and creating new (perhaps provisional) research paradigms or working activities. Rowland (2006: 95) provides a useful summary of the trans-disciplinary approach:

> The value of the trans-disciplinary approach is that it emphasises crossing boundaries and leaving behind familiar disciplinary structures and conventions. It also emphasises the importance of open-mindedness in research that is innovatory and involves working with new people in new ways and on new problems. Conciliation rather than contestation becomes important as attempts are made to reach out across disciplinary boundaries.

One of the researchers and co-authors here involved in delivering this case study exemplified the sort of adaptability advocated, operating as a transdisciplinary research consultant – working in both motorsport engineering (formula one design) and aircraft and aeronautical engineering design. Thus, a rich source of cutting-edge, research-based evidence was provided to construct the case study, contextualising it within the wider discursive field of engineering design. It can be seen that while there are discrepancies specific to the differences in the platform (vehicle) associated with each discipline, there are significant engineering design similarities and overlaps so to have transferable knowledge and skills (see Figure 2.3).

Working with the Case Studies: Implementation

The case studies were delivered over two semesters, and during this time regular post-lab sessions (at the end of critical stages) were introduced to allow students to discuss their experiences and understandings on how the case studies helped to draw attention to and cultivate TSA. Individual face-to-face interviews were conducted between students and lecturers to discuss and evaluate log book reflections and learner contribution towards progressing the case studies. One challenge related to ensuring co-operative learning and levels of individual autonomy and accountability coexisted. In order to facilitate this, lecturers encouraged open debates on critical issues and co-ordinated and guided discussions on potentially problematic areas. Discussions also centred on how learners can recognise impasses and errors and used strategies to gain control over their understanding or performance during the different tasks associated with the case study.

With respect to TSA development, student feedback highlighted that the meta-skills were the most challenging to get to grips with. As discussed previously, meta-skills necessitate critical self-reflection, involving situational awareness and skills

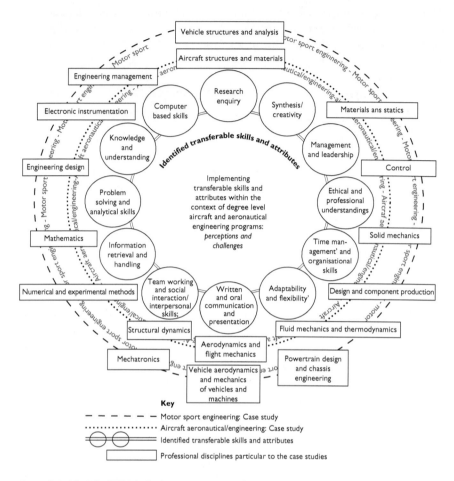

Figure 2.3 Model of TSA linked to two case studies.

mutability: where our thinking and behaviours are customised and reoriented to successfully engage with the new situation. Within the group context, many students found it difficult to jettison or set aside their own ideas to make room for alternative perspectives. Issues of group inter-subjectivity were also acknowledged. For example, it was recognised (and acknowledged in a self-confessional way) that certain individuals within groups were in competition for dominance: for their voice and ideas to be heard. This suggests that critical self-reflection (on the thinking and impact of actions) was not being practised sufficiently at the time. In terms of gaining new insights and enhanced understandings, all students ranked "time management and organisational skills", "adaptability and flexibility", "team-working and social interaction/interpersonal skills" as areas where they felt they developed the most. Measuring outcomes was based on individual reflective accounts, face-to-face progress and evaluations during the case study enactment. Moreover, a final class discussion was conducted, providing individuals with the opportunity to unpack and map their experiences and offer new ideas. All students felt that their sense of identity shifted towards belonging to a professional engineering community. In terms of moving towards the adaptable graduate, defined here as having the capacity to adapt to changing workplace conditions and different employment settings, students did feel the experience provided a valuable starting point on which to build.

Conclusion

The concept of TSA for graduates has moved from the periphery to occupy a prominent place within debates on how the university curriculum should reflect economic imperatives, employer demands and the world of work. Essentially, TSA within the context of higher education aims to provide graduates with the capacity for adaptability. There is an increasing pressure on universities to provide graduates with the intellectual tools, self-efficacy and mental agility to engage with and traverse the challenging and uncertain changes of the employment landscape. This reflects how the advancement of global economic forces has ushered in a new era of heightened awareness of the economic importance of universities. Over the last two decades the sector has operated under a protracted policy drive to justify its contribution to human capital development and economic growth. However, it is important to recognise that the student experience is not homogeneous but is comprised of a multiplicity of experiences contingent on type of institution and associated culture, department, enthusiasm and knowledge of individual lecturers and of course, individual students' academic and social characteristics and their interaction with fellow learners (Barrie, et al., 2009). As such, attempts to introduce TSA for graduates cannot be standardised, but will be influenced by the social and cultural contexts of the learning environment and the dynamics of human interaction within them at a particular point in time.

In many respects TSA can be seen to crystallise around certain core skills such as written and oral communication, presentation skills, time management and organisational skills, and yet with reference to meta-skills and critical self-reflection we cannot ignore that TSA has an ambiguous nature and mutable quality that is difficult to pin down. The findings here yielded favourable conclusions and present what the authors believe to be a good entry point in the efforts to nurture TSA, in this case within degree level aircraft and aeronautical engineering programmes. The set of TSA and problem-based case studies presented here seek to create confident graduates who can manage transition from university into the economy with the requisite skills, attributes, knowledge and confidence to succeed in an ever-changing working environment. For the researchers, the actual experiences gained from enacting the case studies created an essential launch pad from which to reach out in other directions. It is envisaged that these problem-based case studies together with others, still yet to be fully developed, will form a larger project for our graduates – one that ultimately aims to develop the capabilities to respond with flexibility, adapting one's skill set and knowledge to succeed in different work contexts and settings. Feedback has indicated that individual students' sense of identity was influenced by the case studies; there was a stronger sense of belonging to a professional community. Moreover, the results suggest that problem-based case studies offer the potential to engage students in more holistic ways, where social and academic skills are more closely intertwined than in more traditional educational settings, such as the classroom or workshop.

The authors are exploring new directions as well as revisiting earlier assumptions and approaches. This will involve renewed discussions with industry on both updating and refining the set of skills and attributes. These discussions will also include how best to introduce new cases studies, including engineering design modelling within medical applications. The study also found that the student's capacity to critically evaluate and make judgements on the virtues and actual impact of their own thinking and actions (a central feature of Bridges' "meta-skills", 1993) was an important dynamic here. Critically, future investigations will focus on unpacking this further. We are refocusing our attention on introducing new (and refining existing) pedagogical approaches that will assure coherence and structure without losing the all-important organic experiential learning dynamic – an approach where meaningful learning is tested in reality. Learner engagement and the evidencing and recording of learning outcomes are crucial to this process. As stated earlier, the aim is to ensure that TSA plays a role in creating what Bath et al., (2004: 325) refer to as a "living curriculum".

References

Andrews, J. and Higson, H. (2008) Graduate employability, 'soft skills' versus 'hard' business knowledge: A European study. *Higher Education in Europe*, 33 (4): 411–422.

Atlay, M. and Harris, R. (2000) An institutional approach to developing students' 'Transferable' Skills. *Innovations in Education and Training International*, 37 (1), 76–84.

Barrie, S.C. (2012) A research-based approach to generic graduate attributes policy. *Higher Education Research and Development*, 31 (1), 79–92.

Barrie, S. C., Hughes, C., and Smith, C. (2009) *The national graduate attributes project: Integration and assessment of graduate attributes in curriculum.* Strawberry Hills, Australia: Australian Learning and Teaching Council.

Bath, D., Smith, C., Stein, S. and Swann, R. (2004) Beyond mapping and embedding graduate attributes: bringing together quality assurance and action learning to create a validated and living curriculum. *Higher Education Research and Development*, 23 (3), 313–328.

Bennett, N., Dunne, E. and Carre, C. (2000) *Skills Development in Higher Education and Employment.* Buckingham: SRHE/OUP.

Blackmore, J. (2003) The gendering of skill and vocationalism in twentieth-century Australian education, in A.H. Halsey, H. Lauder, P. Brown and S. Wells (Eds) *Education: Culture, Economy and Society.* Oxford: Oxford University Press.

Bowden, J., Hart, G., King, B., Trigwell, K. and Watts, O. (2000) *Generic capabilities of ATN university graduates.* http://www.clt.uts.edu.au/ATN.grad.cap.project.index.html. Accessed: 05.01.06

Brehony, K.J. and Deem, R. (2005) Challenging the post-Fordist/flexible organisation thesis: The case of reformed educational organisations. *British Journal of Sociology of Education*, 26(3), 395–414.

Bridges, D. (1993) Transferable skills: A philosophical perspective. *Studies in Higher Education*, 18 (1), 43–51.

Bridgstock, R. (2009) The graduate attributes we've overlooked: enhancing graduate employability through career management skills. *Higher Education Research and Development*, 28 (1), 31–44.

Candy, P.C. (2000) Learning and earning: Graduate skills for an uncertain future. Paper presented at the International Lifelong Learning Conference. Yeppoon, Australia.

Dearing, R. (1997) *Higher Education in the Learning Society. The Report of the National Committee of Inquiry into Higher Education*. Norwich: Her Majesty's Stationery Office.

Delanty, G. (2001) *Challenging Knowledge: The University in the Knowledge Society*. Buckingham: OUP.

Halsey, A. H., Lauder, H., Brown, P. and Wells, S. (2003) *Education: Culture, Economy and Society*. Oxford: Oxford University Press.

Harrison, R. (1996) Personal skills and transfer: meaning, agendas and possibilities, in R. Edwards, A. Hanson and P. Raggatt (Eds) *Boundaries of Adult Learning*. London: Routledge.

Harvey, L., Moon, S. and Geall, V. (1997) *Graduates' Work: Organisational Change and Students' Attributes*. Birmingham: The University Of Central England, Centre for Research into Quality.

Hesketh, A.J. (2010) Recruiting an elite? Employers' perceptions of graduate education and training. *Journal of Education and Work*, 13 (3), 245-271.

Jackson, D. (2016) Re-conceptualising graduate employability: The importance of pre-professional identity. *Higher Education Research and Development*, 35 (5), 925–939.

Land, R. (2004) *Educational Development Discourse, Identity and Practice*. Buckingham: OUP.

Mason, G., Williams, G. and Cranmer, S. (2009) Employability skills initiatives in higher education: What effects do they have on graduate labour market outcomes? *Education Economics*, (17) 1, 1–30.

Mayhew, K., Deer, C. and Mehak, D. (2004) The move to mass higher education in the UK: Many questions and some answers. *Oxford Review of Education*, 30 (1), 65–82.

Nair, C.S, Patil, A. and Mertova, P. (2009) Re-engineering graduate skills – a case study. *European Journal of Engineering Education*, 34 (2), 131–139.

Nicol, D. (2010) *The Foundation of Graduate Attributes: Developing self–regulation through self- and peer-assessment*. QAA Scotland. Enhancement Themes Qualification Publications, Glasgow.

O'Donnell, P. Rakhshani, B. Rae, A. and Smith, B. (2016) *Adopting Research-Based Case-Studies to Nurture and Develop Transferable Skills and Attributes within the Context of Degree Level Aircraft and Aeronautical Engineering*. Teaching and Learning Academy, University of the Highlands and Islands.

Pagal, M. (2012) *Wired for Culture: Origins of the Human Social Mind*. New York: W. W. Norton and Company.

Peng, L., Zhang, S. and Gu, J (2016) Evaluating the competency mismatch between Master of Engineering graduates and industry needs in China Studies. *Higher Education*, 41 (3), 445–461.

Pritchard, R. (2004) Humboldtian values in a changing world: Staff and students in German universities. *Oxford Review of Education*, 30 (4), 509–528.

QAAS (Quality Assurance Agency for Higher Education Scotland) (2016) Thematic Report on Enhancement-led Institutional Review (ELIR) Reports 2013–16: Employability and Graduate Attributes. Glasgow: Quality Assurance Agency for Higher Education.

Rakhshani, B. (2012) On the Search of New Engineering Curriculum Model for the 21st Century. Annual Enhancement Themes National Conference, Edinburgh Conference Centre, Heriot-Watt University, 7–8 March, 2012. http://www.enhancementthemes .ac.uk/docs/presentation/search-new-engineering-curriculum-model-for-the-21st-century.pdf. Accessed 14.09.16

Rowland, S. (2006) *The Enquiring University. Compliance and Contestation in Higher Education.* Maidenhead, Berkshire: SRHE/OUP.

Takashi, S. and Saito, E. (2013) Unravelling the process and meaning of problem-based learning experiences. *Higher Education*, 66, 693–706.

Tladinyane, R. and Van der Merwe, M. (2016) Career adaptability and employee engagement of adults employed in an insurance company: An exploratory study. *SA Journal of Human Resource Management*, 14 (1), 1–9.

Trede, F., Macklin, R. and Bridges, D. (2012) Professional identity development: A review of the higher education literature. *Studies in Higher Education*, 37 (3), 365–384.

York, M. (2006) *Employability in Higher Education: What it is – what it is not.* York: The Higher Education Academy.

Chapter 3

The Self-Aware Graduate

Ruth O'Riordan and Sophie Morrison

Introduction

In this chapter, a case study of Careers Service–led credit-bearing education at the University of Dundee will be discussed to illustrate that self-awareness is the key to graduate employability and that this essential foundation can be successfully enhanced through careers education in order to ensure that graduates are prepared for their futures. It is written from the perspective of a University Careers Service which delivers a variety of credit-bearing modules designed to enhance careers and employability opportunities. The chapter will seek to argue that a well-developed self-awareness is crucial to enable graduates to reach their full potential.

Having an awareness of one's strengths, weaknesses, interests, abilities and aspirations allows students to make well informed and realistic decisions. While many a career has been launched through happy accident many others have floundered and we believe that career planning is too important to be left to serendipity and chance. The transition from undergraduate to graduate is a process – a process that requires attention and support. Giving students the space, guidance and tools to develop their self-awareness while at university is crucial – a vital part of their learning journey.

Self-Awareness

'Self-awareness' is a term that may be familiar to many who work or learn within the higher education context. However, agreement on what this complex term means and clarity on how to meet the challenges of developing it are less universal. The University of Warwick Counselling Service (2016) asserts that

> self-awareness is about learning to better understand why you feel what you feel and why you behave in a particular way. Once you begin to understand this concept you then have the opportunity and freedom to change things about yourself enabling you to create a life that you want.

Steiner (2014) usefully summarises:

> Self-awareness is generally seen as an inwardly focused evaluative process in which individuals use reflection to make self-comparisons to reality and the feedback of others. The goal of the self-awareness process is to create better self-knowledge, make adjustments and improvements, and accommodate for weaknesses.

In social psychology, discussions relating to self-awareness often refer to Shelley Duval and Robert Wicklund's landmark 1972 theory of self-awareness. Duval and Wicklund (1972) state that self-awareness is the ability to identify, process and store information about oneself. Mead (in Brown, 1998) comments that self-awareness is related to inwardly focussed attention and more specifically how this increased knowledge is used to interact with others with particular reference to the ability to use of perspective (Brown, 1998). Duval and Wicklund (1972) discuss at length the importance of comparing current behaviours to our internal standards. Self-awareness should not be confused with self-consciousness but a level of consciousness of self is necessary to allow someone to become an objective evaluator of themselves (Duval & Wicklund, 1972).

Self-awareness, however, goes further than introspective consideration of one's thoughts, feeling and behaviours. The application of self-awareness and the understanding of the actions we take under different circumstances – for example, students who panic under pressure and bury their heads in the sand versus students who don't enjoy pressure or deadlines but know how to handle such circumstances – are highly valuable. Students lead busy lives with a variety of competing priorities, and taking time to stop and consider where they are now and where they want to go cannot be underestimated. As Leary (2004: 5) highlights, "Perhaps the most important consequence of having a self is the ability to plan. All planning requires the ability to think about oneself so that one can play out various future events and imagine the consequences of one's actions".

The journey towards self-awareness is a process. We purposely use the language of 'process', as it would be unhelpful to assert that someone is 'entirely self-aware' and the progression is complete: "being self-aware is challenging and a lifelong effort" (Guber, 2015). 'Being self-aware' can be true perhaps for a short space in time, but when circumstances, hopes, fears, external influences, priorities, constraints or plans change, then the process resets and the journey of discovery resumes anew. The ability to be introspective in a non-judgemental manner and then apply this knowledge can be bewildering for undergraduates. Supporting students to develop the tools to enhance their self-awareness in times of decision, transition, personal development and future planning is desirable and something that universities, as the producers of graduates, cannot ignore.

Why Does a Graduate Need to Be Self-Aware?

"You will need only half the information you thought you would need about the job market, but twice the amount of information you thought you would need about yourself" (Bolles, 2011: 180).

'Employability' is a well-used term within higher education that is increasingly recognised by students as a vital component in their tertiary education. Employability has been described as being "about having the capability to gain initial employment, maintain employment and obtain new employment if required" (Hillage and Pollard, 1998: 1). For Hillage and Pollard, one's employability depends on four interconnected factors which can be summarised as

• the individual's skills, knowledge and attitudes;
• their ability to deploy these abilities, and the ways in which they choose to do so;
• self-presentation; and
• the social context and personal circumstances the individual is operating within (ibid.).

Yorke and Knight's (2006: 3) definition is widely quoted and still used today:

A set of achievements – skills, understandings and personal attributes – that make individuals more likely to gain employment and be successful in their chosen occupations, which benefits themselves, the workforce, the community and the economy.

To be able to fulfil the above and enhance their employability, it is clear that graduates will need to be able to articulate their key employability skills and graduate attributes to future recruiters/selectors. Long term success depends on how well equipped students are to identify and articulate their own development with respect to personal, academic and career achievements both now as undergraduates and throughout the rest of their lives (Cole and Tibby, 2013). Being self-aware isn't about navel gazing – it's about being able to be flexible in how you respond in different situations (Goleman, 2015) and being able to use this self-knowledge to enhance one's own career aspirations. "If we are not skilled in self-awareness processing we cannot effectively learn about ourselves and our own personal needs, strengths and weaknesses" (Steiner, 2014).

The traditional notion of a 'job for life' has all but disappeared. Graduates need to be prepared to be much more mobile in the workplace. Research carried out by recruitment specialists *LV=* in 2014 reports that "workers have, on average, nine jobs and one complete career change, moving roles every five years" (*LV=*, 2014). Being self-aware will make such transitions between roles, organisations and new learning more straightforward. During the last decade graduate recruiters began to look for graduates with well-developed emotional intelligence. Emotional intelligence is the ability to identify and manage emotions (Goleman, 1995) and is thus clearly linked to self-awareness. However, it is more concerned with emotions (rather than aptitudes and character) and how we react in certain situations alongside how we respond to others' reactions. Self-awareness, along with self-regulation (or self-management), empathy, social skills and relationship management are the key components that make up emotional intelligence (Larizadeh, 2013). It is argued that of these four, self-awareness is the most important construct in emotional intelligence (Steiner, 2014). Thus, a person with high levels of emotional intelligence is more likely to be self-aware.

Employers regularly say they need candidates who are more self-aware, who understand exactly what they have to offer to their chosen industry and how to deliver it. An applicant who is able to articulate their key graduate attributes and unique selling points will clearly stand out in a competitive recruitment process. Hewlett Packard Enterprises involve all their new hires in structured 360-degree feedback which asks the new graduate to think about what they are good at, and their manager and coworkers are then asked to contribute. The Graduate Talent Manager commented:

> At Hewlett Packard Enterprise we are very focused on helping our graduates move from being reflective learners to reflective practitioners and during their initial onboarding and continued support this is a key theme. All staff complete 360° reflection and feedback during their annual performance and career conversations, and we build an awareness and understanding of the benefits of this, for both the individual and the organization, into the graduate development programme. No matter what role the graduate ultimately goes on to perform they will leave the graduate programme with improved emotional intelligence, familiarity with the benefits of becoming self-aware in the professional community, as well as other soft and hard skills ranging from presentation skills to building a Virtual Machine and coding! We believe that this helps them identify what role they want to perform in the business, to stay longer and enjoy what they are doing, as well as understanding what can sometimes be an unwieldy apparatus as we conduct performance and career management on a large scale and lets them be active, aware participants rather than it being done to them!

> (Iain Davidson, Graduate Manager, Next Generation Workforce Programme, HP Enterprise Services Defence & Security UK Limited, 2016)

It is also worth briefly noting the concept of 'mindfulness' which has gained significant currency in recent years. Kabat-Zinn (2003: 145) describe it as "the awareness that emerges through paying attention, on purpose, in the present moment, and nonjudgmentally to the unfolding of experience moment by moment". A clear link to self-awareness can obviously be observed and welcomed but the theory of mindfulness is clear that it is focused entirely on the self and that changes to meet external influences, pressures, directions and perhaps even the requirements of recruiters is not welcomed. Therefore, mindfulness is a useful starting point on the self-aware career planning journey, but the concept of self-awareness goes beyond this to set this journey within a wider context.

For the journey towards career choice and career readiness, Bolles (2011: 181) asserts, "Most job-hunters who fail to find their dream job, fail not because they lack information about the job-market, but because they lack information about themselves". This indicates the direct relevance of self-awareness to career planning but a university module in 'self-awareness' or with such a concept in the title is unlikely to have a broad appeal to today's intrinsic learner. Therefore, students need to have such learning opportunities integrated into modules, where the principle is clearly linked to future employability, is relevant and is therefore of perceived value. As asserted earlier, developing self-awareness is a process and this process will take time. Students need to be supported to make sense of the range of information available (Watts et al., 2002) and to "sense, sift, act" (Gothard et al., 2001: 25).

Can Self-Awareness Be Taught? A Case Study of Credit-Bearing Careers Education at the University of Dundee

The University of Dundee offers a range of credit-bearing careers modules where students engage with a variety of tools to enhance their self-awareness. Using a case study approach this section will discuss the theory underpinning the teaching of self-awareness and will illustrate how self-awareness is taught, assessed and ultimately learned by students. Careers and employability learning are most effective when they are embedded in the curriculum and supported by "structured processes that develop the ability for self-reflection" (Pegg et al., 2012: 27). The Career Planning Module and subsequent modules developed by the Careers Service at the University of Dundee allow students to see the worth of careers learning by giving it the same status as all other modules which contribute towards their degree: required and integrated learning interactions, assessment and credit. If careers learning is not made explicit to students, they may not recognise that they are doing it and therefore may fail to fully grasp this learning. As Knight (2003: 5) puts it, "When employability-enhancing elements are only tacitly present, students' claims to employability are seriously compromised".

The University of Dundee Careers Service's first careers education module, the Career Planning Module, was offered in academic year 2004/5 in response to a desire to embed careers education within the University curriculum and enhance its perceived importance for students by rewarding effort with academic credit. The full range of careers education currently offered by the University of Dundee Careers Service can be seen in Table 3.1.

All the modules in Table 3.1 have been devised with reference to the Joint Association of Graduate Careers Advisory Services (AGCAS) and Higher Education Academy (HEA) Subject Benchmark Statement for Careers Education. This Statement defines careers education as follows and makes a clear link to self-awareness:

> Those formal processes that empower individuals to identify, develop and articulate the skills, qualifications, experiences, attributes and knowledge that will enable them to make an effective transition into their chosen futures, and manage their careers as lifelong learners, with a realistic and positive attitude. (AGCAS/HEA, 2005: 2)

Table 3.1 University of Dundee Careers Service Credit-Bearing Employability Module Provision

Module Name	Student Source	Level of Study	Compulsory or Optional Module	Module Launched
Career Planning Module	Open to any student where their degree pathway permits	2nd year undergraduate	Optional	2005
Internship Module	Open to any student where their degree pathway permits	2nd year undergraduate	Optional	2006
Career Planning Module Online	Open to any student where their degree pathway permits	2nd year undergraduate	Optional	2010
Internship Graduate Certificate	Postgraduate students	Postgraduate Certificate	Compulsory modules form complete programme of study	2010
Business Management Internship Module	BSc Business Management students	2nd year undergraduate	Compulsory	2011
Career Management for Law Student	LLB Law students	2nd year undergraduate	Optional	2013
Careers & Enterprise Module	BEng Engineering students	3rd year undergraduate	Compulsory	2015
Careers & Enterprise Module	BSc Life Science students	2nd year undergraduate	Optional	2016

Theoretical Basis

The University of Dundee careers education model is influenced by the theoretical perspective of Bill Law and Tony Watts, known as the 'DOTS' theory. In the late 1970s, Law and Watts first presented their theory of the four key tasks which careers

Table 3.2 DOTS summary based on the work of Law and Watts (1977)

Decision making:
The skills and knowledge learners acquire in order to increase their decision making abilities. This includes learning about decision making styles and processes, developing decision making skills (e.g. sorting and sifting information, ordering and prioritising and seeing the consequences of their decisions).

Opportunity awareness:
Learners' ability to make sense of the full range of career-related opportunities available to them and identify priorities and constraints related to these opportunities.

Transition learning:
Learners' ability to acquire the skills needed to manage transitions from one phase of their career (school, in Law and Watts' original theory) to another (e.g. work). This could be a range of practical skills to help them secure their next opportunity, for example CV writing skills, interview technique, and communication skills. It can also mean helping the learner to assess and make sense of the differences between stages and to transfer knowledge or skills from one stage to another.

Self-awareness:
The ability of learners to develop their own sense of understanding about themselves; their interests, personal characteristics, desires and needs, personality, strengths and abilities, weaknesses and limitations.

education should set out to achieve: decision-making skills, opportunity awareness, transition learning and self-awareness, which are summarised in Table 3.2 (Law and Watts, 1977).

Self-awareness was seen as crucial to the career learning journey:

> To incorporate a self-awareness component into a careers education programme is to pay attention to the importance of the self-concept in the facilitation of career preferences and choices. (Law and Watts, 1977: 2)

Without this attention to the development of self-awareness in learners, careers education will always remain external to learners – something they have to undertake in order to understand where the world has a place for them, rather than an internalised and empowering decision-making process about where they wish to fit into the world.

This recognition of the importance of self-awareness in careers education led Law and Watts to later present their theory in a different configuration, which made the ordering of and links between the tasks more explicit. Thus, today, these four tasks are more often referred to by the acronym SODT, rather than the original DOTS, with the following being cited as the most useful order to learn these skills:

1   Self-awareness
2   Opportunity awareness
3   Decision–making skills
4   Transition learning

With self-awareness at the forefront of our teaching, the SODT model provides the principal founding theory of Careers Service–led credit-bearing education at the University of Dundee. The AGCAS/HEA (2005: 3) Careers Education Benchmark Statement asserts that the SODT model of careers education is the "most widely used framework in the UK" and that "careers education should be congruent with, and encompass as a minimum, all these four elements, if it is to enable students to implement fully informed and sound career plans" (ibid.).

Since the early days of Law and Watts's original theory, careers education theories have developed and diversified, yet the influence of the SODT model is clearly still evident in several of these. Many of these later developments in careers theory have proved highly useful in developing a nuanced and workable theoretical basis for the University of Dundee Careers Service's education programme. Theories which the University of Dundee Careers Service pays cognisance to are summarised in Table 3.3.

Table 3.3 Supporting Models Recognised by the University of Dundee Careers Service in Addition to the SODT Model

The SOAR Model (Kumar, 2007)	• *Self,* • *Opportunity,* • *Aspirations,* • *Results.* "The focus on Self enables individuals to discover and build their unique identity positively and proactively, through effective participation in learning Opportunities both within and outside the formal curriculum, and to form realistic personal Aspirations based on sound information, achieving more intentional Results as they move towards and beyond transition points." (Kumar, 2007:14)
The USEM Model (Yorke & Knight, 2006)	• Understanding - Appropriate subject knowledge, apprehension and applicability • Skills - Subject-specific and generic abilities • Efficacy beliefs - Awareness and understanding of one's self and one's abilities • Metacognition - The ability to reflect on and regulate one's own learning and behaviour
CareerEDGE Model - A Model of Employability (Dacre Pool & Sewell, 2007)	• Career development learning • Experience (work & life) • Degree subject knowledge, understanding and skills • Generic skills • Emotional intelligence

Even from these brief summarises, it is evident that self-awareness is at the heart of all these theories, demonstrating the central role self-awareness must play in an individual's career planning journey. All careers education at the University of Dundee follows the principle of interactive teaching methods espoused in the AGCAS/ HEA (2005: 5) Careers Education Benchmark Statement: "Facilitative teaching styles that encourage and model an open and honest exploration of the career planning process are often particularly suited to the subject matter". The Statement encourages careers educators to ensure that learners are "personally engaged with learning" (ibid.: 6) by taking account of different learning styles, using content that brings the world of work to life and giving opportunities for experienced-based learning. The University of Dundee Careers Service modules seek to achieve this personal engagement through a wide variety of teaching methods, some examples of which are given in Table 3.4.

Self-Awareness in Action: A Career Planning Journey

"Seek first to understand then to be understood" (7 *Habits of Highly Effective People*, habit 5 [Covey, 1989]).

The value and strengths of integrated careers education are clear, but how does structured careers-focussed learning help students develop their self-awareness? In her brief paper for the Higher Education Academy (HEA), Kumar (2012: 1) invites readers to examine her view "that 'self-concept' is the key that opens the portal to employability development". She goes on to say that "when students identify and appreciate their strengths in a broad, holistic frame, they invariably report an increase in self-confidence and self-efficacy beliefs, resulting in positive energy to deal with personal and professional development needs" (ibid).

Table 3.4 Examples of Learning Approaches undertaken by the University of Dundee Careers Service

Learning Approach:	Example:
Taking account of different learning styles	Small group discussions, class debates, individual reflection, written exercises, informal presentations, practical team-building or communication exercises. Often all occurring within one session.
Bringing the world of work to life	Employer-led mock interviews and employers as guest speakers.
Work-based learning	Short part-time internships and longer full time internships.
Experienced-based learning	Carrying out employer interviews for a job-study report.

"This module made me realise that I have a lot of experience and knowledge on some aspects that I didn't realise I could use" (Second-year Career Planning Student)

Within the credit-bearing careers modules at the University of Dundee a number of interactive timetabled sessions encourage students to explore their 'Personal Factors of Career Choice' and in some cases this exploration of self takes up the first third of the module content. Personal factors of career choice include transferable skills and personal attributes, interests, personality and values. The validity and relevance of the time taken to consider these vital factors is impressed on students by making clear links with future career prospects and long-term career, and ultimately life, satisfaction. The learning in this section is varied in its delivery; students are provided with online interactive materials, paper-based worksheets, thought-provoking discussion starter questions, theoretical concepts and reflective written tasks. It is particularly important when considering self-awareness that students are allowed to explore what is important to them. A directive approach would be detrimental to the students' learning.

When asked to give a message to students considering undertaking the module, a 2015 Career Planning Module student commented: "If you engage in this module fully, you will learn about yourself and your options as well as preparing yourself for your career when you leave university."

Career decision making has to start with self. The first timetabled session in our Career Planning Module for level 2 students is a broad overview of all of these factors alongside consideration of a range of theories of career choice, so that students can understand why we ask them to engage in these topics and also to switch their thinking to these notions over the coming weeks. We ask students to reflect on their decision of subject choice at university; the processes taken to reach this milestone decision are often still fresh in their minds and provide a useful starting point to allow students to reflect on their thought processes and the elements of self-awareness (and external influences) that came into play.

A second-year Career Planning Module student in 2016 commented:

> The most useful part of the course for me was around identifying and doing assignments on your soft skills/employee skills and unique selling point. This is something you just don't think about while at university, so it is good practice to begin developing a Word document that categorises your STAR style strengths, weaknesses, unique points and listing your evidence of things you have done to back each skill up. I can now use this in the future to great effect, as I understand my own skills far better and far more clearly because of this course.

Students are then taken on a supported journey which addresses each of the factors in much more detail. Firstly students consider their interests and values. Using quizzes, worksheets, discussions and card sorts they rank the importance of the different facets of these factors and eventually end up with a list of those interests they wish to capitalise on and those values upon which they will not compromise. Values and interests are factors that many students will have considered in the past, e.g., 'I'm studying Geography as it was my favourite subject at school', or, 'I want a job that pays lots of money'. We ask them to consider where these thoughts and decisions have come from, ask them to quantify them and consider the implications of them for their future. We encourage them to reflect on their choices to date, and we appreciate how they prefer to make decisions and think outside of their comfort zones. In considering their priorities and constraints (whether real or perceived), they start to open up to each other and to their tutors, and valuable dialogues ensue. The ability to articulate their hopes, aspirations, limitations and visions in relation to interests and values is challenging for some, and it is important to recognise that this is not a finite process that ends at a set point of the module. These first steps in self-awareness are hugely supported, and the narrative of employability allows students to see the value in taking time to inwardly reflect.

Students explore their own personality type (using resources including the Myers Brigg Type Inventory and Insights Discovery™) and learn to appreciate the value that a mix of personality types has to a team as well as begin to recognise the strengths they wish to capitalise on and promote to prospective recruiters or post-graduate study providers. This element of self-awareness also allows students to become aware of the differing personality types of others and how this will influence their interactions with them. Students are also encouraged to become more aware of how different situations impact on their actions: for example, stress, conflicting priorities, success or failure.

> It helped me think about how my skills linked to jobs and also how I can frame my personality and qualities towards a job opening too. (Second-year Career Planning Module Student, 2015)

> The Internship Module helped me reflect upon myself and acknowledge the strengths and weakness I have. (Second-year Internship Module Student, 2016)

Next they consider transferable skills and personal qualities. Students are asked to review in groups a varied collection of job adverts and person specifications from across a range of sectors in order to both ascertain why we place importance on this factor and also to discover which skills are asked for repeatedly and which are more niche. The students are then taught about the concept of evidence and the importance of being able to prove their aptitude and ability at their identified skills and attributes. Students then engage with the University of Dundee's Dundee Plus Award (an online tool for enabling students to record, reflect upon and gain recognition for the development of their skills and graduate attributes; more information about the award can be found at http://www.dundee.ac.uk/careers/resources/dundeeplus/). Using Dundee Plus, students are assessed on their ability to write evidence summaries using the STAR technique (Situation, Task, Action and Result).

This is the first step in assessing self-awareness articulation, and for many students will be first time they have had to write reflectively in a structured format. When marking and awarding credit for such an exercise, it is important to be transparent with students and reassure them that we are assessing their ability to reflect and articulate their self-awareness in a structured manner.

> I found the Skills Evidence Worksheet to be really useful. It is now saved on my computer renamed as an 'Employee Skills Profile'. Although I have reformatted it as well so I can continually add in new skills and have a saved document in which I can easily copy and paste to future application forms (obviously with some editing to make them join up with the applicable application form). (Second-year Career Planning Module Online Student, 2015)

> This was a fantastic way to develop skills in career planning. I did not realise just how simple it was to collate all your positive experience to your benefit. Has helped me feel more confident in future. (Second-year Career Planning Module Student, 2015)

Awarding Academic Credit

But why assess reflection and the development of self-awareness at all? At this point it may be valuable to briefly consider the value in awarding academic credit to self-awareness tasks and to employability modules more generally. The value to students of undertaking exercises such as skills reflection is clear from the quotes above from our students. Therefore, it is crucial to ensure this value is recognised by students to ensure their engagement with such activities. As Yorke and Knight (2006: 3) state, success in teaching employability is dependent on "the extent to which students see a 'pay-off' for the effort that they put in". That payoff is most readily understood as achieving grades/awards, and it is the reason why the Careers Service at the University of Dundee strongly believe in the value of summative assessment for careers learning. This view is echoed by Pegg et al. (2012: 33), who state: "It is clear that assessment can be used strategically to motivate and engage students, and carefully chosen assessment tasks can help develop specific employability attributes".

Although "effective development of employability is incentivised by using assessment" (ibid.), it is crucial that this is the right type of assessment, and this may not be the traditional or typical university assessment tools. Pegg et al. urge educators to explore non-traditional types of assessment for employability, voicing a "concern that traditional assessment systems might frustrate the development of personal skills" (ibid). They recommend "realistic tasks" (ibid) as suitable assessment tools for employability. Using Biggs's (2016) theory of constructive alignment, we start with the outcomes we intend students to learn, and align teaching and assessment to those outcomes. The Careers Service at the University of Dundee seeks to ensure its assessment tools are fit for purpose and that they encourage self-awareness.

Thus, we actively seek out non-traditional assessment methods to ensure employ-ability is being taught and learned in the most effective way. Some of these assess-ment methods are explored in the Practice Guide at the end of this chapter.

Teaching Self-Awareness

Just as innovative methods of assessing self-awareness must be sought out, so too must we seek out nontraditional methods of teaching self-awareness and employ-ability (Yorke, 2010). This should mean a move away from traditional lectures to group work, work-based learning and more. However, it is also crucial to foster mutual respect and ensure everyone feels safe and encouraged to engage with their self-aware career planning journey. From observing and interacting with students in university settings, it is clear that self-awareness can be influenced and indeed impacted by a range of external factors. Such factors include an individual mak-ing comparisons with others and then labelling of these interactions; e.g., 'She is much more confident than me'. Feedback from others can have a hugely positive or negative impact on an individual's self-awareness. For example, language used in feedback or comparisons made in tutorials. The development of self-awareness amongst undergraduates can be seen as a personal growth tool which is rooted in developing a resilient mindset. So while it may be true that another person is truly 'much more confident than me', the value in self-awareness training is to recognise this but also appreciate the 'but' or 'and' as a connector in this sentence with the addition of 'I have excellent listening skills that are of value'.

When teaching self-awareness, it must be emphasised that resilience and the abil-ity to cope with change are key components of this. During our modules, we are mindful to regularly tell students that circumstances change, both personally and through external factors. We are careful to ensure that students learn the tech-niques of assessing themselves that can be reapplied as necessary. As Kumar (2012: 1) concludes:

> Self-awareness is a dynamic learning journey as self develops, values, aspirations and circumstances change. We may set a linear collective direction within cur-ricula, informed by generic and relevant employer and tutor requirements, but for each student the journey will also have deviations, revised and re-visited learning outcomes – and reaching 'the destination' will be the point for further goal-setting.

Teaching in our careers modules includes a full session that is dedicated to personal effectiveness – confidence, assertiveness and the ability to perform tasks outside of one's comfort zone. Discovery requires risk (Berkun, 2012: 2). Take the painfully shy undergraduate who finds interacting with peers difficult and speaking in public extremely uncomfortable: having this pointed out, probably not for the first time, in a learning environment does not mean that student will suddenly have the skills to be able to deal with it. Students regularly report to us a perceived 'fear' of delivering presentations, performing in interviews and life after graduation in general, to name a few. Identifying these fears, putting them into context and illustrating a range of coping strategies help students to become more self-aware and allow them to approach decisions with more confidence.

A small longitudinal study undertaken by the University of Dundee which surveyed students in 2014 after they had completed a careers module in academic year 2008/9 asked the question, 'In what ways has the Career Planning Module contributed to your career journey to date?' One response was that

> it gave me a lot more confidence at the time and helped me secure my part time job which helped me get to where I am today.

Additionally, a current undergraduate student commented:

> In my opinion it is a very enriching and unique experience which gives you the opportunity to look inside yourself in terms of the future transition to the labour market.

When done effectively, teaching self-awareness skills will avoid leading students to merely beat themselves up or develop lengthy lists of negative comparisons with others and will instead frame self-awareness as a tool to constructively engage in personal growth. Likewise, group learning environments can be developed in such ways as to empower all students into proactive self-improvement and increased self-awareness.

Practice Guide

A logical starting point for anyone seeking to embed self-awareness into the curriculum is the learning outcomes of the module or interaction. To help students develop their self-awareness, it is crucial to be mindful that every student approaches this from a different perspective and will have a different starting point or level of self-awareness. Self-awareness is not a fixed entity, and learning outcomes should not seek to assess this concept in terms of reaching an end-point – the aim is not for the student to reach a desired level of self-awareness and then desist from self-awareness-developing activities. Rather, self-awareness is a holistic way of thinking and it is crucial to help students develop a picture of themselves that they can use as a foundation to build on as they progress through university and beyond. Students must be encouraged to learn the techniques to understand themselves and to develop the ability to apply and reapply these.

The learning outcomes for the main Careers Service modules at the University of Dundee are given in Tables 3.5 and 3.6.

Writing learning outcomes related to self-awareness is challenging. Being specific and measuring when students have met these outcomes can be complex, as there is a need to acknowledge the personal development and individual starting point

Table 3.5 Career Planning Module Intended Learning Outcomes

I   Identify and articulate your transferable skills and reflect on areas for development

2   Describe the Factors of Career Choice and their personal application to you

3   Research and assess post-graduation options using a range of resources

4   Effectively demonstrate your communication and presentation skills by presenting information tailored to an audience

5   Analyse employer requirements and be able to articulate your skills and experience tailored to this

6   Successfully participate in a mock competency-based interview

Table 3.6 Internship Module Intended Learning Outcomes

I   Evaluate learning from your internship placement

2   Identify and articulate the development of transferable skills and reflect on areas for improvement

3   Analyse employer requirements and be able to articulate your skills and experience in a tailored manner

4   Successfully participate in a mock-competency based interview

5   Effectively demonstrate your communication and presentation skills by presenting information tailored to an audience

of each student. Therefore, the Careers Service at the University of Dundee takes the approach of embedding self-awareness in all our learning outcomes, rather than 'tacking on' a self-awareness criterion to existing learning outcomes. Students are explicitly taught the skills of self-awareness during delivery of the modules, while the ability to be self-aware is implicitly required for success in the assessments. Take, for example, the learning outcome "describe the factors of career choice and their personal application to you". This requires students to understand the importance of the breadth of the factors and to consider in depth how these factors impact their own career choices.

Students are helped to meet this learning outcome through a series of taught classes and assessments. Elements of self-awareness in the taught classes have been explored earlier in this chapter. Here we shall examine one of the key assessments of the Career Planning Module in relation to its ability to support the development of self-awareness – the Job Study. As a foundation to completing this assessment, students are required to understand the factors of career choice and give due consideration to Opportunity Awareness (from the SODT model). Students are given space to consider all the options available to them. Without this scheduled time in the time table, many students leave career choice to their final year or beyond and then find it challenging to understand and meet recruitment requirements, such as the need for work experience and high-quality evidence of skills and graduate attributes. Students spend a full 2-hour class considering professionalism in the workplace and working cultures; what is the world of work actually like, and how do they envisage spending their working career? Enhanced self-awareness gives students the ability to make realistic judgements about their suitability to different career paths.

Following supported self-analysis and career sifting the students then choose one career to investigate in detail. There is a wealth of research available surrounding career decision-making but this is not the place to dissect this. It is, however, relevant to note that recent qualitative research carried out for the Department for Business Innovation and Skills concluded:

> The career decision-making process that individuals used was affected by the extent to which they explored wider options for work and learning, and the extent to which they looked ahead and reflected on and understood their own interests and preferences. (Gloster, 2013: 16)

Students engaging in careers modules at the University of Dundee are encouraged, and indeed required, to reflect on themselves initially and use this improved self-awareness to start thinking about their decisions for the future. We wholeheartedly believe that starting to consider careers without firstly exploring self is pointless.

Once they have chosen a career to investigate, students must then make contact with someone doing this role and carry out an interview to find out what it is like to work within their chosen career. They are required to prepare a factual and reflective report based on their findings. Although many students report feeling anxious at the thought of this exercise, the outputs at the end are highly valuable. Many students gain work experience, work shadowing and a networking contact or a mentor who can help them with choices in the future. For example, a student who interviewed the forensic psychologist at a prison was offered the chance to work shadow; a student who interviewed a zookeeper at a wildlife park successfully gained a prestigious 4-month placement; and a very shy second-year student who lived at home and had never had any work experience secured a one-afternoon-a-week position shadowing a teacher in a local secondary school. Academic credit and marks are awarded for the students' ability to write a comprehensive, structured and factual report. Our external examiner commented in 2014: "This is a highly appropriate assignment, in the context of the aims of the module and students are well supported carrying out the work".

The second element of this assessment is self-reflective; students are asked to reflect on their personal factors of career choice and conclude if the career they have investigated is a good match for them. A significant level of self-awareness is vital for this element of the report – it would be impossible to self-assess without some level of self-awareness. This formalised reflection, which is a key part of the marking criteria, encourages students to set aside how much they enjoyed meeting their interviewee and makes them consider the facets of the role in order to reach a well-reasoned assessment of their suitability for the career. We emphasise to all students that this is not their 'life decision' made; they have learned how to research and assess a career and apply their enhanced self-awareness in a practical situation. These skills can be applied and re-applied as needed as individuals' progress through the different stages of their career.

In the Careers Service we encourage students to be reflective in their writing. The assessment criteria for an A grade in the self-reflective section of the Job Study assessment reads: *Extremely clear evidence of linking of all five factors of career choice to the suitability of the job. Extremely clear understanding of the requirements of the job. Excellent in-depth reflection on suitability/interest (or lack of) in the career area.* Thus, students are not assessed on their ability to pick a career to investigate that suits them, or on the level of abilities they have that match this job, but rather they are assessed on the extent to which they reflect upon the chosen career, their awareness of their abilities and their capacity to reflect upon these abilities.

The requirement for self-reflection continues into the more practical section of the module which focusses on presentation skills, CV and cover-letter writing, application form completion and interview techniques. We regularly link back to the factors of career choice and illustrate to students the importance of articulating their strengths, interests, skills, abilities and chosen career choice in a focussed and positive manner. Written recruitment-style submissions are required to be targeted with a clear focus on strengths and evidence thus again requiring high levels of self-awareness for success. The Application Form assignment involves the completion of a personal statement which requires students to carefully demonstrate the suitability of their skills, personal attributes and experiences for the job applied for. The final assessment is a face-to-face graduate interview with a real graduate recruiter. We use a range of volunteer recruiters from an assortment of industries who take the students through a videorecorded 25-minute competency-style mock interview for a vacancy chosen by the student and using the student's completed application form. For both these assessments, success is dependent on the accumulation of self-awareness and the ability to articulate personal strengths and skills to potential employers.

Given the opportunity to reflect upon the module five years after completion, former students commented:

> I have looked back on the notes from the session a couple of times to help me with applications.

> I remember the mock interview being particularly helpful.

> The assessed interview as the most valuable session – it was great to have the interview without the pressure of it being real.

> The mock interview – it gave me some pointers which I used in my first proper interview.

Similar benefits are understood by students immediately upon completing the modules too. Final comments in 'End of Module' evaluations demonstrate this:

> In my opinion it is a very enriching and unique experience which gives you the opportunity to look inside yourself in terms of the future transition to the labour market.

> The course is a great confidence builder.

> I would 110% recommend this module. It is so helpful in preparing you for applying to Graduate Schemes and jobs and understanding how to make yourself employable.

These words, from just some of the undergraduates who have participated in our modules since their inception in 2005, demonstrate the very real, highly practical and continually applicable benefits of a self-awareness-focused approach to careers education.

Conclusion

As can be seen from the student voices above, students grasp the importance of self-awareness in relation to their future career planning. This chapter aimed to present a case study of Careers Service–led credit-bearing education at the University of Dundee, detailing its development and the theoretical underpinning of the Law and Watts SODT model. By setting out in detail the typical learning activities and assessments of Careers Service–led education at the University of Dundee, we have demonstrated that through a combination of highly interactive learning material, work-based and work-related learning opportunities and nontraditional assessment tools, self-awareness can be explored and developed with the result of enhancing students' abilities to plan and manage their career decision making and career transitions as they progress from undergraduate to graduate.

References

AGCAS/HEA (Association of Graduate Careers Advisory Service / Higher Education Academy) (2005) *Careers Education Benchmark Statement*. Sheffield: AGCAS/HEA.

Berkun, S. (2012) *Can Self Awareness Be Taught?* Available: http://scottberkun.com/2012/can-self-awareness-be-taught/. Accessed 28.06.16.

Biggs, J. (2016) *Constructing Alignment*. Available: http://www.johnbiggs.com.au/academic/constructive-alignment/. Accessed 23.06.16.

Bolles, R. N. (2011) *What Color Is Your Parachute? A Practical Manual for Job-Hunters and Career-Changers*. Berkley: Ten Speed Press.

Brown, J. D. (1998) *The Self*. Boston: McGraw-Hill.

Cole, D. and Tibby, M. (2013) *Defining and Developing Your Approach to Employability: A Framework for Higher Education institutions*. York: HEA.

Covey, S. R. (1989) *The 7 Habits of Highly Effective People*. London: Simon & Schuster UK Limited.

Dacre Pool, L. and Sewell, P. (2007) The key to employability: Developing a practical model of graduate employability, *Education + Training*, 49 (4), 277–289.

Duval, S. and Wicklund, R. (1972) *A Theory of Objective Self-Awareness*. Oxford: Oxford University Press.

Gloster, R. (2013) Adult Career Decision-Making: Qualitative Research. *BIS Research Paper* 132. Available: https://www.gov.uk/government/uploads/system/uploads/attachment_data/file/252087/bis-13-1183-adult-career-decision-making-qualitative-research.pdf. Accessed 06.08.16.

Goleman, D. (2015) *How Self-Awareness Impacts Your Work*. Available: http://www.danielgoleman.info/daniel-goleman-how-self-awareness-impacts-your-work/. Accessed 28.05.16.

Goleman, D. (1995) *Emotional Intelligence*. New York: Bantam Books.

Gothard, B., Mignot, P., Offer, M. and Ruff, M. (2001) *Careers Guidance in Context*. London: SAGE.

Guber, P. (2015) *Self-awareness is the most important skill for career success*. Available: https://www.linkedin.com/pulse/i-were-22-self-awareness-most-important-skill-career-success-guber. Accessed 25.05.16.

Hillage, J. and Pollard, E. (1998) Employability: Developing a Framework for Policy Analysis. *Research Brief DFEE*. Available: http://webarchive.nationalarchives.gov.uk/20130401151715/http://www.education.gov.uk/publications/eOrderingDownload/RB85.pdf. Accessed 06.08.16.

Kabat-Zinn, J. (2003) Mindfulness-Based Interventions in Context: Past, Present, and Future. *Clinical Psychology: Science and Practice*, 10 (2), 144–156. Available: http://www-psych.stanford.edu/~pgoldin/Buddhism/MBSR2003_Kabat-Zinn.pdf. Accessed 28.05.16.

Knight, P. (2003) Briefings on Employability 3: The Contribution of Learning, Teaching and Assessment and Other Curriculum Projects to Student Employability. ESECT. Available: http://www.qualityresearchinternational.com/esecttools/esectpubs/knightlearning3.pdf. Accessed 28.05.16.

Kumar, A. (2007) *Personal, Academic and Career Development in Higher Education: SOARing to Success*. Available: http://cw.routledge.com/textbooks/professional/978041542360-1/data/Kumar-Chapter1.pdf. Accessed 14.05.16.

Kumar, A. (2012). Threshold Concepts in Employability Curricula. The Higher Education Academy. Available: https://www.heacademy.ac.uk/system/files/artikumaremployabilityarticle.pdf. Accessed 28.05.16.

Larizadeh, A. (2013) *Forget Business School: Why an Emotional Education Is Indispensable*. Available at: http://www.forbes.com/sites/avidlarizadeh/2013/07/08/forget-business-school-why-an-emotional-education-is-indispensible/#6e85f51f6d70. Accessed 28.05.16.

Law, B. and Watts, A.G. (1977) *Schools, Careers and Community: A study of some approaches to careers education in schools*. London: Church Information Office.

Leary, M. R. (2004) *The Curse of the Self: Self Awareness, Egotism, and the Quality of Human Life*. Oxford: Oxford Scholarship Online.

LV=. (2014) *Goodbye to the Job for Life: We Take 9 Jobs over 50 Years*. Available: http://www.lv.com/about-us/press/article/job-for-life. Accessed 28.06.16

Pegg, A., Waldock, J., Hendy-Isaac, S. and Lawton, R. (2012) *Pedagogy for Employability*. York: Higher Education Academy.

Steiner, P. (2014) *The Impact of the Self-Awareness Process on Learning and Leading*. Available at: http://www.nebhe.org/thejournal/the-impact-of-the-self-awareness-process-on-learning-and-leading/. Accessed 29.05.16

University of Warwick Counselling Service. (2016) *Self Awareness*. Available: http://www2.warwick.ac.uk/services/tutors/counselling/informationpages/selfawareness/. Accessed 25.05.16.

Watts, A. G., Law, B., Killeen, J., Kidd, J. M. and Hawthorn, R. (2002) *Rethinking Careers Education and Guidance: Theory, Policy and Practice*. London: Routledge.

Yorke, M. (2010) Employability: Aligning the message, the medium and academic values. *Journal of Teaching and Learning for Graduate Employability*, 1 (1), 2–12.

Yorke, M. and Knight, P. (2006) *Learning and Employability Series One: Embedding Employability into the Curriculum*. York: HEA.

Chapter 4

The Resilient Graduate

Jill Shimi and Gaye Manwaring

Introduction

This chapter explores the concept of resilience as a graduate attribute, structured under the four strands of resilience in the Robertson Cooper model: confidence, adaptability, purposefulness and social support (Robertson and Cooper, 2013). Our understanding of resilience comes from our experience as lecturers in higher education, our personal philosophies and our study of relevant literature. We believe resilience combines inner strength with the ability to deal positively with challenges. We are concerned with all students and with the processes leading to their personal growth and development. We consider how staff members in different disciplines foster resilience among their students, discussing how students can be empowered to understand and develop their own resilience to enable them to react appropriately to change and uncertainty.

Definitions of Resilience

Many common phrases refer to resilience: Keep calm and carry on. Out of your comfort zone. Hang in there. Suck it up. What doesn't kill you makes you stronger. We use metaphors when discussing support: safety nets, apron strings, helping hands. The boingboing resilience project uses the telling phrase "Beating the odds whilst also changing the odds" (Hart, 2013).

Mansfield et al. (2012: 35) say, "Resilience involves dynamic processes that are the result of interaction over time between a person and the environment and is evidenced by how individuals respond to challenging or adverse situations." They discuss the importance of personal strengths, coping skills and the role of professional context in the development of resilience. However, Aburn et al. (2016: 1) conducted a literature review on resilience and concluded that "there is no universal definition of resilience adopted in the research literature."

Our operational definition is: resilience is the development of the skills and abilities to transform challenges into opportunities for growth.

Resilience as a Graduate Attribute

Universities are under increasing pressure to provide graduates who are not only proficient in their subject areas, but who also have the skills to navigate their way through a world of continuous change. The Higher Education Academy (2015) organises these skills into the following categories: literacies, competencies and character qualities. Resilience features as a character quality alongside curiosity, initiative, persistence and adaptability. According to Stallman (2011: 121), "students must develop the ability to handle future situations ... To cope effectively in a changing world and also think creatively and innovatively it is therefore imperative that students are resilient." Resilience is a complex quality which includes several components and which overlaps several other named attributes. Considering the links between the different aspects, resilience could be seen as overarching, underpinning or interconnecting.

Resilience is often regarded as the ability to do well in the face of adversity and is linked to recovery from trauma (Windle, 2011). It involves the fostering of a positive response in times of major challenge and threat. Indeed much of the literature related to the topic focuses on the ability of individuals to overcome the most devastating of world events and serious personal tragedy: surviving the harsh reality of captivity in wartime, escaping and assisting others as the Twin Towers crumbled to the ground and the rebuilding of lives after the ravages of a tsunami. The resilience of individuals who have to cope with these extreme situations and the more common issues such as redundancy, serious illness and bereavement are just some examples in which the resilience of the individuals concerned has been stretched beyond the norm.

Resilience is, however, much more than the ability to bounce back after major crises and personal grief. It is a dynamic process of positive adaptation that can be developed and enhanced in everyday situations. Resilience is the ability to accept the reality of any challenging situation, to overcome it and to experience personal growth as a result. It is an important graduate attribute which will empower students to become stronger individuals who can respond positively to their particular challenges such as failing an assignment, tension with peers, pressing deadlines, managing change and dealing with uncertainty.

We talked to colleagues about resilience as a graduate attribute and received these comments:

> The ability to bounce back. Life doesn't go on an even keel and it's dealing with that. If something bad happens, dealing with it positively. (Human Resources manager)
> We need people who can function in the real world. It's the ability to cope with unexpected things, stresses at work or in the personal life. (History lecturer)

Students need resilience to get through uni and to equip them to survive in the workplace. (Education lecturer)

Many universities provide lists of graduate attributes, and terms such as 'flexible', 'independent', 'confident', 'adaptable', 'mental resourcefulness', 'autonomy', 'motivated', 'perseverance', 'reflection' and 'awareness of personal strengths and weaknesses' are common. These relate to the importance of resilience in the face of new and changing contexts, and to the self-knowledge needed by graduates.

Some vocations have identified resilience as being especially relevant to their profession. Medical educators have been encouraged "to consider their role in nurturing the '3Rs' in future doctors: responsibility, resilience and resolve" (Eley and Stallman, 2014: 835). They discuss the need for resilience in medical students and its link with wellbeing which helps them to bounce back from challenges. Mansfield et al. (2012) discuss the importance of resilience as an attribute for graduating and early career teachers. McAllister and McKinnon (2009: 1) argue that resilience theory should be part of the curriculum for health professionals to give students "strength, focus and endurance in the workplace".

Resilient students approach challenges with confidence and determination, overcoming obstacles with a variety of strategies which they can then transfer to meet the demands of new situations. Resilience is transformative and empowering. The challenge for academic staff is how to teach, support and assess it. Most tutors can readily conjure up an image of a student who lacks resilience: the student who has failed an assignment, cannot cope with the experience of failure, responds negatively to advice and feedback and who may eventually drop out. The resilient student, however, when faced with a similar situation, accepts the reality of a failed assignment, responds positively, rises to the challenge of passing in the future and seeks guidance to improve the outcome. The following example illustrates a very resilient student:

> A lecturer provided a job reference for a student. The student was interviewed but did not get the job and sent the following email to the lecturer. "I was initially very disappointed, however if this particular role had been meant for me, the outcome would have been different. There is absolutely no point in dwelling on a decision that I cannot change, and instead will use my energies and seize the courage to change the things I can." A few days later the student met the lecturer and explained that she had requested feedback from the interview panel. This had led to an informal chat which had generated the opportunity for work shadowing which might in turn lead to future employment in the organisation.

Models of Resilience

We examined a range of models of resilience and selected a model which identifies four strands of resilience: confidence, adaptability, purposefulness and social support (Robertson and Cooper, 2011). These four aspects relate to our interpretation of resilience being for all students in their daily lives, rather than for damaged individuals in response to trauma. This model incorporates most aspects from other models that are pertinent to university education. The additional elements refer to stress management and spirituality. We also recognise that this model comes from the world of business into which our graduates will enter.

The American Psychological Association (2016) lists ten ways to build resilience:

- Make connections
- Avoid seeing crises as insurmountable problems.
- Accept that change is a part of living.
- Move toward your goals.
- Take decisive actions.
- Look for opportunities for self-discovery.
- Nurture a positive view of yourself.
- Keep things in perspective.
- Maintain a hopeful outlook.
- Take care of yourself.

Some resilience models focus on the connectedness of individuals to the social environment, the physical environment and their inner values (Denz-Penhey and Murdoch, 2008). Staying positive, being reflective, developing emotional insights, taking action and seeking support occur as common features of many lists of resilience factors (Levine, 2011). Stallman (2011) has used a resilience-building program with psychology students based on six components: realistic expectations, balance, connectedness, positive self-talk, stress management and taking action. Mansfield et al. (2012) describe a framework of four dimensions of teacher resilience: profession-related, social, emotional and motivational which relates closely to the Robertson-Cooper model. A study of work-based students identified four aspects related to their success: capacity, collaboration, capability and congruence (Martin, 2016) and an analysis of these terms showed they included purposefulness, personal resilience, social connections, confidence and managing change. A project, carried out at the University of Birmingham's Jubilee Centre for Character and Values, looking at character development in school children includes resilience as a performance character virtue alongside traits such as determination, confidence and creativity, and Walker (n.d.) discusses the importance of personal strength, emotional supported and belongingness.

The Cynefin framework (Mindtools, 2016) looks at four types of systems: simple, complicated, complex and chaotic, yet most higher education courses focus on only the first two. They provide no preparation for dealing with complex or chaotic situations that students may have to face in employment; resilience training could help. Robertson et al. (2015) have shown that training in the workplace can improve personal resilience especially when based on individual needs.

Empirical Study: Eliciting the Views of University Staff

We interviewed a range of staff across the University, adhering to the guidance provided in our institutional ethics policy. We talked to ten academics from vocational and non-vocational disciplines and to six support staff from different services. We asked how they defined resilience and whether they thought it was important as a graduate attribute, and if so how they taught and assessed it. We recorded the interviews and then carried out a thematic analysis of key ideas and a trawl for quotes and vignettes. Some respondents regarded resilience to be the same as stress management whilst others thought resilience was only needed by students with major crises. However, the majority felt it was an important attribute for all students at university and beyond. We have indented quotes from interviewees and have boxed some of the stories they told. Our interviewees used phrases such as "empowered, confident, outward-looking", "blossoming" and "tolerance". They saw resilience as not just a response to problems but a transformative approach to challenges:

> Employers need self-starters who can accept change and challenges and who know themselves. (Work-based tutor)
> Employers need you to think beyond … find a new approach. (Academic advisor)
> Student will need to function in a high stress career: clients are emotional, things do not go smoothly. (Law lecturer)

Confidence

Confidence and self esteem are essential components of resilience (Robertson and Cooper, 2011). Confident individuals have faith in themselves and in their abilities. They respond positively to challenge with the awareness that they possess the personal power required to deal effectively with situations they encounter. They predict that their actions will result in positive outcomes. If they do not achieve their desired results immediately, confident people adjust to their new situations quickly and modify their behaviours appropriately to meet their new challenges. They tend to be solution-focused and highly motivated. Confident students believe that they have the ability to meet their course requirements and to pass assignments. They anticipate success. If they meet with failure, they quickly view the experience as an opportunity to enhance their learning, modifying their approach until they achieve their desired outcome.

> *A student handed in assignment with the words "I am confident enough to pass and self-confident enough to fail." When asked to explain this enigmatic epigram she explained "I think I have met all the criteria but if I fail it will not knock me as I know I can do it on resubmission."*

Biggs and Tang (2007: 32) encourage tutors to motivate students by teaching them to "expect success when engaging in the learning task". The expectation of success is deemed to generate confidence which results in the student engaging in deep learning, and developing a belief that future successes are possible. Feedback is an especially powerful tool in shaping the expectations of students. Biggs and Tang point out that feedback which involves students reflecting on their performance can be extremely useful in promoting positive expectation, particularly when using criterion-based assessment. The tutor is encouraged to help the student to explore what they did, to look at how it could have been done differently and to consider how a better result could be achieved. The student's confidence is developed in this way because they have accepted the reality of their own work and modified it to achieve an even higher standard. Unfortunately, feedback does not always result in the promotion of positivity among students. Those lacking confidence tend to focus on negative feedback, even if it is accompanied by constructive comments.

Norm-referenced feedback in particular, in which students are graded in relation to their peers, has the potential to damage a student's confidence. Being assessed as below average when compared to others on the same course can be discouraging and demotivating and especially for the student whose confidence was low from the outset. It is the responsibility of the tutor to make sure that feedback is delivered in a sensitive and constructive manner. "A valuable act of self-reflection as a teacher is to monitor what you say, how you say it and what comments you write in students' assignments" (Biggs and Tang, 2007: 34).

Staff interviewed in our study spoke of confidence building as an integral part of their programmes. We learned of design students, who have to present their work to a public critique from their peers. Some can find the criticism they receive too harsh and personal. Tutors respond to this by guiding the students to avoid unhelpful thinking habits and to provide supportive advice. The confidence of students was said to rise if the challenges presented were incremental. One lecturer spoke of how unreasonable it would be to expect a student to work at dissertation level without previously providing the necessary scaffolding to foster confidence. In her course, students were taught how to complete a literature review in their first year, carried out fieldwork in the second year and engaged in staff-led research in year three. By their final year, tutors were able to remind them that they already had the skills and abilities required and this was said to boost confidence and improve performance.

Confident students are generally reflective students. They use reflection as a tool to assess their own performance and to improve upon their own personal best. Ghaye (2011) discusses the building of a reflected best-self portrait which links to confident optimism. The Chartered Institute of Personnel and Development (2016) suggests the following reasons for reflection: to encourage individuals to accept responsibility for personal growth; to enable them to see a clear link between the effort invested and the benefits gained; to help people to see value in each learning experience and to assist people to learn how to learn and add new skills over time.

Reflection is undoubtedly a valuable tool in the world of work and the inclusion of opportunities for reflection in academic courses equips students with a very useful transferable skill.

Mentoring is becoming an increasingly popular strategy for building confidence within both academic institutions and the workplace. Mentoring is a supportive relationship which seeks to bring about positive change: "a sophisticated relationship between two people whereby experience and wisdom is used to enable a person to reflect, question and construct actions while being able to tap on doors that would otherwise be closed" (Owen, 2011: 10).

Common features of the mentoring relationship in education include: learning conversations, sharing and reflecting upon practice and a focus on teaching and learning. Mentors are in a position to listen and understand their mentees and it is that connection that leads to change. The mentoring relationship is useful to promote personal growth, professional competence and to foster a deeper understanding of one's potential. In the words of Connor and Pokora (2007: 11): "The central principle is that the learning and change occur through the relationship with a coach or mentor". Mentoring can provide students with an opportunity to build their confidence by assessing their current situations, encouraging reflection, adaptability and goal setting.

The following vignette illustrates the impact that confidence can have on student learning.

> The case of two teacher education students who both received two 'unsatisfactory' grades whilst on professional practice placement demonstrates the difference between a resilient student and one who lacks confidence. Susan and Amy were both just one 'unsatisfactory' grade away from completely failing their first placement. Both met with their tutor prior to their second placement to reflect on their situation with a view to preparing them for their next session in school. Susan had made a note of the two criteria she had failed. She had accessed and read literature related to the criteria and asked the tutor to recommend additional texts. She planned to link the theory to her next professional practice placement and was sure that this would assist her in gaining a pass in these areas in the future. She acknowledged that her performance had not been up to standard but she was enthusiastic about her forthcoming placement and predicted that the work she had done to prepare for it would stand her in good stead.
>
> Her fellow student, Amy also attended her tutor meeting, but with a very different attitude. When Amy was encouraged by the tutor to reflect on her previous experience, she gave a list of the class teacher's failings and blamed her lack of success on a 'personality clash' with her mentor. She felt defeated by her failure to meet the criteria but had done nothing to address her failings. She was not optimistic that the next placement would be better as she feared she would encounter another clash of personalities and that this would result in further failure.
>
> Amy's tutor responded to her negativity using coaching techniques. The tutor acknowledged that personality clashes had happened before, but not often. She accepted that they were unpleasant experiences and that they did have the potential to result in an

unsatisfactory grade. She asked Amy to consider how she would cope if she experienced the something similar in her next placement. With the tutor's guidance Amy devised three strategies she could use: she could explain to the class teacher immediately that she perceived a problem and ask for her help; she could contact her tutor for support and, if the situation continued to deteriorate, she could ask to be transferred to another school. Amy's dread lessened and she no longer felt powerless. She began to consider how she would meet the criteria in her future placement.

Adaptability

Adaptability is one of the cornerstones of resilience as identified by Robertson and Cooper (2011). It includes a range of attributes such as flexibility, perseverance, responsiveness, initiative-taking, autonomy and being proactive. There are also strong links to external motivation, positivity and coping well with change. Ghaye (2011: 76) discusses reflection-for-resilience and talks about people who "are proactive problems-solvers … tackle issues rather than avoid them … keep things in perspective and … know where to look for assistance." Such people have a positive self-image based on self-awareness, self-motivation and self-affirmation, all elements that can be encouraged in students.

The literature contains a plethora of terms related to adaptability but they are not used consistently. Martin et al. (2013) discuss buoyancy and self-regulation and they regard resilience as a sub-attribute of adaptability. They refer to adaptability in regard to uncertainty and novelty, whereas buoyancy and coping relate to adversity. Buoyancy is developed in response to common challenges which link to our interpretation of adaptability as a set of strategies to deal with everyday challenges such as failing an assignment, or arguing with a friend. In a longitudinal study of adolescents, Martin et al. (2013) found that adaptable students were more likely to have positive academic outcomes as well as higher self-esteem.

The idea that adaptability is a positive and active response involving strategy building is explored by Walker et al. (2006). They discuss the importance of the ability to trust oneself and others and that cooperative learning can help students to become more resilient. They recommend encouraging critical debates in class, using problem-based learning and giving speedy formative assessment to facilitate adaptability. Some courses need to foster creativity. Students of design need to develop lots of ideas and see it as a process.

> They need to iterate versions of ideas. Do not settle with one thing but come up with lots of ideas: a fecundity of creativity so if one is rejected they have others to fall back on. (Design lecturer)

Staff that we interviewed used the following terms to explain this aspect of resilience: "cope with unexpected", "need to focus during change", "tenacity", "overcome challenges", "need to think in new ways" and "be proactive not reactive".

Deal with what happens. Cope with the unexpected. Get on and manage complexity. (Humanities lecturer)

Student employability profiles (Rees et al., 2007: 140) identify the following personal capabilities:

The ability and desire to learn for oneself and improve one's self awareness and performance. To be a self-starter (creativity, decisiveness, initiative) and to finish the job (flexibility, adaptability, tolerance to stress) … Maintains effectiveness in a changing environment … Initiative – Identifies opportunities and is pro-active in putting forward ideas and potential solutions. Employers need adaptable workers.

The Enhancement Themes initiative describes several key transition skills including independent learning (QAA, 2015). Staff can structure activities that encourage autonomous learning. Self-directed learning does not mean abandonment by the tutor, but a shift in role and responsibilities. As well as dealing with subject content, it is important to help students to develop generic skills. These include strategies to find resources, to know when to seek help, to plan, prioritise and manage time well. It is essential to persuade the student that these are transferable skills that will help them at university, in their career and in their life. Some feedback sheets are designed to highlight comments related to the specific learning outcomes and content of an assignment as well as the generic learning which can be fed forward to future situations.

Asking questions is a valuable learning tool. Non-resilient students ask tutors about the simplest aspects that they could easily discover for themselves. Academics need to resist the urge to answer the questions but to advise the student about how to find out. One way is to allow students a limited number of questions they can ask. This encourages them to sort the easy ones themselves, work in teams and identify the most important questions to ask the tutor. Apart from saving the tutor time, this builds confidence in becoming an independent learner. Dynamic lists of questions (Cowan, 2003) encourage students to list all the questions they have at the start of a course. As they learn, they tick off some questions, realise that some do not matter or are unanswerable, and add others. The list acts as a measure of their learning and ensures that the items remaining are important aspects that can be discussed with the lecturer. This again builds independence and confidence.

Many students focus on negative feedback rather than positive comments. Tutors try to sandwich constructive criticism between complimentary points, but some students ignore the praise and obsess about the problems. This has less to do with the student's ability or the quality of the work and more to do with the student's need to think positively about how to turn problems around. Tutors need to help the students see that a poor grade is not a disaster but a challenge. With a positive and calm attitude, the student can address the shortcomings and plan a specific way to improve. Staff can use a coaching approach to help students confront problems and learn from failure.

Adaptable learners are more prepared to take risks and realise that they learn out of their comfort zone. Senniger's model of concentric circles has the middle as the comfort zone surrounded by the learning zone, with the panic zone on the outside (CPD, learning development, 2016). The learning zone is exciting, challenging and scary but allows for transformative growth. Sue Watling (2016: 26) describes her response to a changing and challenging situation: "Everything in life is a duality of opposing forces. The skill is finding the balance between them." Watling improved her self-awareness of her own abilities by doing a personal audit and was surprised at how much she had already achieved. This gave her confidence and motivation. The skill for academic staff is to give students experiences that challenge them without panicking them and then provide tools that evaluate and evidence their accomplishments.

One of the authors of this chapter interviewed a distant learner whose grades had dropped after two years of high marks. She explained that she now had a young baby and her priorities had changed. She knew exactly how hard she had to work to pass but did not do anything extra. She was a strategic learner who had adapted her approach to study to suit her changed circumstances.

Academic work can be structured to provide situations that force students to deal with change and unexpected problems. A course on planning gives students a project lasting several weeks. Each week the initial brief is modified as the planning regulations are modified or the client makes changes or key materials are delayed. The final assessment looks at how the student reacts to the changes without getting too stressed or being rude to people involved. Professional behaviour in a difficult situation is a key employability attribute, every bit as important as design skills. The success of this approach is partly down to the way the tutor explains that obstacles will be introduced to simulate real life, and that students need to be self-aware of their reactions and responses.

Social work students may face ethical stress while on placement when they feel disjuncture between their own values and the managerialist approach they are expected to follow. Tutors model appropriate behaviour and encourage students to discuss their moral courage and to consider how far they can put their values into practice by positive action and confronting issues. This approach should be more explicit in terms of learning outcomes and assessment criteria in the course documents.

Law students engage in mock interviews with actors portraying emotional clients with difficult legal issues. Here their soft skills are tested as much as their legal knowledge. The interviews are captured on video for review by peers and tutors, and the students keep a reflective blog of the whole experience. The students find they are uncomfortable in this unpredictable situation but they appreciate the benefits later. Time management is also essential in training for such a high-stress profession, and this means students cannot be perfectionists.

Students respond to stress in different ways. Resilient learners understand their stressors and deal with them by taking action rather than ignoring the problems (Richardson et al., 2012). Some students ask for mitigating circumstances to be considered time and again. These habitual users are resilient in that they have learned to work the system, but this will not help them when the systems are different when they are in a job.

Extra-curricular activities often provide challenges such as The Duke of Edinburgh's award scheme, and students return from abseiling or camping in the rain feeling energised and able to tackle new unrelated challenges. The Dundee Plus Award (University of Dundee, 2016) encourages students to engage in activities such as running societies and volunteering to develop skills and enhance their employability. They collect evidence and gain the award, which adds to their CV. This personal skills development programme recognises and adds value to activities outside the degree courses. It helps students to develop key transferable skills employers are looking for and build self-management, including resilience, adaptability and drive.

The Centre of Entrepreneurship (2017) at the University of Dundee offers a range of activities which develop flexible and adaptable approaches that are transferable and required by future employers. It is managed by students for students and supported by experienced business patrons and runs free workshops and events to develop enterprise skills. An enterprising individual is regarded as active, confident and purposeful – not uncertain and dependent. The Centre helps students to see change as an opportunity rather than a problem and to develop a determined, confident and effective manner.

Purposefulness

Purposefulness was identified by Robertson and Cooper (2011) as an important component of resilience. Having a purpose, being determined and resolute, can propel the student to success. Few individuals would embark on even a short trip without choosing a destination, planning a route, arranging accommodation and having at least a rough idea of an appropriate return date. So it is with student life. The start date of the course is established, the university campus is in a fixed location (even if it is accessed through distance learning), student accommodation is available for those who require it, exam timetables are planned well in advance and graduation is in sight, albeit perhaps 4 years away. The higher education institution has planned a journey for the student. The challenge for the student is to muster the resilience to cope with their new environment and to rise to the rigours of academic life.

In the interviews we carried out it became apparent that tutors were particularly concerned about students who failed to complete their academic journeys. They identified reasons for students failing to complete their courses: "Coming to uni is a huge step which can cause loneliness"; "Students who don't stay on campus are particularly vulnerable"; "Starting university can be overwhelming". Students start their courses with a sense of purpose. They want to get a degree. But many become overwhelmed by the challenges student life presents. Those with a strong sense of purpose, however, weather the storms and achieve their desired result. Students who are purposeful keep their end goal firmly in sight. They tend to use proactive language (Covey, 1992). Instead of the reactive "There is nothing I can do", "That's just the way it is" and "I can't", purposeful people say, "I can choose a different approach", "I will choose an appropriate response" and "I will complete".

Tutors recognised that they have a role to play in facilitating and supporting purposefulness. Some spoke of the support they could give the student on a personal level whilst others considered how they promoted it within their courses. There is much the tutor can do to help the student to maintain their sense of purpose. Encouraging them to clarify their ambitions is a useful starting point. According to Cottrell (2003: 21), "It is the vision that keeps us going when the inevitable unexpected setbacks occur". Students are more likely to maintain their engagement with their studies if they have a picture of the end in sight. Cottrell (2003) encourages students to consider long term goals to foster deferred gratification. They are also urged to create short-term goals along the way to provide opportunities to celebrate success as the student journey progresses. The short-term goals are designed to provide steps to the ultimate goal and help students to maintain their motivation. Similarly, students can be prompted to devise personal mission statements where they identify their main objectives and how they intend to achieve them. They can be encouraged to visualise future success and guided to work towards making their vision a reality. One tutor encourages students "to create self-imposed targets and to tell someone about them so they can chase them up".

Lecturers spoke about the importance of explaining the relevance of course tasks, with one tutor advising, "[D]on't just throw the students in". This tutor advocated the use of small projects at the beginning of the course with bigger challenges later. He presented his students with incremental challenges noting that "at dissertation they have developed all the necessary skills and are implementing them altogether". The students were aware of the purpose of the tasks and that they were leading up to an important piece of work. This knowledge kept them focused and engaged. Another said that he promoted purposefulness within his course through the use of problem solving which mirrored the tasks students would be doing in professional life after graduation. He described putting them under pressure, encouraging them to work together to find a solution. He made sure that the task was time-limited, to add to the pressure. The group had to appoint their own leader and make decisions collaboratively. They were encouraged to "evaluate risk and reflect upon it to build their resilience". These students reported that when they went for job interviews they had high levels of confidence because they had been prepared well with meaningful and relevant tasks throughout their course.

Several tutors in our study discussed the importance of monitoring student attendance. Students who were disengaged and who lacked purpose were identified as those who tended to miss lectures and tutorials. In the words of one tutor, "People struggling drop out, miss deadlines. If we spot this early we can intervene and help". There was general agreement that early identification of failing students, and prompt interventions were vital to get students back on track.

Support

Robertson and Cooper (2011) talk about the importance of building good relationships to enhance resilience. This includes both relationships within the university with staff and other students, and personal relationships with friends and family. Resilience comprises internal protective factors such as self-esteem and confidence that can be enhanced, and external protective factors such as supportive relationships (Jindal-Snape and Rienties, 2016). They explain that good social support can buffer negative academic experiences so universities need to provide opportunities to enhance such positive arrangements. People we spoke with felt that supporting students on an individual basis was important for all and crucial for some. Staff talked of the importance of building supportive relationships with students and of treating them as individuals:

> Recognise their specific contexts and understand the constraints and enablers for each person. (Work-based tutor)
> Reinforce that they learn from experience; even failure. (Careers advisor)
> They need space to learn to cope. (Student advisor)

There was also a strong sense that too much support was counterproductive. Phrases such as "spoon-feeding" and "molly-coddling" were accompanied with a look of disapproval, since discomfort and dissatisfaction are useful spurs to action. The metaphor of a tightrope walker seems appropriate: a harness is too restrictive but a safety net gives confidence as well as protection. If we push the analogy further, tutors also provide the rope (the learning experiences), the ringmaster (facilitation and supervision) and the audience (encouragement).

Resilient students know when and how to seek support. They are aware of their own abilities and know when it is the right time to ask for help. They also realise that working together is a strength, not a weakness. Tutors and peers give immediate feedback on ongoing product design but these conversations are not seen as feedback by the students as the comments are not written down. The tutors should encourage the students to make notes of the key points. One course for work-based students asks them to set up their own support network and to consider the best person to provide each type of support (see Table 4.1). This analysis is a valuable training.

Distance learning offers many advantages but can cause students to feel isolated, so online courses are usually designed to include peer discussions and support. Students are encouraged to share ideas and comment on the views of others. For some, this provides a welcome feeling of community, while others do not engage but focus just on the content of the learning materials. Some more strategic learners become lurkers, observing the interactions without contributing.

Tutors try to move students from dependence to independence, but it is important to go further and to nurture interdependence (Covey, 1992). Employers want recruits who can work collaboratively as part of a team. The resilient student develops the power to know when to be dependent, when to be independent and when to be interdependent. Some courses include group projects and include teaching and assessment linked to effective teamwork. Learners need to know how to monitor their own behaviour and the performance of the team. Preparatory tasks can include the identification of preferred roles, yet the greatest learning and resilience come when students deliberately take on a non-preferred role.

Many courses encourage buddies when older students support those in earlier years in the programme. Distance learning programmes encourage students to find their own local mentor. These individuals offer both support and challenge, helping the students to develop their full potential, gain confidence and feel empowered. The importance of social networks in helping international students cope with transitions is discussed in depth by Rienties and Jindal-Snape (2016). They have compiled some recommendations for practice and suggest they apply equally to all students. They include the following approaches that may alleviate stress and help students adapt more easily:

- Provide information about academic life in advance with, e.g., videos of places and people, interviews with current students, clear handbooks, regulations, expectations.
- Offer help with daily life related to accommodation, shopping, travel, food, medical care etc.
- Set up a buddy system with peer learners, students already on the course, alumni and local residents.
- Provide appropriate training for tutors so they can recognise the individual difficulties their students face.

The University of Dundee offers a scheme called Peer Connections in which trained student volunteers provide a welcoming and mentoring service to help students settle in. The mentoring process is valuable to all involved and helps the mentee, the mentor and the organisation. Motivation theory shows how important it is to have a sense of being accepted into a group, and the boingboing resilience framework (Hart, 2013) has "belonging" as a key strand.

The Financial Services advisors at the University of Dundee (n.d.) find that money worries can get in the way of academic success. They have developed an ingenious tool called Oscar the Pig which stimulates conversation and problem solving (see Practice Guide Table 4.4). The acronym OSCAR stands for Objective, Situation, Choices, Action and Reflect as a process to structure discussion and planning. It not only deals with the immediate challenge but helps students to develop a flexible approach to crisis management and self-management.

Developing appropriate social interactions helps students to become more emotionally intelligent. Clubs, societies and student union events can be crucial in helping students fit in and find friends. There have been suggestions that activities such as attending religious services regularly and group events like laughter yoga can improve well-being and resilience largely due to the social interactions and positivity. Technology and social media allow interactions to be global and asynchronous, so that support is ongoing and isolation should be avoidable. Social support is a key aspect of resilience, and this needs to be recognised by all parties. A wide range of support is required to meet the differing needs and students need to know how and when to access help. The support systems work much better if they are built on a personal relationship, which takes time and continuity. Jindal-Snape and Rienties (2016: 11) explain that

> resilience is dynamic and changes across context and time … educational and life transitions can incur stress … it is the responsibility of the university to provide opportunities to develop strong social and academic networks to enhance students' resilience.

Implications for Practice

It seems to be generally accepted that resilience is an important attribute both at university and in a career. Universities provide a wide range of support services that help students with a range of academic and personal challenges. Yet these systems often tend to be reactive rather than proactive, and to provide interventions rather than foster empowerment. We believe that resilience should be part of the formal curriculum and that the aims, learning experiences and assessment should be aligned to develop resilient practices. For this to be effective, the whole notion of resilience needs to be made explicit. Students should appreciate that there are skills and strategies that they should understand and practise. Metacognition is required to understand their strengths and weaknesses, so they are empowered to take appropriate decisions and make relevant plans.

Metacognition (i.e., thinking about thinking) can be taught, and students can be encouraged to analyse their behaviour, emotions and motivations and to develop effective strategies. The Resilience Audit (see Practice Guide section below) has been used with several groups of student who found it useful and empowering, leading to practical action plans. Covey (1992) explains techniques of time management and prioritisation to deal with challenge. The Johari Window is a powerful self-awareness tool that can help students develop their emotional intelligence. Lecturers can encourage students to reflect on their experience and their learning and to record their ideas using journals and blogs. These methods can make students more resilient and make them more aware of their resilience; i.e., meta-resilient. This was summed up by a member of support staff:

> Students do not know about the support systems that are available and they do not know when to ask for help. The University needs to become serious about resilience. (Academic supporter)

McAllister and McKinnon (2009) suggest that educational experiences can be designed to help students be more creative and to think more critically, that senior colleagues should discuss decision-making and ethical issues and that approaches such as mentoring and shared storytelling can facilitate reflection. Such strategies would require changes in policy, practice and culture but could lead to organisational development. We have included a Resilience Grid in the Practice Guide together with some of the collated suggestions from members of staff.

We would like to make the following recommendations about resilience as a graduate attribute:

For the institution

- Provide coherent resilience training for staff, both for personal development and to help them support their students.
- Build resilience into the curriculum content.
- Continue to provide relevant inputs for students such as stress management.
- Continue to offer a range of coordinated student support services that are well advertised.

For the staff

- Teach resilience as a topic and as a set of skills within courses.
- Make it explicit in learning outcomes and assessment criteria.
- Develop supportive individual relationships with students.
- Relate teaching, assessment and support to students' strengths, needs and contexts.

For students

- Learn about resilience as a topic.
- Develop your own resilience.
- Help your peers to become more resilient.
- Find ways to demonstrate your resilience to prospective employers.

Conclusion

We have tried to represent resilience development as a diagram (Table 4.1) which shows the process and progression from entry into higher education, through the four facets of resilience, leading to a person who is fully aware of his or her own

Table 4.1 Resilience as a Transformative Process

>>>>> INCREASING RESILIENCE >>>>>		
Previous experiences	Confidence	Metacognition
Personal characteristics	Adaptability	Self esteem
Current challenges	Purposefulness	Personal growth
	Social support	Professional development

potential and uses a range of strategies to function effectively in an uncertain world.

Resilience is a holistic attribute which affects all aspects of a student's life: academic, professional, personal and interpersonal. Resilient students strive, survive and thrive on challenges and are aware of the transferable strategies they have. The University of Dundee provides various approaches to encourage resilience (see Table 4.4) but falls short of including resilience as a feature of the core curriculum.

Many approaches to resilience training are designed to help combat disadvantage. There are programmes and initiatives for looked after children, ethnic minorities and young offenders, but few strategies for whole institutions or whole communities. The boingboing project (Hart, 2013) in partnership with the University of Brighton has developed a resilience framework and designed a variety of training materials for use with disadvantaged groups. The University of Birmingham's innovative approach to character education in schools (Wright et al., n.d.) has created useful resources on resilience and other virtues. These ideas could be translated into higher education, but they will be effective only if they are accompanied by a cultural change that regards resilience as a key attribute for all and plans resilience training and assessment as an integral part of the main curriculum. An elastic waistband needs to become a Lycra garment.

Helping students become more resilient will help them to become authentic and critical learners and "develop visions of themselves that are strong enough to sustain them throughout all their lives" (Walker et al., 2006: 262). "The challenge for higher education is to help and enable learners to become agile in the way they view and respond to the world ... they will encounter disruptions that require them to be resilient" (Jankowska, 2016: 48). Confident, purposeful, adaptable, socially supported people create confident, purposeful, adaptable, socially supported organisations, and resilient organisations create resilient people.

Our final quote comes from the authors of the resilience model we have used in this chapter, Robertson and Cooper (2013: 2) "We must keep a focus on graduate resilience and wellbeing throughout degree programmes ... encouraging individuals to develop and reflect on their coping techniques." Students need to become meta-resilient, staff need to integrate resilience training into the core curriculum, and the institution needs to become a resilient community.

References

Aburn, G., Gott, M. and Hoare, K. (2016) 'What is resilience? An integrative review of the empirical literature'. *Journal of Advanced Nursing* 72 (5): 980–1000,

American Psychological Association. (2016) *The Road to Resilience*. Washington, DC: American Psychological Association.

Biggs, J. and Tang, C. (2007) *Teaching for Quality Learning at University*. Maidenhead: Open University Press.

Chartered Institute of Personnel and Development, The. (2016) *What is reflective learning?* http://www.cipd.co.uk/cpd/reflective-learning.aspx. Accessed 22/09/16.

Connor, M. and Pokora, J. (2007) *Coaching and Mentoring at Work*. Maidenhead: Open University Press.

Cottrell, S. (2003) *Skills for Success: The Personal Development Planning Handbook*. London: Palgrave Macmillan.

Covey, S. (1992) *The Seven Habits of Highly Effective People*. London: Simon & Schuster.

Cowan, J. (2003) *Curriculum Development*. http://www.control.aau.dk/~lpj/PBL/PhD2012e/Cowan-bookletCD.pdf. Accessed 22/09/16.

CPD, learning development (2016). https://digitalacademicblog.wordpress.com/tag/senningers-learning-zone-model/. Accessed 03/02/17.

Denz-Penhey, H. and Murdoch, C. (2008) 'Personal resiliency: serious diagnosis and prognosis with unexpected quality concerns'. *Qualitative Health Research* 18 (3): 391–404.

Eley, D.S. and Stallman, H. (2014) 'Where does medical education stand in nurturing the 3Rs in medical students: Responsibility, resilience and resolve?' *Medical Teacher*, 36 (10): 835–837.

Ghaye, T. (2011) *Teaching and Learning through Reflective Practice*. London: Routledge.

Hart, A. (2013) *Resilience Framework*. www.boingboing.org.uk. Accessed 22/09/16.

Higher Education Academy. (2015) *Literacies, competencies and character qualities*. https://www.heacademy.ac.uk/search/site/literacies%2C%20competencies%20and%20character%20qualities. Accessed 22/09/16.

Jankowska, M. (2016) 'Pathways through life: Development at the junctions, inflections, disruptions and transitions of life'. *Lifewide Magazine* 16: 43–48.

Jindal-Snape, J. and Rienties, B. (2016) 'Multiple and multi-dimensional transitions of international students to higher education: Setting the scene'. In D. Jindal-Snape and B Rienties (Eds) *Multiple and Multi-Dimensional Transitions of International Students to Higher Education* (pp. 1–17). London: Routledge.

Levine, I.S. (2011) *Mind Matters: Resilience*. http://www.sciencemag.org/careers/2011/06/mind-matters-resilience. Accessed 22/09/16.

Mansfield, C. F., Beltman, S., Price, A. and McConney, A. (2012) '"Don't sweat the small stuff": Understanding teacher resilience at the chalkface'. *Teaching and Teacher Education* 28: 357–367.

Martin, A.J., Nejad, H.G., Colmar, S. and Liem, G.A. (2013) 'Adaptability: How students' responses to uncertainty and novelty predict their academic and non-academic outcomes'. *Journal of Educational Psychology*, 105 (3): 728–746.

Martin, K. (2016) *Work, think, learn: Crossing boundaries in continuing professional learning*. University of Dundee Doctoral Thesis.

Mindtools (2016) *The Cynefin Framework*. https://www.mindtools.com/pages/article/cynefin-framework.htm. Accessed 22/09/16.

Owen, H. (2011) *The Complete Guide to Mentoring*. London: Kogan Page.

QAA (Quality Assurance Agency). (2015) *Transitions Skills and Strategies*. Glasgow: QAA.

Rees, C., Forbes, P. and Kubler, B. (2007) *Student Employability Profiles: A Guide for Higher Education Practitioners*. (2nd ed). York: Higher Education Academy.

Richardson, A., King, S., Garrett, R. and Wrench, A. (2012) 'Thriving or just surviving? Exploring student strategies for a smoother transition to university. A practice report'. *The International Journal of the First Year in Higher Education*, 3 (2): 87–93.

Rienties, B. and Jindal-Snape, J. (2016) 'Multiple and multi-dimensional transitions of international students to higher education: A way forward'. In D. Jindal-Snape and B. Rienties (Eds) *Multiple and Multi-dimensional transitions of international students to higher education* (pp. 259–283). London: Routledge

Robertson, I. and Cooper, C. (2013) *Resilient graduate series – 3. Recruitment, development and resilience.* http://www.robertsoncooper.com/blog/entry/resilient-graduate-series-3-recruitment-development-and-resilience. Accessed 22/09/16.

Robertson, I. and Cooper, C. (2011) *Well-Being: Productivity and Happiness at Work.* Basingstoke: Palgrave Macmillan.

Robertson, I.T., Cooper, C.L., Sarkar, M. and Curran, T. (2015) 'Resilience training in the workplace from 2003 to 2014: A systematic review'. *Journal of Occupational and Organizational Psychology*, 88 (3): 533–562.

Stallman, H. M. (2011) 'Embedding resilience within the tertiary curriculum: A feasibility study'. *Higher Education Research and Development*, 30 (2): 121–133.

University of Dundee. (2016) *Dundee Plus Award* http://www.dundee.ac.uk/careers/resources/dundeeplus/. Accessed 22/09/16.

University of Dundee. (n.d.) *Oscar the Pig.* University of Dundee Student Services.

Walker, C., Gleaves, A. and Grey, J. (2006) 'Can students within higher education learn to be resilient and, educationally speaking, does it matter?' *Educational Studies*, 32 (3): 251–264.

Walker, D. (n.d.) *How can resilience be developed in UK schools?* Birmingham: The Jubilee Centre for Character and Values, University of Birmingham.

Watling, S. (2016) 'Changing jobs, changing institutions, changing my future: The ecology of transition, learning and development'. *Lifewide Magazine*, 16: 24–27.

Windle, G. (2011) 'What is resilience? A review and concept analysis'. *Reviews in Clinical Gerontology*, 21 (2): 152–169.

Wright, D., Morris, I. and Bawden, M. (n.d.) *Character Education: A taught course for 11 to 16 year olds.* Birmingham: The Jubilee Centre for Character and Virtues.

Practice Guide and Resources

1. Student Resilience Audit

Table 4.2 can be used by students on an individual basis to monitor their resilience development.

Score yourself on each aspect from low (1) to high (6). Find ways to make the low scores higher. The high scores may contribute to a lack of balance in your life, so think of ways to reduce them slightly.

Table 4.2 Resilience Audit Grid

	1	2	3	4	5	6
Independent						
Making plans						
Conscientious						
Confident						

	1	2	3	4	5	6
Collaborative						
Positive						
Sociable						
Motivated						

2. Resilience Grid

This tool can be used by individual members of staff or by course teams. It can be an audit or a planning aid.

Complete the grid in Table 4.3 with your own examples and discuss it with your colleagues and students.

Table 4.3 Resilience Grid

Resilience attribute	Student	Staff	Organisation
Confidence			
Purposefulness			
Adaptability			
Social support			

Table 4.4 shows a compilation of some of the responses from staff members.

Table 4.4 Resilience Grid Completed by Staff

Resilience attribute	Student	Staff	Organisation
Confidence	Reflection Peer interaction Social media Build a list of achievements	Mentoring Reflection tools and tasks Feedback and feedforward Be positive Acknowledge distance travelled Formative comments Clear tasks and guidelines	Academic Skills Personal development planning Optional workshops on stress management, procrastination, time management. Encourage self care Mentoring schemes

(continued)

Table 4.4 Resilience Grid Completed by Staff (continued)

Resilience attribute	Student	Staff	Organisation
Purposefulness	Set goals Short term goals Weekly planner Use the library	Action plan tools Feedback Learning log Examples of planning Increase independent learning	Online portfolios Academic Skills Career guidance Volunteer opportunities
Adaptability	Take risks Manage stress Keep an open mind Challenge self-perceptions Tolerance of change Reflect on strengths and weaknesses	Challenging tasks Role play Incremental challenges Relaxation techniques Clear expectations. Clear notice of change	Allow for risk Flexible delivery Tailored assignments Appeals & mitigating circumstances board Varying exit points Resits & extensions, Cater for different study styles Provide open spaces and quiet areas
Social support	Identify own network Ask for help Join societies and clubs Develop hobbies	Group tasks Peer networks Support network tool Build relationships Communication skills Be approachable	Time for staff Social spaces Counselling Disability Service Chaplaincy Students' union Peer support system

Although you are studying at a distance, you are not alone. There are numerous people, resources and activities to help you. Each of you needs to identify and develop your own support network which meets your needs and suits your lifestyle and workplace.

This diagram shows some possibilities but you should draw your own network and be as precise as possible. Put the names of specific people and consider the role they will play. Talk to them about it. There is a lot of skill in knowing how to use the different elements in your network efficiently. Identify three particular types of support you might need during your course, and choose where you would seek the specific support within your network. Store it in your Journal.

3. Developing and Using a Support Network (Figure 4.1)

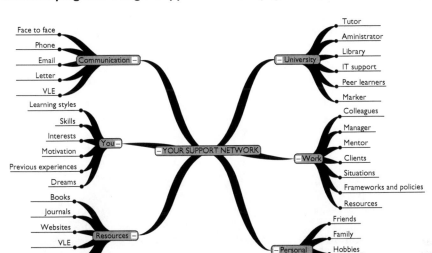

Figure 4.1 Network Diagram.

This is an extract from an online module

4. Oscar the Pig

Table 4.5 shows online advice offered to students supported by face-to-face discussions by Student Services at the University of Dundee. Apart from being a cute pig, the *Oscar* name is an acronym for a standard set of coaching skills: Objective, Situation, Choices, Action, Reflect.

Table 4.5 OSCAR

Objective	*Identify what you want to achieve*
Situation	*Consider all possible ways of achieving your goal*
Choices	*Identify the best solution for your situation*
Action	*Create a written plan of how your choices will meet your goal*
Reflect	*Reflect on your actions within your situation to determine if you have achieved your goal or not. If necessary revise your choices and try again*

Chapter 5

The Agile Graduate

Glynis Gibbs and Jackie Malcolm

Glynis ✓ Gibbs

Introduction

Increasing diversity and participation from under-represented groups is a key tenet of Further Education (FE) policy in the UK today. In Scotland this is supported through the Post-16 framework established in 2012 to signpost and facilitate pathways for every young person in the country, identifying key responsibilities for all stakeholders (Scottish Government, 2012). As a result, six articulation hubs were established throughout Scotland to aid the movement of learners from school to colleges and onto universities, with universities taking a more active role in the transition process, providing additional routes into higher education (HE) (Universities Scotland, 2013).

There is a growing literature linked to both the general transition to university (QAA, 2008) and more specifically the transition between the FE and HE sectors. Emergent themes include the role of identity (Briggs et al., 2012) and student expectations, hopes and fears (Christie et al., 2006). In particular, the differences in learning, teaching assessment and feedback are well documented in several studies, for example, Briggs et al. (2012), Yorke and Vaughan (2013) and the Higher Education Academy (HEA, 2012). In several studies the fear of isolation, the need for tailored help and a support structure to aid the smooth transition are also noted (see Leese, 2010).

In this chapter we consider the experiences of a group of learners progressing from FE colleges to levels 2 and 3 of a Graphic Design course at Duncan of Jordanstone College of Art and Design (DJCAD), University of Dundee. Firstly, we will examine some of the theoretical discourse around 'Learning Agility' (De Meuse et al., 2010; DeRue et al., 2012; Lombardo and Eichinger, 2000) and discuss the concept, important to the transition of the individual. Secondly, we discuss the relevance of Further Education as a 'steppingstone' to Higher Education (HE) and examine the skills perceived by students to be valuable when preparing them for study at tertiary level. The chapter then discusses, through the lens of reflexivity, the individual intent to 'change' and be 'different' through a transformation of the 'self' across space and time.

Methodology

This empirical study adopted qualitative methods to examine and identify key themes emerging from the transitioning into HE of students from FE colleges. Interviews were conducted with seven graphic design undergraduate students at DJCAD: two students, Isaac and Simon, had been direct entrants to level 2 within the Graphic Design pathway and had recently completed their first year at HE; two students, Gill and Keith, had been direct entrants to level 3 and had completed their first year of study at HE; and three students completed their honours degree, with Billy and Kevin having been direct entrants at level 2 and Theresa at level 3. Names have been changed to provide anonymity to the students who participated in this study.

The limitations of this study are acknowledged; however, due to the nature of the course, there is a long history of direct entrants from FE into HE, and it is understood there are significant differences in skills at level 2, between those students who have progressed from level 1 into the Graphic Design pathway, and the direct entrants from FE. This experience provided the research study with a rich source of data from which to draw contextual information relating to pedagogical approaches in both FE and HE, drawing comparisons from core skills development, whilst observing the way in which individuals can transform the 'self' through such a transition in their educational journey.

Interviews were conducted with each participant, with a set of predetermined questions framing the conversation:

1 Before joining college, what were your expectations regarding studying at college?
2 How did you find the transition from college to University, and did you encounter any difficulties?
3 How did your 1st year of study at University compare to your expectations?
4 Do you expect 2nd year to be any different? If Yes, explain in what ways you expect study to be different.
5 What skills do you think you have gained during your studies?
6 Looking forward to next year and study at university, do you foresee any differences in the following:
   - Your expectations
   - Your tutors' expectations of you
   - The level of study
   - The amount of effort and work needed by you
7 What additional skills do you think university level study will give you that you feel you didn't get at College?

Use of Giddens's (1984) Theory of Structuration as the theoretical framework, provided the research with a rigorous understanding of constructs affecting the transition of participants through institutional spaces. Anthony Giddens's theoretical framework provides us with an understanding of society and how its institutional constructs such as education, working environments and communities enable the individual to act. *The Constitution of Society* (ibid.) offers an explanation for social scientists to process the ways in which 'social life' exists. Understanding what triggers human action and interaction within institutional environments, has provided this study with an insight into the landscape of modern society and the individual, as he or she transitions through space and time. Giddens's focus is very much given to the "understanding of human agency and of social institutions" (ibid.: xvii). Social life is a process, from birth to death, but what influences the ways in which we live our lives, as we transition from home to education, from education to work, and the social constructs that shape the interactions that occur within this landscape, is conceptualised by Giddens in his 'theory of structuration'. The flow of day-to-day life and the capacity of the individual, or in Giddens's term the 'human agent' (ibid.: xxii), to be reflexive within the context of social interaction, provides the 'human agent' with knowledge that can impact on his or her ability to act and respond. Such actions will be influenced by the social structures in which the individual is engaged, either through conscious acts or through 'practical consciousness'. Giddens suggests that the 'practical consciousness' is immersed in the routines of day-to-day life; that is to say, they are conscious acts that the human agent conducts due to habit. In other words, a set of circumstances that happen as a direct result of the routine of everyday life means the human agent or individual will automatically act without thinking in a particular way. This is knowledge that is acquired over 'time' and within social 'spaces'.

Giddens's notion of the duality of 'time and space', shaping the way in which we 'act' within a particular social space, in our case, educational landscapes, allowed us to analyse the research findings and acknowledge the impact of temporal dimensions. Giddens suggests that "time in this case is the time of the body, a frontier of presence quite different from the evaporation of time-space inherent in the duration of day-to-day activity" (ibid.: 35). This notion of 'time-space' in relation to the 'self', shaped the observations analysed through the interviews, and allowed us to consider ways in which the 'self' is transformed through the lived experience of the participants. This empirical research provides a rich examination of individual transformations through the design landscape of further education and higher education, as they move into the professional arena.

What Do We Mean by 'Agility'?

The concept of 'agility' within the context of the FE and HE learning environment can be associated with Lombardo and Eichinger's concept of 'learning agility', which they defined as "the willingness and ability to learn new competencies in order to perform under first-time, tough, or different conditions" (2000: 323). The individual's ability to learn relies on a set of characteristics that are defined by the individual and the way in which they will respond to a set of triggers within the learning environment in which they exist (DeRue et al., 2012: 259). By characteristics we mean attributes the individual has acquired due to the experiences that have informed their development, for example, personal attributes or knowledge based skills. Lombardo and Eichinger's concept of 'learning agility' has been critiqued by DeRue et al. (2012: 259), and they suggest it is a new phenomenon that relies on the individual's "willingness to learn and ability to implement the lessons of experiences as they move through the constructed environments and institutions of learning and work".

DeRue et al. (ibid.) examine the various interpretations of 'learning agility' and suggest it should be related to "speed and flexibility within the learning process". They define 'learning agility' as "the ability to come up to speed quickly in one's understanding of a situation and move across ideas flexibly in service of learning both within and across experiences". This definition is crucial to the context of this study where we investigated an individual's ability to move from one learning environment into another, and reflect on previous learning experiences to enable them to 'quickly' adapt to this change. Billy discusses the fact he "gets on with [his] stuff quite fast" and "when [he] works on screen [he's] very fast". These statements support the notion that being agile does relate to the speed at which people adapt and accept change. Isaac however, acknowledges there is a difference between FE and HE suggesting that "when you're in University, it's like another level. You try and push yourself". Isaac also states that "knowing the software skills helps you to push yourself a little bit further and produce more creative work". We can observe that Isaac has already differentiated the technical skills he has acquired at FE, with the creative process he is now experiencing in HE. Given the opportunity to reflect on these experiences, the students all acknowledged a change within the learning environments of FE and HE, and have made reference to the need to drive or 'push' themselves rather than be driven. This requires an individual to be agile, making necessary changes to the ways in which they learn.

In understanding the above definition of 'learning agility', it allows us to consider the relevance of students' experiences within the structural constructs and routinisation of daily life. It is important we understand the meaning and relevance of such experiences and their relationship with agility. DeRue et al. (2012: 263) suggest, crucially, the duality of space and time enables the individual to quickly acknowledge what they are learning within an experience, as well as drawing "connections between the lessons of that experience and future experiences". We must therefore consider the 'self' and how such experiences can become transformational through an ability to be agile.

Anthony Giddens (1984: 34) suggests that 'time' is 'the most enigmatic feature of human experience', however it is the situational relationship of the human experience within a space which must be considered, to provide context to our understanding of agility within the landscape of FE and HE. Levitt and March (1988) discuss the duality of 'history' and 'routine'. They suggest that this relationship shapes the behaviour of the individual and their ability to learn within an organisational framework. If we consider Giddens' notion of time and space through the flow of daily life, we can begin to understand the way in which an individual might behave within such constructs. Some will react quickly to tasks and engage with creative processes, however those not able to be 'agile' might lack the drive to succeed, becoming unsettled within the same environment. Indeed, within this research one student became 'panicked' initially as a response to the changed learning framework.

Giddens (1984: 36) states that "all social systems … express and are expressed in the routines of daily social life, mediating the physical and sensory properties of the human body". To be agile within an institutional learning framework requires the individual to be consciously aware of his or her surroundings and respond quickly to change. It is worth noting here that DeRue et al. (2012: 264) specify a separation of "one's willingness to engage in agile learning" from agility and one's "ability to learn from experiences through being flexible and fast". They suggest that "defining learning agility independent of any particular experience type" allows us to investigate the "type of experience" that could "accentuate (or attenuate) the value of learning agility". They also question the validity of 'success' as a dimension of agility and the definition by Lombardo and Eichinger (2000: 323) whereby they state that "learning agility is relevant for performing in first-time, tough, or different conditions".

Throughout life we experience many different situations: in education, in work and personal lives, resulting in many different experiences. In order to adjust to these different situations and experiences we need to be able to adapt, often quickly to these changes in order to be able to fit in, to perform and to succeed. Being agile is an attribute that enables people to make changes to themselves and their practices, enabling the transition between different learning experiences, and is ultimately a life skill that will help enable progression beyond study into employment, helping them to cope with the multitude of different experiences that they will face during their life-time. According to Lombardo and Eichinger (2000), highly learning agile individuals learn the 'right lessons' from experience and apply those lessons to 'novel situations'.

> People who are highly learning agile continuously seek out new challenges, actively seek feedback from others to grow and develop, and tend to self-reflect, evaluating their experiences and drawing practical conclusions (De Meuse et al., 2010: 120).

As such, agility is not a single attribute but a series of attributes and skills that enable learners to move, grow and succeed from school based education into further and higher education and ultimately into employment. These attributes can be linked to Schlossberg's Model for analysing human adaptation to transition (2011) and in particular can be seen to link to the 'self' within the 4S's model (Goodman et al., 2006). These attributes include the following:

- self-awareness – and the ability to know what they do not know
- self-efficacy (Chemers, 2001)
- adaptability – the ability to change thinking and practice and self-direction (Grow, 1991)

The associated skills include; digital and conceptual skills, time management and professional practice. Being agile also includes the ability to form and utilise peer bonds – developing a working knowledge and understanding of group roles, structures and norms, often within pre-existing groups (Tuckman and Jensen, 1977; Levine and Moreland, 1994). We can see that agility is a theme reflected in guidance to students in some universities; for example, in the *Quality Handbook* of Nottingham Trent University (2015):

- Aptitude for independent, critical thought and rational inquiry, alongside the capacity for analysis and problem-solving in multiple contexts.
- An enterprising and creative mind-set, able to thrive in rapidly changing work and social environments.
- Intellectual curiosity, enthusiasm for learning and an aptitude for self-directed learning.

This ability to thrive in a changing work and social environment is evidenced in the learners' move into further and higher education and agility is a much sought-after skill in the world of work, where the ability and willingness to learn from experience and then apply that learning to perform successfully under new situations is a highly valued attribute.

De Meuse et al. (2010: 126) note that to date, research into 'learning agility' has remained within a professional landscape and they suggest that "many conceptual, empirical, and theoretical issues remain to be explored". This chapter will go on to examine some of the theoretical debates relating to 'learning agility' through our empirical study with design students, transitioning from further education into higher education, and the ways in which this relates to the development of graduate attributes. Firstly, we will consider the life experience of further education and how this has influenced their learning journey.

Agility and Further Education

A striking feature of the study was the role that further education played in helping learners to define their future journey. They all left school unsure of their futures, some as a result of a failure to achieve entry into their first choice of institution: Isaac suggested that "it was a last minute choice because [he] didn't get into University". Kevin acknowledged that he had not "fully decided" what he would do, but recognised his intention was to "go on and do more education, unless something amazing [came] along". Gill's ambitions lay elsewhere – "I always wanted to do dance when I left school".

For others, it followed a period of employment before entering college. Further education was a place to 'find themselves' with less commitment than a 4-year university course, but with a structure that was more akin to school, less onerous and less of a jump into the unknown (Christie et al., 2006; HEA, 2012). As Theresa, one of the students, related, "[I]t was a stepping stone, cause I wasn't ready at all to like jump into university, it was quite daunting … it was a nice stepping stone".

Further education was a space that allowed the acquisition and development of specific skills, such as technical skills. Learners were instructed how to use specific software in a supportive environment where there was always someone on hand to help. Many of the respondents spoke at length about the importance of their experiences at FE college in the acquisition of the practical software skills: Billy described it as being

> dead methodical. You're getting taught how to be a draughtsman, not a designer. You get taught how to use the tools, the principles of typography and stuff like that.

And Issac suggested that

> in college, yes, it was good because they teach you the fundamentals first, the software basics and so everything you need to get started … I wouldn't know much software if it wasn't for college.

We can therefore observe that further education facilitated a deeper knowledge and understanding of a specific subject that then allowed the learners to decide which avenue to pursue in the future. This is an important aspect of agility – self-knowing (Wenger, 1998). This is exemplified by Gill who stated that "in the end it came down to" the fact she "wanted a change because a lot of people [were] in the class, they were lovely people, but I felt I could not always get my work done" and Simon suggested that "if you want to get a bit better, then obviously you should go to uni, especially an Art school" as "it's only going to make you better".

Further education also facilitated the development of other key skills, deemed to be aspects of agility: developing as people, learning about themselves and who they are, and developing a sense of self-awareness. Gill spoke of realising the need to work in addition to class and that class time alone would not be sufficient to achieve the level of work that she aspired to:

> I've always put a lot of work and effort [into it] cause at college you could get away with just going in on the day, you were only in 3 days a week. You could get away with just going in on those 3 days and doing the work and not doing anything else – there were people in my class that would, but I always liked to take my stuff home and work on it more and like improvements and stuff.

Learning to become more self-directed (Grow, 1991) and increasing self-efficacy (Bandura, 1977; Chemers, 2001) was also found to be an important part of the FE experience. Self-direction can be viewed as a series of steps and a trait that is acquired at different times as learners become more self-directed at their own pace (Grow, 1991), but can sometimes feel held back by those who are less self-directed: as Gill states,

> I just went and played with it. A lot happened, a lot of people said how did I do that, I just said I hit a button or deleted something and this happened and then it

would work, but a lot of people would like – would you help me with this and that? So that I felt that I couldn't get my stuff done because I had to help out.

This growth in self-direction is however limited in some areas, due to the structure and ethos that underpins the FE sector. The courses are all competency based (SQA, n.d.) and learners are, in most instances, awarded for competency of execution rather than originality of thought. This leads to a more process driven learning experience, with learning contained within the classroom and within the subject, rather than the interdisciplinary and more creative approach adopted at university. Therefore, learners need to be agile to effectively make the move from FE to HE. Billy spoke of his experiences:

> [H]ere it's like a proper hierarchy, here at uni it's more like what's your concept, there seems to be a lot more focus on a concept – to elevate your execution, whereas in college it seemed more like better typographic practice and sort of Photoshop skills.

Kevin, speaking of his college experience in comparison with that at university, commented that

> they feel more like teachers. It's like an air of authority with them that, it's not that I didn't enjoy them coming up, but they come into a space and then they feel like they're in charge, or they feel like they think they're in charge, and I think that's just the nature of the style of teaching that they have to do because of the people who are at college.

Learners also reported that this culture led them to use their time less effectively and not to push themselves, but all realised that this would not be the case in HE and that they would need to push themselves more and work harder, as the expectations would be very different at university. Billy expressed the view that was shared by many of the respondents:

> College doesn't motivate you. If you only come into the place for 16 hours a week, which is nothing, you're not motivated to value it, there's no requirement to do well at college, because you are there a tiny amount of time.

The learners' experiences gained through their time at college were then transferred and used to enable them to transition successfully into the higher education environment.

Agility and HE: Transitioning the Self

We have acknowledged the role played out by further education colleges, in that they provide essential technical skills valued by students, when transitioning to higher education. It should also be acknowledged that this appears to set them apart from students progressing from level 1 within the University, to specialise in their chosen subject. Billy describes how he "let his ambitions of a project far surpass the reality" of his ability, and that considering what is possible within a specific timescale was "an attitude to work [he] didn't have in second year". Ian describes himself as "panicking" but then he "realised that they [students coming from level 1] didn't know so much web design and things like that". He also states that he felt he "knew more of the tech side of things and I think they knew more of the process". Kevin also acknowledged that "college taught [him] how to be kind of ok at using the programmes".

This was a recurring theme by all further education students, but when defining a difference between further education and higher education, Kevin stated that college "taught us how to do the technical stuff and expected the creativity to come from ourselves, whereas here you teach us how to think". This notion that higher education can teach individuals to 'think' is a very powerful statement to make, but one which can be aligned with Giddens's notion of institutional constructs and the routinisation of daily life. In this case further education is referred to as "clockworking and your life is structured around you" through the routine of everyday life. Kevin suggests however that university provides you with a "space" to "break the way you think and build it back up again" and that coming out of a 'school like' environment offers the students an opportunity to 'become more set in the real world'. Kevin felt that "before, [he] didn't have to think about being an adult with a job" but then he "[came] to University and then [he] became more serious". Agility, within this context, suggests that it is a transformational experience of the 'self'. The ability to reflect on such differences, acknowledging a change across time and space, through the institutional landscape of educational constructs is insightful, and allows us to observe the powerful transition that occurs through the lived experience of a student.

Such experiences however are also driven by the relationships students make and sustain, not only at university, but also beyond, often enhancing their path through education into employment. Schlossberg discusses Erik Erikson's theory for an "eight-stage progression in ego development, each characterized by a crucial issue that must be successfully resolved before the individual can move on" (Schlossberg, 2011: 4). We can suggest that this is evident in students who have progressed from college into university, where they have a choice to remain within a 'school-like' environment, where structure is rigid and constraining, and then move into an environment, which is more open and free allowing them to nurture relationships that help them define their own identity and 'ego'. Billy is proud to say that "we love each other in class. It's such a tight group and it's because that thing is cultivated here". Billy also values the fact that he has "25 peers who will be working in the industry who [he] can call on at any time … in terms of work and career".

The notion that university provides you with friendships that will last a lifetime suggests that higher education can provide relationship networks that form ecosystems, supporting and constructing the identity of that individual, nurtured across time and space. Learning agility therefore requires a holistic process to coexist with workload and new skills. This reflects the view of Lombardo and Eichinger

(2000: 324) where they developed a strategic set of measurements for evaluating 'learning agility'. This is based within four dimensions: People Agility, Results Agility, Mental Agility and Change Agility. Throughout these dimensions they refer to the way in which an individual might engage with 'others', inspiring them, communicating effectively with them and treating others 'constructively'. Billy reflects on the challenge of "being able to communicate with people who don't necessarily share the same ideas as you" and yet acknowledges that they have "grown to know each other and know each other's nuances". We can observe that Billy's ability to reflect on his experiences gives him a deeper awareness of his situational relationship with others and the value this brings to him, across space and time.

The environment in which students learn in higher education plays a role in the way in which they engage with their studies. This supports Giddens's theory (1984), whereby he considers the way in which institutional constructs impact on the 'self' whereby it "cannot be understood outside 'history'". Billy expresses his environment as 'a second home', suggesting the routine of the studio and its availability constructs his life and the way in which he organises his time. Giddens refers to this as 'systemness' whereby it is 'achieved largely through the routine reflexive monitoring of conduct anchored in practical consciousness' (ibid.: 36). Billy prefers the learning environment of university due to the 'self-directed' approach to study. He acknowledges the method of teaching within the landscape of further education and suggests "it is not how you learn", due to the rigidity of tutorials and the limited use of space. Billy states "you learn through doing, not through being told a set of moves, because you're not going to learn the nuances of those moves through that". We can observe the duality of time and space whereby Billy refers to the access he has to the learning environment where he "can come here [studio] from 9 in the morning to 9 at night and just work".

If we examine some of the terminology used by students to describe their experience of higher education, such as, 'home', 'love', 'think', 'value' we can begin to understand how learning agility is embedded within the 'practical consciousness' (ibid.: 36) of the self. The student's ability to be agile depends upon the environment and the social interactions that occur within that time and space. This therefore takes 'learning agility' to a new context not yet discussed by previous researchers. Learning has not been referred to within the context of home, value, thinking and love prior to this empirical investigation, and we would suggest that agility can rely upon the ability of the individual to transform the self within the environment of higher education where they feel emotionally attached to people and place.

The transformation of the self can only be realised through reflection and an understanding of previous life experiences. This can facilitate agility, as an attribute, to have relevance within this context. Billy reflects on the transformation in himself and acknowledges that "he has changed a lot". He also refers to a change in values whereby certain interests that he "valued before" he has seen "disappear and other interests take favour". Billy now feels they are the qualities in life that now "motivate [him] with regards to personal things to better [himself] as a person". The Learning Agility process is outlined in Figure 5.1.

Figure 5.1 Learning agility process.

Agility and Community

When acknowledging change in one's self we can see that the relationships you create and sustain have value. Billy states that you've "got to have the right attitude" and that he specifically wanted to "be a different person to the person [he] was", and that meant "embracing opportunity". Agility therefore requires an approach to learning that is reflective, embedded within the history of life's experiences up to that time, and that transformation of the self can occur through a process of reflective agile learning. Lowe and Cook (2003: 53), through their research of first year university students, found that the abrupt shift from the controlled environment of school or college and family to an environment in which students are expected to accept personal responsibility for both academic and social aspects of their lives will create anxiety and distress, undermining their normal coping mechanisms.

This study suggests that the ability of the student to be agile by reflecting and understanding their 'self' can help and encourage them to grow and mature as an individual, thereby applying a rigorous work ethic to their studies within the higher education landscape. This has the potential to help them cope with any stress and anxiety attached to the social and academic dimensions, and that the relationships they create and sustain can impact on their life experience beyond higher education. Throughout our interviews, learners often referred to the importance of social interaction outwith their learning environment, suggesting this encouraged them to bond as a community. Billy, however, does feel this was his biggest challenge when moving to university, and he "didn't really expect" the "social aspect"; however, this is seen as being exceptionally important for the development of his career beyond university. Billy acknowledges that he is now in the "fortunate position" of having "a network of peers who will always be there, certainly into the immediate future within [his] professional career".

Reflectively Billy considers his relationship with the university and he suggests he "has been nurtured here", but he also acknowledges this is a dual pathway and he has "given [him]self to the university as well". He describes this as being "a nice relationship" where he is "not just a young student … getting brought up", but he is a "student who does things for the University", which means he is now "very well prepared" for life beyond the confines of higher education. Billy also discusses his future with confidence, and he discusses his vision of not just "being a cog in the wheel" within a design company, but that he aspires to "make the big decisions that [his] business puts out in the world". Admirably, he aspires to "be in a position where [he] can alter the effects of what that company [is] doing to the world". What is insightful is that Billy also considers the prospect of "coming back to education" and teach; however, his short-term goal is "to embrace everything that [he] can and learn". Billy has realised he now has "short term goals and long term goals" and that "university makes you ambitious". He was a "different person 3 or 4 years ago" and is now a "different character altogether".

Nancy Schlossberg (2011: 5) proposes in her Model for Analysing Human Adaptation to Transition that "a transition can be said to occur if an event or non-event results in a change in assumptions about oneself and the world and thus requires a corresponding change in one's behaviour". There is evidence within this study to suggest that this transition is very much aligned with the change, as a result of students' own lived experiences, when moving from further education into higher education. Schlossberg refers to Parkes's proposal of the term 'psychosocial transition' (Parkes, 1971: 103, cited by Schlossberg, 2011), which he defines as a change that necessitates "the abandonment of one set of assumptions and the development of a fresh set to enable the individual to cope with the new altered life space". Our research has evidenced this 'transition' of the 'self' where one moves one's values and expectations. It is clear that some individuals require this transitional phase, as Theresa explains that "she wanted to understand more about [her]self" and that further education was a "nice stepping stone for [her] to figure out" her "life and what design was". She acknowledged she "wasn't ready at all to jump into University, it was quite daunting". Theresa therefore required the duality of time and space for her to make the transition to further education and suggested she needed to be "more open" to "change and be different".

This reflection and understanding of their 'self' can also be linked to the theory of emotional intelligence, "the ability to reason with emotion" outlined by Peter Savoy and John Mayer (1990: 187) and further developed by Daniel Goleman, who broadened this definition of emotional intelligence, defining it as "understanding one's own feelings, empathy for the feelings of others and the regulation of emotion in a way that enhances living". Goleman (1995) also identified what he called the "the five domains of emotional intelligence", namely:

- knowing one's emotions
- managing one's emotions
- motivating oneself
- recognising emotions in others
- handling relationships

These five domains can be recognised within the discussions with all seven students as critical to their ability to adapt to and grow within the different learning environments that they have encountered in their learning journeys to date. The emotional aspect to their learning – their ability to know themselves and to understand their feelings, make adjustments and integrate into new groups through their understanding of others has been an important part of their journey.

Conclusion

In setting out this empirical study we predicted some of the attributes highlighted by the students who engaged with this research. The way in which they attained specific technical skills at FE and more creative skills at HE, enabling them to develop the way in which they 'think'. However, we were surprised by the deep and emotional references that were made to the ways in which they related to their experiences as higher education students. Becoming agile was not evident through learning in FE, but to realise the potential of HE and the expectations the students had of the learning journey meant they needed to reflect on their experiences at FE and adapt quickly to the changing processes they encountered. Students also appeared to develop an emotional intelligence that enabled them to create and sustain a network of peers, facilitating a transformational change in their idea of 'self' and the values that were important to them.

Recognising emotional attributes such as 'love', 'community' and 'value' suggests there is further research to be undertaken to truly understand the full impact of social interaction, and whilst this research documents the positive aspects through the experiences of our learners, we must acknowledge the flip side, where learners who cannot be agile and adjust to change may become remote and withdrawn from studies and the learning community. We would suggest there is new knowledge to be gained that might help us understand the landscape when an individual cannot become agile. David Orr (2004: 43) writes about the importance of "emotional bonds, fight and love", suggesting they are "not typical of polite discourse in the sciences or social sciences" and that, sadly, it appears that "good science and emotion of any sort are incompatible". Orr asks whether we now require a "different kind of education" due to the changing nature of the environmental and societal issues the world now faces. Considering love as an important aspect of learning, Orr suggests (ibid.: 44) it could "set limits on knowledge or on the way in which knowledge is acquired". He does, however, recognise that these are "difficult issues", and that it requires a "serious and sustained discussion about love in relation to education and knowledge". Orr (ibid.) goes on to suggest that "emotions in relation to intellect" must be considered as a duality for the future of our education system. The evidence from our empirical research suggests that 'love' is intertwined with 'value', 'community' and 'intellect', and that together they become very important assets when the learner is becoming agile within the learning landscape of higher education.

Practice Guide – Reflexivity and Love

Within this chapter we have suggested that further education is a 'steppingstone' to higher education, as the learning environment gives birth to the individual through a transformational process, and that the reflexive process of learning from prior experiences is crucial across temporal and spatial dimensions. However, we would like to suggest within this chapter that nothing can be more powerful than the recognition of emotional intelligence and the relationship with the 'self' through what is 'valued', and how 'love' can encourage a sense of community within and beyond higher education.

We would like to suggest you explore how to help the development of emotional intelligence of your learners, perhaps by exercises linked to an emotional competence framework such as that suggested by the Consortium for Research on Emotional Intelligence in Organisations (n.d.) to enable your students to help understand where agile learners can enhance the learning journey, not only for themselves, but for their peers.

Some suggestions of how this might be achieved follow:

1   Ask students to produce a learning map.

Students should highlight the key points within the learning journey, making connections from one point to the next. This should be quite simple and very visual.

It can be hand-drawn or computer generated, depending on what the student feels most comfortable with. This will highlight to the student the entire learning process and what has happened along the way.

If students are working in groups, it is important that each member produces their own learning map. Each student might highlight different points that mattered to them, and no two maps will be exactly the same, even though the students have experienced the same project.

Examples of learning maps can be seen below in Figures 5.2 and 5.3.

2   Ask students to produce a 500-word reflexive article of their learning journey.

Students should reflect on their learning map, which documents the process, and critically reflect on this experience. It is important the written article is critically reflective of the experience, presenting what skills they have learned, what they felt worked and what didn't, and most importantly what they would do differently next time. This is very much the nexus between one learning experience and the next and should help the student understand what the value has been throughout that experience.

One word of caution: if students are working in groups, the written article should not be a naming and shaming exercise, nor should it be a list of what they, or members of their group, have produced. This should be a very personal reflection of the individual learning experience. It should be confidential to enable the student to feel comfortable imparting emotional response to the project.

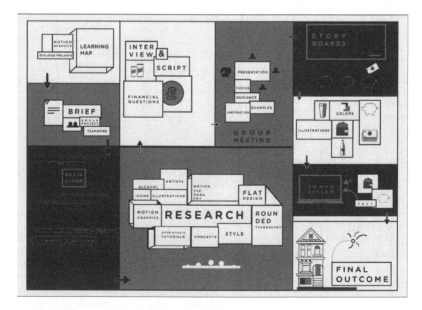

Figure 5.2 Learning map (Stelianos Ypsilantis).

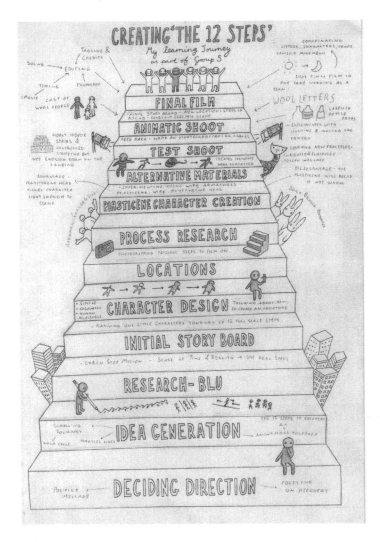

Figure 5.3 Learning map (Connie White).

References

Bandura, A. (1977) Self-efficacy: Towards a Unifying theory of behavioural change. *Psychological Review* 34 (2), 191–215.

Briggs, A., Clark, J. and Hall, I. (2012) Building bridges: Understanding student transition to university. *Quality in Higher Education*.

Chemers, M. M. (2001) Academic self-efficacy and first-year college student performance and adjustment. *Journal of Educational Psychology* 93 (1), 55–64.

Christie, H., Cree, V., Hounsell, J., McCune, V. and Tett L. (2006) From college to university looking backwards, looking forwards. *Research in Post-Compulsory Education* 11 (3), 351–365.

Consortium for Research on Emotional Intelligence in Organizations, The (n.d.) EI Framework *www.eiconsortium.org*. Accessed 20.08.16.

De Meuse, K. P, Dai, G. ana Hallenbeck, G. S. (2010) Learning agility: A construct whose time has come. *Consulting Psychology Journal: Practice and Research* 62 (2), 119–130.

DeRue, S. D., Ashford, S. J. and Myers, C. G. (2012) Learning agility: In search of conceptual clarity and theoretical grounding. *Industrial and Organisational Psychology* 5, 258–279.

Giddens, A. (1984) *The Constitution of Society*. Polity Press: Cambridge.

Goleman, D. (1995) *Emotional Intelligence*. Bloomsbury: London.

Goodman, J., Schlossberg, N. K. and Anderson, M.K. (2006) *Counselling Adults in Transition: Linking Practice with Theory*. 3rd ed. New York: Springer.

Grow, G. (1991) Teaching learners to be self-directed. *Adult Education Quarterly* 41 (125).

HEA (2012) Learning journeys: Student experiences in further and higher education in Scotland. http://scotland.heacademy.ac.uk/assets/documents/nations/scotland/Learning_Journeys_2013.pdf. Accessed 08.06.16

Leese, M. (2010) Bridging the gap: Supporting student transitions into higher education. *Journal of Further and Higher Education* 34 (2), 239–251.

Levine, J. M. and Moreland, R. L. (1994) Group socialization: Theory and research. *European Review of Social Psychology* 5 (1), 305–336.

Levitt, B. and March, J. G. (1988) Organizational learning. *Annual Review of Sociology* 14, 319–340.

Lombardo, M. M. and Eichinger, R. W. (2000) High potentials as high learners. *Human Resource Management* 39 (4), 321–329.

Lowe, H. and Cook, A. (2003) Mind the gap: are students prepared for higher education? *Journal of Further and Higher Education* 27 (1), 53–76.

Nottingham Trent University (2015) *Quality Handbook*. Nottingham Trent: Nottingham.

Orr, D. W. (2004) *Earth in Mind: On Education, Environment, and the Human Prospect*. Island Press.

QAA (2008) *Quality enhancement themes: The First-Year Experience*. QAA: Glasgow.

Savoy, P. and Mayer, J. (1990) *Emotional Intelligence*. www.unh.edu/emotional_intelligence/ … /EmotionalIntelligenceProper/EI. Accessed 20.08.16.

Scottish Government (2012) *Post 16 Transitions* http://www.scotland.gov.uk/Publications/2012/11/3248. Accessed 08.09.14.

Schlossberg, N. (2011) A model for analysing human adaptation to transition. *The Counselling Psychologist* 9 (2).

SQA (n.d.) A guide to HNs www.sqa.org.uk/sqa/files_ccc/CD6482_SQA_Guide_to_HNs_A4_8pp_L2_leaflet_Web.pdf. Accessed 11.06.15.

Tuckman, B. W. and Jensen, M. A. C. (1977) Stages of small group development revisited. *Group and Organizational Studies*. 2, 419–427.

Universities Scotland (2013) *Access all areas*. http://www.universities-scotland.ac.uk/uploads/ACCESS%20ALL%20AREAS%20final.pdf. Accessed 08.09.14.

Wenger, E. (1998) *Communities of Practice: Learning meaning and identity*. Cambridge University Press: Cambridge.

Yorke, M. and Vaughan, D. (2013) The expectations and experiences of first year students in Art and Design. *Journal of Higher Education Policy and Management* 35 (2), 215–228.

Chapter 6

The Empathic Graduate

Carey Normand and Christine Kingsley

with fondness & respect

Carey

Introduction

The complex and conceptual environment of the 21st century requires the graduate to think in new and creative ways. The previous emphasis on those graduate attributes (GAs) where proficiency is defined by knowledge acquisition and/or skills aptitude may be insufficient for the task. Recent studies stress the importance of different types of thinking and polarise logical-deductive thinking from intuitive-creative thinking, considering the latter to be essential in a conceptual age (Pink, 2008; Kress, 2008). Consequently, in this chapter we will explore conceptualisations of graduate attributes that focus on the affective domain, though still incorporating cognition and practice, and examine the construct of *empathy* as a graduate attribute for the 21st century.

It is argued that empathy "is one of our most valuable natural resources" (Baron-Cohen, 2012). Definitions of empathy have centred on it as a social competence and note its relation with emotional intelligence. One's ability to empathise with the needs of others has, until recently, been defined as a *soft skill*; however, recent evidence defines one's empathetic aptitude as both financially and politically beneficial. One reason for the shift in perspective is empathy has multiple dimensions that can be combined with other attributes, for example, leadership. If we consider empathic leadership we would expect to see inspiring, creative and effective collaboration with others through collective goals. Within the political sphere, this might manifest as the ability to navigate and negotiate, to influence, manage and develop others, while cultivating change. Empathy can be seen as the ultimate attribute as when used effectively people relate and flourish, working relationships grow and businesses are successful (Goleman, 2007; Patnaik and Mortensen, 2009). Further, research shows that empathy can improve with practice (Baron-Cohen, 2012), which is significant for educators. Therefore, in addition to conceptualisations of empathy as a GA, this chapter also explores how we recognise and foster empathy within the curriculum and the role that higher education institutions can play in the alchemy of empathy.

Empathy as a Concept

'Empathy' is one of those words that generate a range of responses and definitions. Its etymological route is from the Greek word *empatheia* "meaning to enter feelings from the outside"; "to be with a person's feelings, passions or suffering" (Howe, 2013: 9). This illustrates the nature of empathy is to understand rather than explain another's feelings. Being empathic is to see and feel the other person's point of view and attempt to understand it and, perhaps, to convey that understanding to those around us. Often it is referred to as standing in someone else's shoes or "the ability to share someone else's feelings or experiences, by imagining what it would be like to be in that person's situation" (Cambridge Dictionary, 2016). This decentring is essential to empathic behaviour, and it enables insight and understanding into another person's beliefs, values, emotions and behavioural codes. Empathy entails some degree of action, connection and emotional sharing, arguably, as a prerequisite to truly understanding someone else's inner world. Crucially, empathy is quite different from sympathy, which can be seen as a passive engagement that does not necessarily illustrate understanding, though may be an expression of "care for someone else's suffering" (ibid.). This can be illuminated through the Greek word for feeling, *pathos* that acts as a suffix for a number or related words: 'apathy' (without feeling), 'sympathy' (with feeling, together feeling), 'antipathy' (feeling against) and 'empathy' (into feeling or feeling into) (Howe, 2013: 9). The definition of empathy above illustrates its immersive quality: "into feeling" or "feeling into" (ibid.). Hoffman defines empathy as the "involvement of psychological processes that make a person have feelings that are more congruent with another's situation than with his own" (Hoffman, cited in Rifkin, 2009: 13). To have a fuller understanding of the concept of empathy, it is necessary to explore the interpretations posited by different disciplines and philosophical perspectives.

Origins of Empathy as a Concept

It is argued that the precursor of empathy was sympathy; popularised during the European enlightenment in the eighteenth century by Adam Smith, the Scottish economist, in his book, *Moral Sentiments* (1759). In the book he devoted attention to "human emotions" and "feeling sorry for another's plight" (Rifkin, 2009: 12). German philosophers from the mid-to late-19th century used the word *einfuhlung:* a single noun meaning 'feeling into' to discuss aesthetics (DeWaal, 2010: 65). This term is attributed to the German philosophers Theodore Lipps (1851–1914), Robert Vischer (1873–1994) and Wilhelm Dilthey (1833–1911). Theodore Lipps described being in suspense while watching a high-wire artist and said, "[W]e are on the rope with him" (DeWaal, 2010: 65), though he stated that he knew that he himself was not high above the ground (Stueber, 2010: 8). He also used the Greek equivalent, *empatheia*, meaning experiencing strong affection or passion in a similar context by projecting himself into another's experience (ibid.). Vischer used *einfuhlung* "to discuss the pleasure we experience when we contemplate a piece of art" (Howe, 2013: 6).Vischer explored the positive emotional connection, and the immersive effect experienced from having empathy with another's idea or expression; while Dilthey began using the term outside aesthetics to describe "the mental process by which a person enters into another person's being and comes to know how they feel and think" (Rifkin, 2009: 12). It was early in the 20th century that E. B. Titchenener, an American psychologist, translated *einfuhlung* into the word 'empathy', after studying introspection – the study of one's inner drive, feelings and thoughts – to form selfhood and identity. Consequently, empathy's entry into our vocabulary began when modern psychology began to explore human selfhood and the human journey (ibid.: 11).

Empathy as a concept, within a psychological paradigm, spanned social, cognitive and neurophysiologic psychology. Empathy was understood by scholars as a cognitive function, wired to the brain requiring cultural attunement; an instrumental value with a social function; an emotional state with a cognitive component. Most psychologists agreed that both emotion and cognition play a pertinent role in empathy, and stress the increasing importance of this on our "consciousness and social development" (Goleman, 2007: 58).

There is a leaning by psychologists towards a Romantic view of empathy as essentially an affective or emotional state with a cognitive component (Rifkin, 2009: 13). In this model, the empathic observer doesn't lose their sense of self in observations or fuse into other person's experience; neither do they coolly and objectively read the experience of the other as a way of gathering info. Empathy runs deeper (Rifkin, 2009: 13). Daniel Goleman (2007) describes the science of empathy through the lens of social psychology and neuroscience in his book *Social Intelligence*. Within social intelligence, he defines two categories: social awareness, "what we sense about others", and social facility, "what we then do with that awareness" (Goleman, 2007: 84). Social awareness, he posits, is a spectrum that spans innate or "primal empathy" to the more complex and situated "social cognition" (ibid.). Social facility builds upon social awareness through a spectrum of "effective interactions" (ibid.).We all have primal empathy, the initial feeling of another, sensing non-verbal emotional signals.What we chose to do thereafter is determined by our levels of empathic accuracy: understanding the needs of that person, and our social facility, whether we influence, act or show concern relates to our empathic attunement (Hoffman, cited in Rifkin, 2009: 13). The observations of young children have found that they can understand others' feelings early in their second year of life from "affective tuning" to the emotions of others and that they can differentiate their responses as appropriate to the relationship, for example, responding differently to siblings and parents (Dunn, 1998: 111). However, empathy was also shown to have an instrumental value that was used to advance one's own social interest and maintain appropriate social relations (Rifkin, 2009: 13). Goleman considered the following three senses to be pertinent: "*knowing* another person's feelings; *feeling* what that person feels; and *responding compassionately* to another's distress" (Goleman, 2007: 58). The term 'wired to connect' is recognised as the first stage, primal empathy or biological predisposition to care: feeling with others, sensing nonverbal emotional signals. This three-phase sequence deepens through increased connection, a combination of social awareness and action through social facility; "I notice you, I feel with you, I act to help you" (ibid.).

Neuroscientific research has identified that mirror neurons in the brain are in operation when we experience empathy. Mirror neurons are the "mechanisms that make seeing someone hurt, really hurt you" (Goleman, 2007: 57). A shared emotion or experience shows identical circuitry in both person's brain activity: mirroring occurs whenever our perception of someone automatically activates an image or a felt sense, when what's on their mind, occupies ours. Preston found that if someone brings to mind one of the happiest moments of her life, then imagines a similar moment from the life of one of her closest friends, the brain activates virtually the identical circuitry for those two mental acts. In other words, to understand what someone else experiences, to empathise, we utilise the same brain wiring that is active during our own experience (Preston, cited in Goleman, 2007: 58;59). From a cognitive perspective, neuroscientists observe that when we share a moment of empathy we have a mental 'representation', or set of images, associations, about the other person's predicament that we may feel their pain and act to help them. Mirroring happens when our perception of another person activates an image, in our own brain because we are wired to connect (Goleman, 2007).

Empathy in Education

The psychological constructs have influenced educational practices, and, in the contemporary period, we witness educators adopting empathic attunement and social intelligence as innovative pedagogy. The 20th-century conception that saw 'knowledge as power' has been replaced by the notion that "knowledge is an expression of the shared responsibilities for the collective wellbeing of humanity and the planet as a whole" (Goleman, 2007: 15).

Higher Education (HE) in the 21st century functions within a complex and challenging environment. The current educational landscape is a consequence of external drivers, including operating within a competitive global market and a neo-liberal policy context; and internal drivers, for example, a shift towards efficiency in teaching and learning. This landscape also reflects changes in the composition of the student body, which has changed as a consequence of new technology; the massification of HE and widening participation. Educators in HE have been responsive to the needs of the diverse learners they work with, and the curriculum has subtly shifted from one that is focused on content (the what) to one with an emphasis on processes (the how, why, who and when) (Kingsley and Normand, 2013). A highly diverse student body requires a curriculum that is 'transformative' and one that "develops dispositions, skills and other capabilities which enable graduates to challenge culture-bound knowledge and to produce new knowledge in a global context" (Appadurai, 2001, cited in Caruana, 2012: 11). This internationalised curriculum is now present in the Scottish school system known as The Curriculum for

Excellence, with its focus on "the development of knowledge and understanding of key concepts" (SQA, 2013).

Scottish education, at all levels and in all sectors, favours a 'generalist' tradition, with a curriculum that is broad and interdisciplinary rather than narrow and subject specific (Davie, 1961). Drawing on this cultural tradition, the authors of this chapter have used the breadth of the interdisciplinary lenses of Design and Education to illuminate ways of teaching and learning in the 21st century. Our Journey Mapping in the Landscapes of Learning (JMapLL) approach accentuates the processes inherent in curricula, and how these are illuminated by reflecting on and applying the lens of another discipline; in this instance, between Design and Education. We have found that one of the most effective ways to do this is through 'conversations' and agree that "conversation is the means by which existing knowledge is conveyed and new knowledge is generated" (Dubberly and Pangaro, 2016: 4). Our JMapLL approach utilises multimodal literacies, allowing for conversations to happen through a mix of methods, including digital, mapping and drawing.

Empathy in Design

Design Thinking

The design domain is multidisciplinary, interconnected with many other disciplines, contexts and stakeholders. As a result it has learned to communicate with diversity. What is distinct are motivations to design empathically, depending on the role designers, engineers or business people have in the design process. Moggridge (2011, cited in Lupton, 2014) highlights that empathy is keenly integrated into designers' practice; he compares roles thus:

> Engineers start with technology, and look for a use for it; business people start with a business proposition and then look for the technology and the people. Designers start with people, coming towards a solution from the point of view of people." (Moggridge, 2011, cited in Lupton, 2014: 21)

This latter point is pertinent and gives meaning to the choice of participants in our empirical study and analysed in this chapter on empathic graduates. The changes in higher education and the curriculum as well as characterisations of design thinking from a historical overview are also explored.

In 1955 Henry Dreyfuss, the American industrial designer, published his book *Designing for People*, promoting his philosophy of "fitting the machine to the man rather than the man to the machine" (Lupton, 2014: 23) demonstrating that people come first. His design office defined the terms 'ergonomics', 'human factors' and 'human engineering' to explain the connections between the measurements of the human body, human psychology and the industrial world we live in. In the 1940s and '50s, the Dreyfuss office pioneered *interface design*, a crucial study of how people interface with devices, the software and hardware between humans and machines.

This knowledge has expanded to be known as *Interaction design* today. By the 1970s 'human-centred design' was a widely accepted term that encompassed this knowledge. Developed over the next 40 years, a parallel practice of collective empathic methods was emerging in Europe as *participatory design*.

Participatory design originating through research projects in the 1970s in Norway, Sweden and Denmark, the collective resource approach, was established to "increase the value of industrial production by engaging the workers in the development of new systems for the workplace" (Sanders and Stappers, 2008: 9). Crucially, this design movement demonstrates the active role of empathy that design researchers employed to transition change for all stakeholders in the system of design. Twentieth-century design is defined by Dreyfuss's maxim 'designed *for* people', while the 21st century is dominated by the collective creativity that the Internet has enabled: we now design *with* people (Lupton, 2014: 21). The language of engagement with people has moved from clients, customers and consumers, to participants, users, designers and people.

The term 'design thinking' is used to connect the innovation, strategy and business of design activity. It is a methodological approach which combines empathy for the context of a problem that incorporates multiple perspectives in iterative problem-solving (Wildevuur and Van Dijk, 2013: 207). The goal is to focus on potential needs and desires of users rather than on predetermined outcomes. Often working in interdisciplinary teams, proponents of design thinking generate multiple solutions and then create, test and revise prototypes in an iterative process (Lambert, cited in Lupton, 2014). Design thinking encapsulates participatory design, human-centred design and the terms 'collective creativity', 'co-design', 'co-creation', 'user-centred design' and 'universal design'. Design empathy underpins the design process. In 2009 Stanford University's Institute of Design launched their design thinking toolkit/guide, *d.schoolbootcampbootleg*, under a creative commons licence. This open sharing of design thinking methods and processes is a downloadable set of approaches, highlighting "vital attitudes for a design thinker to hold" (Stanford, 2016). The Stanford Institute of Design school explain seven parts of the D.Mindset, one being a "focus on human values – empathy for the people you are designing for and feedback from these users is fundamental to good design" (ibid.).

Research Methodology

Empathy Formation: Empirical Case Studies

In this study the authors were driven to find out if empathy was learned/taught or caught and to explore salient factors in its development. We were interested in empathy formation and wanted to research its origins with the individual, their natal family and in formal and informal learning. As educationalists we were motivated to examine the role that educators have in empathy formation and development. This enquiry led us to choose a case study methodology, as it provided the level of focus that was required to ascertain empathy formation, development and learning.

Our approach is to use participants' life-histories as a vehicle for conveying empathy's formation, learning and development within specific contexts. Our overarching research question is, How is empathy formed, learned and developed?

Participants

The participants of our study that completed the empathy cultural probes and the contextual interviews are three female graduates, ranging in age from 23 to 45, at different stages in their careers. To maintain anonymity, objectivity and rigour, we named the case studies CS1, CS2 and CS3. The following life experience of all participants contextualises their appropriateness for this study. Participant CS1 has an MSc in Product Design; and is also qualified as an occupational therapist, with one year's post-qualification experience. Participant CS2 has a degree in Textile Design; qualified in primary education with four years' experience, then graduated with a Master's degree in Service Design. Participant CS3 is a qualified secondary teacher specialising in behavioural guidance, though she was initially qualified as a home economics teacher. Significantly, all three have facilitated behavioural change in participants using design thinking methods, visualised alternative ways of seeing problems and solutions, and demonstrated enterprise in their interactions, observations and prototyping with people. Two participants were educated in design, working with one of the authors (Kingsley), a design academic, firstly as students, then as colleagues in separate co-design research projects. The relationship emerging with both participants demonstrates Wildevuur and VanDijk's 3Es of relationships (encounters, expectations and exchanges) and the life stories common to educational research (2013: 73). The competences captured through the interviews and evidenced in the completed cultural probes explore the perceptions of empathy as a graduate attribute.

Research Design

A cultural probe is a set of activities, designed and thoughtfully put together to engage participants in a conversation with a design activity. They are used as part of a qualitative research process. Cultural Probes, in design research, are seen as a collection of "evocative tasks" that are used for obtaining inspirational responses from people (Muratovski, 2016: 67). The cultural probe method is useful for conducting rapid ethnography and to collect contextually sensitive information (ibid.).

> Like astronomic or surgical probes, the probes were part of a strategy of pursuing experimental design in a responsive way. (Gaver et al., 1999: 22)

To investigate this we designed an Empathy Cultural Probe that invited participants to do a three-part activity: the probes included three activities combining textual and graphical modes of communication to elicit life and learning histories.

The empathy probe we assembled for our participants was designed to enable them to engage with three questions that examine aspects of empathic graduate ability. The tasks were sent by mail in purple packaging.

> We've brought you a kind of gift … they're a way for us to get to know you better, and for you to get to know us. (Gaver et al., 1999: 22)

This was pertinent, and we explained to the participants the cultural significance of the colour purple and, for us, its analogous qualities to empathic ability. Purple is a colour compatible with all other colours: it works with both warm (red) and cool (blue) colours. Our initial conversations as researchers of empathy led us to associate the colour purple with the concept of empathy. For us, the colour purple was the mix of red and blue, and this, we felt, encompassed the attributes of empathy: empathic people are able to work with all types of people, including those who are warm and cool, in a synergic way that creates a whole. We framed the activity by stating our research position, that empathic ability is 'powerful, compassionate and strategic' (Kingsley and Normand, 2013; see Figure 6.1: photo of probe and questions).

At this point we specifically ask the participants to consider the constructs of empathy:

1   To what extent have you recognised empathy in your learning environment?
2   To what extent can you recognise empathy as a graduate attribute you have?
3   What value do you consider empathy to hold as a lifelong attribute?

We anticipated that this design methodology would enable a big-picture perspective.

We have previously developed a model to unfold thinking called Journey Mapping through the Landscapes of Learning (JMapLL) and decided that this approach would enable our participants to think through drawing and mapping. Our rationale is that in creating a visual image, participants can encapsulate complex and multiple concepts, in this instance in relation to their learning journey and empathy formation (Kingsley and Normand, 2013). For the maps we drew on Sibbet's (2010) method for visualisation facilitation. In Cultural Probe Activity 1, participants were invited to think about their learning journey and visually map it.

In Cultural Probe Activity 2, Participants were asked to create another map, but this time it was in the form of a family tree: an example of a family tree was provided by Normand. The task was to invite participants to consider aspects of their life history and illuminate facets of their identity. By creating a life history and focussing on relatedness and connections, we hoped that the participants would recognise personal influencers and empathic relationships.

Following from this, in Cultural Probe Activity 3 as a natural extension of Activities 1 and 2, participants were given the opportunity to probe constructions of learning empathy by addressing three self-reflective questions. First, they were asked to show how they understand empathy as a concept, then to explore the extent to which they recognise empathy as a graduate attribute, and the value they hold for empathy as a lifelong attribute. This Empathy Cultural Probe was followed up with semi-structured interviews to interrogate participants' responses in more detail, in relation to the research questions.

We also included a participant information sheet and an ethical consent form. In addition, strengthening the cultural probe, we included a purple pen and herbal tea with an invitation to "put the kettle on and make yourself a cup of tea to accompany you completing the tasks" (ibid.).

On return of the empathic cultural probes, a follow-up contextual interview was undertaken. The Interviews and Directed Storytelling methods were used in the design research inquiry as immersive methods of observing and interviewing: "Interviews are a fundamental research method for direct contact with participants, to collect first-hand personal accounts of experience, opinion, attitude and perception" (Lidwell et al., 2003: 102). Directed storytelling was used in conjunction with the interview: "Directed storytelling allows designers to easily gather rich stories of lived experiences from participants, using thoughtful prompts and guiding and framing question in conversation" (ibid.). Interviews were conducted following the same sequential questioning as the probe, affording participants the opportunity to clarify points arising from the probe answers and expand on the answers submitted.

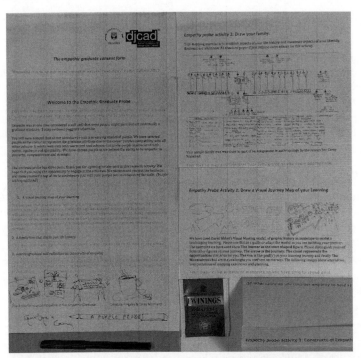

Figure 6.1 Contents of the cultural probes illustrating selected returned examples.

The interviews varied, in that CS1 was an extended Skype interview, CS2 was undertaken in the home of the participant and CS3 in a local café. All interviews were undertaken and transcribed by Kingsley, the design educator, and analysed by both researchers using methods from their discipline of study. The use of directed storytelling in the interview process allowed the design researcher to probe the use of empathy in the contexts familiar to both researcher and participant to share empathy-related stories.

It is worth noting that, while both researchers agree that the transcribed interviews expand on the probe answers, they do not add significantly to the results of the research findings, showing that the construction of the empathy cultural probe was robust in harvesting appropriate data. In hindsight, the design researcher, knowing all participants in both an educational and personal capacity, has found the interviews to be valuable in clarifying specific points in the probe answers, but more in consolidating the deepening relationship between participant and researcher, professionally and socially. The life stories that the transcripts have provided from the interview activity have no further insights to the findings but exemplify the existing relationship through "exchange, expectation and encounter" (Wildevuur and VanDijk, 2013: 70) as indicated in development of relationships.

Research Analysis

Two forms of analysis were used: Affinity Diagramming and Discourse Analysis.

Affinity Diagramming

Affinity diagramming or mapping was used by Kingsley, the design researcher, to "externalise and meaningfully cluster observations and insights from the research" (Lidwell et al., 2003: 13). Figure 6.2 shows the emerging insights from the affinity mapping method.

Discourse Analysis

The other methodological and conceptual framework employed in this study is Discourse Analysis. This approach has been chosen by Normand as it enables the education researcher to analyse the language in texts – the 'talk' (discourse) – not merely as an objective entity, dislocated from context, but as a social practice or medium for interaction, 'action' between people, and what they do. The discourse-analytic perspective allows researchers to analyse how language is used representationally, i.e., culturally constructed.

Discourse analysis has many forms but is essentially a research methodological tool to analyse 'text', be that written or spoken, and sometimes the non-verbal aspects of language; that is analysing what is not said but can be inferred from body language or inferred through the spaces between thought and 'text'. It is best understood as a "field of research rather than a single practice" (Taylor, 2001: 5).

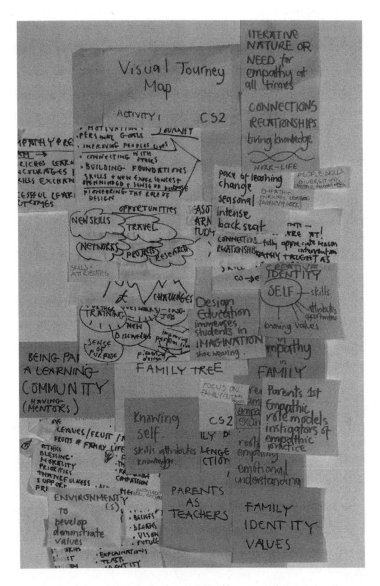

Figure 6.2 CS2's story emerges about the nature of her empathic experience.

That is because there is no one right way to undertake this research, although there are methodological and ethical frameworks of practice. This study will focus on written text, though cognisance of action that both preceded and resulted from the texts will undoubtedly provide a context, lens or framing reference from which the texts will be interpreted.

This will be done following the framework of cultural models as the tools of enquiry as outlined by Gee (1999). This framework and approach examines how language (words and phrases) is used and the types of meanings they have within a particular situation or context. The framework recognises that, beyond the situated meaning of the words-in-use, they also have more general meanings, storylines and theories that are "shared by people belonging to specific social and cultural groups" (ibid.: 81). Further, that these 'storylines' or 'theories', within cultural models, "link to create bigger storylines" (ibid.). This framework will lead me to read the texts and ask 'what I must assume' about the views, values, and beliefs of the people who wrote the text, be they conscious or not, implicit and explicit? Of these beliefs, what differences can I detect between the values and beliefs espoused and those effecting actions, practices and outcomes? Finally, I will question how these cultural models have arisen and what discourses they are creating, helping to reproduce or transform (ibid.: 78).

Findings

Analysis of the Empathy Cultural Probe illuminated how our participants conceptualised empathy, how they developed empathy, how they use empathy in their life and work and how they value empathy as a graduate and lifelong attribute.

Empathy is conceptualised by participants in a range of ways, and the following words/concepts/characteristics are pivotal in their understanding and can help us, as researchers, to garner meaning around the concept.

Affinity Mapping

Analysis of the responses in the Cultural Probe Activity 1 shows that participants felt comfortable with mapping their learning journey. We suggested using Sibbet's Visual Meeting model, with the big arrow showing the direction of travel; however, only one of the participants used this method. Participant CS1 chose the Kawa model, and participant CS2 created a hybrid of Sibbet and Kawa models, having used both methods previously as an Occupational Therapist. Both models are effective in mapping challenges, strengths, influences, barriers and motivations in the learning journey. The emerging themes are that learning is not just about the cognitive domain but also the affective domain. Feelings, emotions and connections with others are all vital to successful learning and achievement.

Cultural Probe Activity 2 also illustrated a divergent response to the probe, with only one participant (CS1) using the anthropological family tree model, as illustrated by Normand. Participant CS2 chose to represent her familial relationships by drawing a tree with her family lineage on the trunk, family values in the roots ("faith, hope, joy, love, trust"), the branches as "fruits of family life" and leaves symbolising mental states ("identity, compassion, value, communication"). Participant CS3 represented her family tree through three lenses: historical, parents, siblings.

The Cultural Probes generated rich data and can be summarised thus:

- Findings from the visual journey map were rich in detail, proving that the JMapLL method of multimodal communication is a rich method of obtaining social cultural data.
- All three participants show through the family trees and learning map activities, that family have been highly influential in their empathic preparation, concurring with other research, namely, Howe (2013), Goleman (2007) and Baron-Cohen (2012).
- All three participants show that their education has prepared them for empathic engagement when working with people, through reflection, case study and observation of other significant teachers and collaborative working in professional settings.

Discourse Analysis

In response to Cultural Probe Activity 3, which is text based, and the interview transcripts, the participants showed concordance in the words and phrases they chose to discuss constructs of empathy. All three participants understood the concept in relation to their personal and professional lives. From the narrative texts the following ten key words/concepts provide illumination on the characteristics of Empathy:

Respectful (of all perspectives and needs)
Mindful (of process, sense-making)
Reflexive (time to think, metacognitive)
Appreciative (value others)
Relatable (relationships, credible)
Self-aware (and other-aware)
Collaborative (team working, participation, engagement)
Understanding (of needs, compassionate, decentring)
Active (interactive, proactive, reactive)
Grounded (aware of the context and situation)

All three participants viewed empathy as a lifelong graduate attribute and considered having it a strength in both their personal and professional lives.

> [K]nowing you are a pro-active, engaged and compassionate person is a much more vital skill to have. (CS2)

This statement is in response to CS2's perception that knowledge acquisition and displays are less important in the 21st century. She refers to the competitive job market for designers and says that "the value of a degree is not as high as it used to be" and that graduates need "to show other skills ... evidence of people skills".

The participant in CS3 considered empathy to be a "turning point and malleable which contributes to a person's journey" in personal and professional contexts and "life long learning".

In relation to empathy formation, participants proffered insights into whether it is caught or taught. CS1 participant thought it "comes from before education in some respects" and linked it to moral development and beliefs learned implicitly within the family. CS3 participant believes that empathy is taught and refers to her own university education as a designer but says that "the learning of 'how to be' empathic is … related to a person's ability to be self-aware".

Conclusion

From our research it is clear that empathy is an important construct and is essential when working effectively with people. The data suggest that it is caught and taught but that learning to use it is dependent upon the person's self-awareness and ability to decentre to consider another person's perspective. The ten characteristics of empathy to emerge from our study – respectful, mindful, reflexive, appreciative, relatable, self-aware, collaborative, understanding, active and grounded – are useful in understanding the types of behaviour associated with being empathic, but, for us educators, it gives the insight needed to design curricula that can foster such ways of thinking and being, leading to the empathic graduate.

Practical Guide – Embedding in Curricula

This study has illustrated the potency of the cultural probe methodology in eliciting rich data and enabling participants to think creatively and independently. Our method can be replicated to suit most learning environments. From this study and our JMapLL research, we have found that enabling participants to reflect on their story, to share it with others and create larger stories results in shifts in thinking and empathic behaviour. We have found that participants get more out of the experience if multimodal opportunities are available, e.g., social media, conversation, drawing, visualisation and collaboration. We suggest that this approach should be built into curricula planning with the same credence as learning outcomes.

Practice Guide – Cultural Probes

In our research we used cultural probes to evoke responses from our participants. The colour was important in our thinking about empathy and was important to this cultural probe. Essentially, we created a purple pack, which included purple paper, purple pen, purple envelope and purple teabag (see Figure 6.1). We set the scene with this purple package, which was functional and aesthetically pleasing. The teabag also symbolised our intentions for this to be a calm and reflective activity but also that it was an immersive activity. The activities in the cultural probe used questioning effectively and invited participants to engage through text and drawing/diagramming. From our research we have found that it is important to use a variety of modes to elicit and unfold thinking.

This approach could be used in many different contexts and with different disciplines. From this example, we hope that you can envisage how you could create a cultural probe to foster empathy within your curricula, or to explore other themes.

Resources could include cameras, colours, postcards, maps, packaging, grouping items, coloured Post-it notes and social media tools (e.g., Pinterest or Storify).

References

Baron-Cohen, S. (2012) *Zero Degrees of Empathy: A New Theory of Human Cruelty and Kindness*. St. Ives: Penguin.

Cambridge Dictionary (2016) http://dictionary.cambridge.org/ Accessed 06/09/2016.

Caruana, V. (2012) 'Appreciatively Inquiring into the Internationalised Curriculum – A model for CPD'. *Educational Developments*. Staff and Educational Development Association. 13.2. (13).

Davie, G. E. (1961) *The Democratic Intellect*. Edinburgh: Edinburgh University Press.

De Waal, F. (2010) *The Age of Empathy: Nature's Lessons for a Kinder Society*. London: Souvenir Press.

Dubberly, H. and Pangaro, P. (2016) *What is conversation? How can we design for effective conversation?* Dubberly.com. Available at: www.dubberly.com/articles/what-is-conversation.html Accessed 14/09/2016.

Dunn, J. (1998) 'Young children's understanding of other people: evidence from observations within the family'. In M. Woodhead, D. Faulkner and K. Littleton (Eds.) *Cultural Worlds of Early Childhood*. London: Routledge.

Gaver, B., Dunn, T. and Pacenti, E. (1999) 'Cultural probes'. *Design Interaction Magazine*, January/February http://www.m-iti.org/uploads/Ga99.pdf Accessed 11/9/2016.

Gee, J. P. (1999) *An Introduction to Discourse Analysis: Theory and Method*. London: Routledge.

Goleman, D. (2007) *Social Intelligence*. Croydon: Arrow Books.

Howe, D. (2013) *Empathy: What It Is and Why It Matters*. Houndmills, Basingstoke, Hampshire: Palgrave.

Kress, G. (2008) *Social, Educational and Semiotic Change: Learning in a World Marked by Provisionality*. Conference paper from the Media Art Culture with reference to Documenta 12, Kassal University Presseries [online] http://www.uni-kassel.de/upress/online/frei/978-3-89958-410-3.volltext.frei.pdf Accessed 31/01/2013.

Kingsley, C. and Normand, C. (2013) *Co-Curriculum Design in a Conceptual Age: Engaging Students in the Landscapes of Learning*. International Enhancement Themes Conference, Conference proceedings publication, Quality Assurance Agency Scotland, June 2013.

Lidwell, W., Holden, K. and Butler, J. (2003) *Universal Principals of Design*. Beverly, MA: Rockport Publishers.

Lupton, E. (2014) *Beautiful Users Designing for People*. New York: Princeton Architectural Press and Cooper Hewitt, Smithsonian Design Museum.

Lupton, E., Carpentier, T., Lambert, T. and Cooper-Hewitt Museum (2014) *Beautiful Users: Designing for People*. New York: Princeton Architectural Press.

Muratovski, G. (2016) *Research for Designers: A Guide to Methods and Practice*. Sage.

Rifkin, J. (2009). *The Age of Empathy*. New York: J.P. Tarcher/Penguin.

Patnaik, D. and Mortensen, P. (2009) *Wired to Care: How Companies Prosper when They Create Widespread Empathy*. Upper Saddle River, NJ: FT Press.

Pink, D. (2008) *A Whole New Mind: Why Right-Brainers Will Rule the World*. Croydon, UK: Marshall Cavendish Business.

Sanders, E.B-N. and Stappers, P.J. (2008) 'Co-creation and the new landscapes of design'. *CoDesign*, 4 (1): 5–18 Taylor & Francis Online http://dx.doi.org/10.1080/15710880701875068 Accessed 19/09/2016.

Sibbet, D. (2010) *Visual Meetings: How Graphics, Sticky Notes & Idea Mapping Can Transform Group Activity*. Hoboken, NJ: John Wiley & Sons.

Smith, A. (1759) *The Theory of Moral Sentiments*. Printed for Andrew Millar, in the Strand; and Alexander Kincaid and J. Bell, in Edinburgh.

SQA. (2013) *New Qualifications – New Opportunities: A Guide for Universities to the New National Qualifications*. Scottish Qualifications Authority.

Stanford Institute of Design (2016) *D. Mindsets, d.school bootcamp bootleg*. https://dschool .stanford.edu/wp-content/uploads/2011/03/BootcampBootleg2010v2SLIM.pdf Accessed 15/09/2016.

Stueber, K. R. (2010) *Rediscovering Empathy: Agency, Folk Psychology, and Human Sciences*. Cambridge, MA: MIT Press.

Taylor, S. (2001) 'Locating and conducting discourse analytic research'. In M. Wetherell, S. Taylor, and S. J. Yates, *Discourse as Data: A Guide for Analysis*. London: The Open University, Sage.

Wildevuur, S. and Van Dijk, D. (2013) *Connect: Design for an Empathic Society*. Amsterdam: BIS.

Chapter 7

The Ethical Graduate

Kate Martin

Introduction

The concept of graduate attributes can be extended to encompass awareness and application of ethical values and principles that are transferable across contexts and disciplines in relation to the contributions which graduates will make to society. This chapter considers the relevance of ethical learning to completing students from perspectives of purpose, theory and practice. The chapter examines what is meant by the idea of an ethical graduate and why this concept is significant to 21st-century students as they prepare to enter an expanding range of professional settings. Theories of ethical learning and ideas about the development of moral perspectives will be reviewed, followed by a discussion drawn from case studies of two professions which present practice examples of ethical teaching and learning. The chapter concludes with examples of individual and collective ways in which learners can develop ethical awareness, skills and capabilities as academic graduates, professional practitioners and global citizens.

As an increasing range of occupations seek professional status, growing numbers of students in higher education will join professions that act on behalf of society to enhance well-being. In this respect, an important aspect of graduate learning relates to ways in which ethical agency is developed as part of professional practice for public good. It is recognised that students come into higher education with existing sets of norms and values, socially constructed through interaction within and between kinship groups, sociocultural communities and networks (Bronfenbrenner, 1994). In the interests of fostering diversity and inclusion in higher education, concern about ethical practice does not propose culturally situated principles for students to follow, but rather considers opportunities for students to explore, discover and develop ethical approaches through learning.

Western societies are influenced by three main sets of beliefs about ethics: Aristotle's virtue ethics, Kant's deontological ethics and John Stuart Mill's utilitarianism (Vardy & Grosch, 1999). Aristotle's view of ethics was that virtues of justice, altruism and equality were dispositions that benefited both individuals and their societies. Kant's ideas were that duty is central to moral behaviour and that humans have a responsibility to respect all sentient beings, whereas John Stuart Mill's ideas concerned the consequences of moral judgement for justice, guided by a maxim of 'the greatest good for the greatest number'. These three philosophies can be identified in contemporary professional principles, such as egalitarianism, responsibility and social justice. Describing ethics in social work professional practice as broadly concerning 'conduct, character, relationships and the good society', Banks (2014: 5) assertsed that these factors tended to focus on deontological duty and 'greatest good' responsibilities, with an increasing contemporary interest in virtue ethics as moral agency. In Banks's interpretation, ethical practice in professions related to all three key philosophical approaches, in upholding professional principles, engaging in processes of deliberation, decision-making and responsibility for societal benefit. In biomedical ethics, these ideas are reflected in four moral principles of 'respect for autonomy; beneficence; non-maleficence and justice' (Beauchamp & Childress, 2001: 13). In the latter account, autonomy relates to the rights of both service providers and users to make decisions about matters that affect them; beneficence concerns benefit to society through services; non-maleficence involves doing no harm; and justice means taking responsibility for promoting equality and fairness in practice.

What Does It Mean to Be an Ethical Graduate?

In terms of ethical outcomes of tertiary education, Bowden et al. (2000) defined graduate attributes as qualities which extended beyond knowledge or skills acquisition in preparing students as 'agents of social good'. For these authors, graduate attributes represent

> the qualities, skills and understandings a university community agrees its students should develop during their time with the institution. These attributes include but go beyond the disciplinary expertise or technical knowledge that has traditionally formed the core of most university courses. They are qualities that also prepare graduates as agents of social good in an unknown future.
>
> (cited in Barrie, 2004: 262)

For contemporary Scottish graduates, the Quality Assurance Agency for Higher Education in Scotland (QAA Scotland, 2011) proposed eight generic attributes as common elements threaded through the principles, ethos and strategic priorities of Scottish higher education institutions. Drawing on a sector-wide investigation, these were outlined as the following:

- Lifelong learning
- Research, scholarship and enquiry
- Employability and career development
- Global citizenship
- Communication and information literacy
- Ethical, social and professional understanding

- Personal and intellectual autonomy
- Collaboration, leadership and teamwork

(QAA Scotland, 2011: 2)

Of particular interest to ethical learning in higher education were QAA Scotland's aims to foster global citizenship, lifelong learning, collaboration and ethical, social and professional understanding. Reviewing the graduate attributes devised by the Australian universities of Melbourne and Sydney, Nicol (2010: 2) identified common aims of enhancing knowledge, capabilities and personal qualities, in a process of 'preparing students for lifelong learning in a complex world'. Attributes developed by the University of Technology Sydney (UTS) were linked to a model for learning which focused not only on what attributes students can develop, but also on where learning is located and what methods are used to develop capabilities for future practice (UTS, 2011: 2). In the model, headings of 'personal, professional and intellectual' attributes were cross-referenced to learning contexts, described as 'research-inspired and integrated, practice-oriented and situated in [the] global workplace' (ibid.: 2). In the latter goal, international mobility and cross-cultural engagement were fostered as key aspects of ethical learning for global citizenship.

QAA Scotland's (2011) compilation of graduate attributes shows similarities to processes of determining traits as characteristics of professions. Anglo-American authors Flexner (1915), Sullivan (1995) and Carr (2000) identified key traits of professions as including specialist knowledge and expertise, autonomy, association and altruism. Comparisons among these factors and the QAA Scotland attributes of learning can be determined in collaboration and associative professional membership and between personal autonomy and professional responsibility. In particular, aspects of professional altruism are apparent in aims of citizenship and ethical understanding, and in Bowden et al.'s (2000) notion of 'preparing graduates as agents of social good'. The QAA project of determining attributes recognised qualities of critical thinking as central to academic study, but added a need to establish 'flexible competencies needed for a knowledge economy' and the contribution of higher education to 'culture, citizenship and intellectual growth in Scotland' (QAA, 2011: 1). In this analysis, higher education has interests beyond individual accreditation, towards the good of society. As a transforming influence in society, an ethical perspective of academic study indicates ways in which education contributes to society, balanced against individualised acquisition of credentials for the advancement of social and economic capital (Bourdieu, 1986).

Why Is Ethical Learning Important for 21st-Century Graduates?

Challenges for 21st-century graduates include a decline in public trust of professions and in the autonomy of professionals (O'Neill, 2002). Arguing that accreditation of pre-qualifying professional practice is driven by a reductionist standardisation of competency, O'Neill suggested that this approach focused on sufficiency rather than excellence, and on compliance rather than the development of critical awareness of what constitutes good practice. In this respect, Maslow (1943) had described responding to preset targets as a deficit approach to learning, where over-reliance on extrinsically determined motives could restrict growth of autonomy or self-governance. As an alternative to standardised competency, O'Neill endorsed a need for professional practitioners to develop 'intelligent accountability', which incorporated self-efficacy and agency in taking responsibility, making decisions and carrying out professional judgements in order to regain public trust. Proposing trust as key to professional practice, O'Neill explained that those holding public office in the UK were required to conform to the seven 'Nolan' principles of 'selflessness, integrity, objectivity, accountability, openness, honesty and leadership' (Committee on Standards in Public Life, 2015: 23). Evetts (2013) argued that in response to neo-liberal managerialism, agency and ethical judgement have declined and been replaced by professionalism as a normative construct of identity. In this respect, ideas of 'being ethical' as a graduate attribute suggest that completing students and their potential employers have a common understanding of applicants as responsible and trustworthy, able to demonstrate commitment and integrity in their approach to practice. For most professions, ethical decisions are considered to involve reference to a relevant code of practice; for example, professional principles of education or social care.

In response to challenges of declining agency and trust in professions, Cough (2002) suggested Aristotle's concept of *phronēsis*, or practical wisdom, as a necessary factor of being an ethical professional. Cough (ibid.: 12) described phronēsis as 'not just wisdom of knowing that, but wisdom of knowing how to do the right thing, in the right place at the right time'. In Greek philosophy, Aristotle argued that well-being is the goal of humanity and for individuals to achieve this, development of moral character, as a combination of knowledge, experience and ethical judgement, is required. Flyvbjerg (2001: 57) explained that Aristotle had used the terms *techne* to describe skill, craft or 'know how'; *episteme* as scientific, universal knowledge or 'know why'; and phronēsis to identify moral understanding of knowing the right judgement to make. Flyvbjerg considered that, in contrast to Foucault's (1984) concern about ethics of the self, Aristotle was concerned with ethics in relation to society:

> Foucault ... talks about 'aesthetics of existence', that is, the relationship you have with yourself when you act. Aristotle, in discussing phronēsis, is mainly talking about ethics in relation to social and political praxis, that is, the relationship you have with society when you act.
>
> (Flyvbjerg, 2001: 55)

In this sense, if professions have a pact with society to deliver specialist services and maintain levels and standards of quality, it follows that understanding ways in which ethics are perceived, shaped and learned is a necessary factor of preparation for professional practice. Yet it seems that ethics play a restricted role in professional learning. In UK social work, Banks (2014) indicated an expanding interest in ethics from the 1990s, but argued a tendency towards responding to codes of practice and regulation of conduct, resulting from influences of neo-liberalism and organisational managerialism in public service professions. This latter process of managerialism in professions, Banks argued, had increasingly taken precedence over a moral agency perspective of autonomous ethical practice towards equalities and social justice.

From their research with medical students, Monrouxe et al. (2011: 527) considered that individual and collective discourses of professionalism did not encompass the complexity of 'wise application' stemming from Aristotle's ideas of phronēsis, but viewed wise application as emerging over time through competent practice and effective communication, set within ethical and legal procedures. As a professional aspiration, wise application became the pinnacle of 'excellence, humanism, accountability and altruism' (ibid.). Hilton and Slotnick (2005: 61) argued a similar emphasis for ethical practice as a domain of professionalism in medicine. The authors saw phronēsis as a central feature of the 'mature professional', who knew 'which rules to break and how far to break them' in responding to situated dilemmas. Monrouxe et al. (ibid.) suggested that this level of insightful judgement could be achieved only through significant and accumulated experience in dealing with 'paradox, complexity and uncertainty'. In this respect, phronēsis required development through experience over time, with opportunities to make deliberative ethical judgements, both individually and collectively, about complex matters of the 'greatest human concern' (Schön, 1987: 3). To expand on these ideas, the next section examines some theories and models of ethical learning and development.

Theories of Ethical Learning and Development

Aristotle's *Nicomachean Ethics* (Cahn, 1990) described the process whereby phronēsis could be achieved through experience, artistry, teaching others, mastery and deliberation. First, Aristotle suggested that skills learned through experience were more valuable than theoretical knowledge and that the combination of theory and practice, termed artistry, had even more value. Repeated integration of theory and practice as artistry then led to a stage of mastery, which enabled and was enhanced by the experience of teaching others. Beyond mastery, Aristotle suggested the highest aspiration of learning to be phronēsis. He believed that the *phronimos*, or person of practical wisdom, developed this state through mastery derived from an ability to determine what is good, to deliberate and to act on that deliberation towards societal well-being. By repeating this approach in a range of situations, habit would be formed, and through habit, disposition. Aristotle suggested that virtues such as loyalty, generosity, trust and courage were learned through interaction with others and that this contributed to a virtuous disposition, formed through the habit of experience and by deliberation towards a common good. Knowing the right approach to take, Aristotle argued, came from deliberation based on these intentions, which in professional practice might be interpreted as professional judgement or ethical decision-making. Deliberation in Aristotle's construct has similarities to reflection as a means of investigative experiential learning (Schön, 1983; Kolb, 1984), where critical analysis of a situation is followed by new action. Explaining deliberation as concerned with matters of complexity, Aristotle stressed the importance of collective decision-making in the proposal that where a problem was too great for individual resolution, dialogue and debate with others would be necessary.

> Deliberation concerns what is usually one way rather than another, where the outcome is unclear and the right way to act is undefined. And we enlist partners in deliberation on large issues when we distrust our own ability to discern the right answer.
>
> (Aristotle, cited in Cahn, 1990: 246)

In this interpretation, participation with others in debating moral action becomes a necessary factor of ethical learning. According to Sfard (1998: 6), ways in which new learning is developed can be described as metaphors of acquisition or participation, and that a balance between the two forms is necessary for effective practice. As acquisition, Sfard suggested that knowledge is received, interpreted and internalised as concept development, in a process of 'gaining possession over some commodity'. As participation, Sfard proposed that learning involved becoming a member of a community, assimilating and contributing to norms through apprenticeship, moving from a peripheral position to situated membership (Lave & Wenger, 1991). In this view of participative learning, ethical understanding may be developed through observation, modelling and replication, as in Aristotle's initial stages in development of phronēsis. Whereas practical examples of participative learning communities are discussed later in this chapter, the next section examines three models of developmental ethical learning.

Three Models of Ethical Learning

Recognising that individually and culturally formed values and principles underpin the student experience, ideas about agency and responsibility based on self-reliance, mutual trust, respect and integrity underpin learning, teaching and assessment principles of university education across disciplines. How do these concepts relate to developmental processes of student learning? In this section, three models of ethical learning are considered, drawing from the work of Perry (1970), Kohlberg (1986) and King and Kitchener (1994). In the United States, Perry conducted over 400 interviews with university students about ways in which ethical behaviour was learned. From this data, Perry (1970: 16) proposed that students moved through stages of ethical learning as a developmental process from duality to multiplicity and relativism, resulting in personal commitment. A summary of Perry's key ideas is presented in Figure 7.1.

In Perry's research, students' moral development commonly began at a point where knowledge and values were perceived as absolute, and behaviour would be either right or wrong. In a second stage, multiple perspectives were recognised, within a parameter that 'everyone might be entitled to their own view' (ibid.). From this stage, awareness of ethical perspectives as relative to specific contexts emerged. A position of relativism, Perry (1970: 259) explained, represented 'a plurality of points of view, interpretations, frames of reference; value systems and contingencies in which the structural properties of contexts and forms allow various sorts of analysis, comparison and evaluation in multiplicity'. This process of critique, comparison and evaluation led to a position of ethical commitment, where the students' personal views took shape. Perry stressed that personal commitments were continually 'expanded or remade in new terms as growth', and that balances of diverse perspectives were determined through the 'tensions of polarities', in particular through alternating processes of reflection and action (Perry, 1970: 262).

King and Kitchener (1994: 44–74) drew from Perry's ideas in developing their model of reflective judgement. The authors proposed a seven-stage progression of assumptions about knowledge, from a position where acquired knowledge is believed as true, to a position where knowledge is assumed to be subject to interpretation, and solutions could be formed through critical reflective inquiry, as shown in Table 7.1.

| Duality (right or wrong) | Multiplicity (multiple perspectives) | Relativism (context specific) | Commitment (personal beliefs) |

Figure 7.1 Four stages of ethical learning (adapted from Perry, 1970).

Table 7.1 Stages of Reflective Judgement (Adapted from King and Kitchener, 1994)

Stage	Development	Assumptions about knowledge
1	Observed	What is observed is considered to be true and justification is not required – all problems have true responses.
2	Received	Knowledge held by those in authority is true. The task for individual is to determine which authorities to believe.
3	Justified	Assumption that while ultimately all knowledge can be validated, some problems are presently unsolvable and solutions are justifiable on basis of personal feelings or understanding.
4	Abstracted	Individuals recognise uncertainty of knowledge and are sceptical of role of authority figure in determining what is true.

(continued)

Table 7.1 Stages of Reflective Judgement (Adapted from King and Kitchener, 1994) *(continued)*

Stage	Development	Assumptions about knowledge
5	Contextual	Assumption that knowledge must be considered within a context to achieve interpretation relative to particular circumstances.
6	Reasoned	Knowing involves arguments, evaluation, comparison of evidence and opinions.
7	Reflective Judgement	Recognition that although knowledge is subject to interpretation and uncertainty, critical reflective inquiry can construct reasoned solutions.

Table 7.1 outlines a developmental approach to ethical learning, which for students might represent progression from an accepted acquisition of knowledge, to a perspective that differing views can be validated or justified, then to knowledge as relative to particular contexts. As students develop skills of questioning, investigation and argument through academic study, a stage of reasoning, evidence and justification is achieved. In the seventh stage of reflective judgement, the process of critical reflective judgement might be compared with a move from relativism as analysis of a specific context to a commitment to personal professional autonomy.

In a third framework, Kohlberg's (1986: 34–35) model of moral development proposed a similar six-stage progression from rule-dependency to self-efficacy in selecting ethical principles, structured in levels described as 'pre-conventional, conventional and post-conventional'. In Kohlberg's construct, the learner moved from an initial 'pre-conventional level', first adhering to rules, then appreciating different interests, to a 'conventional' level that incorporated stages of both self and societal regard. Here, the learner responded first to the expectations of others as a means of determining self-regard, and then complied with societal norms in order to perpetuate a particular social system. Kohlberg's 'post-conventional' level involved stages of relative rules towards impartial welfare and the eventual development of self-selected universal ethical principles, which, Kohlberg explained, may represent conflict with rules or laws. In Kohlberg's final stage, self-determination of ethical values corresponded to Perry's (1970) idea of personal commitment. In Kohlberg's model, stages were similar to transformative ideas of learning, where knowledge is first assimilated, then critically reviewed in order to surface contradictions, leading to transformative change (Freire, 1970; Habermas, 1971).

These three models are useful in explaining individual and interpersonal processes of moral learning as socially constructed, in relation to the received knowledge, to expectations of others in workplace contexts, and to professional principles. For students undertaking a professional degree, such as teaching, nursing or social work, experiential learning forms a significant aspect of study. A move from university to workplace as the location for learning provides students with opportunities to develop situated ethical understanding, for example, Perry's (1970) relativist and commitment stages, or King and Kitchener's (1994) contextual, reasoned and reflective judgement stages. From theoretical ideas of ethics and ethical development, professional codes of practice and frameworks of practice competence are used to inform and assess students in practice experience. In the next section, examples of theoretical and profession-specific ways in which ethical learning has been developed in the curriculum are considered.

Teaching Ethics: Three Approaches and Two Case Studies

From a UK research project on teaching and learning ethics in higher education, Illingworth (2004: 9) identified the three main approaches applied in universities as 'pragmatic, embedded or theoretical'. In a theoretical approach, key ideas of moral philosophies; for example, Kant's deontology, Aristotle's virtue ethics or John Stuart Mill's utilitarianism might be introduced, with discussion of ethical dilemmas in relation to each set of ideas. A pragmatic approach, Illingworth explained, would introduce ethical considerations through profession-specific values, principles and codes of practice, and through ethical requirements for conducting research. An embedded approach addressed ethical learning through situated examples of practice dilemmas, using processes of 'reflective critical thinking, narrative or dramatisation' (Illingworth, 2004: 35). Following the UTS (2011) suggestion that not only method, but also location of learning has significance in developing attributes, the theoretical, pragmatic and embedded approaches relate to the academy, profession and workplace as primary learning locations. In relation to models of development, Kohlberg's (1986: 35) 'pre-conventional stage' of rule-dependency might correspond to the pragmatic approach of first identifying required standards, whereas 'conventional and post-conventional' (ibid: 36) stages of self-efficacy in selecting ethical principles could be developed through ongoing embedded approaches of critical reflective analysis. Illingworth explained that the three approaches were routinely integrated, in that a theoretical approach would underpin and enhance the development of critical debate and analysis of principles and practices examined through pragmatic and embedded learning approaches.

To illustrate Illingworth's (2004: 9) three 'embedded, pragmatic and theoretical' approaches, two case studies are presented as examples of ethical learning in Scottish nursing and social work undergraduate programmes. The case studies use first-person accounts drawn from semi-structured interviews with two lecturers from a Scottish university whose work involved devising and delivering ethical teaching and learning. The semi-structured interviews were conducted and transcribed during 2014 by the author, who described the respondents as 'Nursing Lecturer' and 'Social Work Lecturer'. In the first case study, shown in Case Study 7.1, the Nursing Lecturer explained methods used for teaching and learning in an undergraduate programme and the significance of ethical practice in nursing.

Case Study 7.1 Teaching Ethics in Nursing

Ethical practice is essential in situations where practitioners are working with people, respecting the individual, and from a nursing perspective, ensuring not only correct treatment but also compassion and care. Ethics are taught in an interdisciplinary module, shared between about 450 nursing and medical students. The students are given an online profession-specific reader which outlines ethical theories and precepts such as justice, non-maleficence, beneficence and autonomy – this can form a sort of moral compass for decision making. For example, 'is my decision fair, does it respect the autonomy of the individual, will it do no harm, or will it do good?' Then there is a lecture for all students. At a later stage, students undertake problem-based learning sessions in interdisciplinary groups of 20, jointly facilitated by nursing and medical lecturing staff. In sub-groups of 6-7, the students work through a series of ethical dilemmas in clinical practice, and based on the theoretical materials, they come up with perceptions of the problem and justify their decisions and actions. They present their proposed decisions and actions to the larger group of 20, followed by a Q & A session and then evaluation. Examples of scenarios might be: i) a dementia patient in a nursing home, previously active, has become agitated, and his family are now concerned that he has been over sedated; or ii) a woman from an ethnic group requires urgent medical attention at a time when no female practitioner is available, and her culture would not permit her to be examined by a male doctor.

In the nursing case study, lectures were used to deliver theoretical ideas to large groups of students. Advantages are that this can be an effective and administratively efficient way to deliver information to a large audience. Disadvantages might include limited opportunities for active engagement in learning on the part of students, which may affect attention span and retention of ideas, and may not suit all learning styles. To address these concerns, self-directed study materials were provided online prior to lectures, which allowed students to prepare for lectures and undertake follow-up activities. An embedded approach of debating practice dilemmas in groups was introduced, using a problem-based learning approach. Interdisciplinary learning groups were selected to ensure a balance of gender, culture and discipline. Dilemmas were prepared by staff and presented to each group. The facilitation of groups by staff members ensured that ground rules were set, all participants were encouraged to contribute, discussion was not dominated by individuals and conclusions were communicated to the wider group. The example indicated that teaching ethics was shared by multiple staff members across programmes, rather than being delivered by individual lecturers, or as separate modules. In terms of assessment, where ethical practice learning in nursing was mainly assessed through supervised evidence-based practice, embedded methods of reflective analysis and dramatisation contributed to this.

An example of ethical learning in practice assessment might be to select a critical incident from a clinical placement, deconstruct the incident using a model of reflection and refer to ethical theories. In another example, learning about suicide risk used an assessment called 'Observable Simulated Clinical Examination' (OSCE) as a way of testing skills, observations, verbal skills and ethical engagement with a patient. In this format, a simulated patient has a script, and the student works through a dialogue to determine a profile of suicide risk.

(Nursing Lecturer)

This latter technique of semi-scripted dramatisation might be suited to situations where students would be expected to demonstrate particular ethical behaviours in response to set procedures; for example, in history taking or client interviewing. The approach might represent Perry's (1970) initial idea of duality, where there is an expectation of a right or wrong way to act (Hilton & Slotnick, 2005). In a second case study, shown in Case Study 7.2, a combination of theoretical, pragmatic and embedded approaches to teaching ethics is described as part of a module on reflective practice in an undergraduate social work degree.

Case Study 7.2 Teaching Ethics in Social Work

Currently, ethics are taught as part of a second year reflective practice module. With programme review, this will change – more theoretical lectures will be introduced, and more ideas about reflective practice will be examined, in preparation for students going out on placement. That will allow more emphasis on moral thinking and decision making. Part of the reason for change is that ethics was 'squeezed in'; there wasn't sufficient time to explore ethical ideas and relate these to practice. Teaching ethics from a theoretical perspective can be quite challenging; second year undergraduate students might not fully engage with this – they might listen to lectures but not fully appreciate what this has to do with their practice. So the approach is making sure that ethical ideas are meaningful to students. They have a summary outline of key theories and recommended reading in initial lectures, then we would look at what ethics would mean in practice, encouraging the students to draw from practice examples, and engaging in debates within the classroom. It does need the students to work as a group, to be open to discussion and respectful of different perspectives. Examples of issues from students included whether or not foster carers should be paid, or if a student on a short-term placement be involved in personal care with elderly people. In discussions, students were encouraged to present reasoned arguments, listen to differing viewpoints and think about the wider ethical theories. Another format used in the module was to ask students to watch a Harvard University

(continued)

Case Study 7.2 Teaching Ethics in Social Work
(continued)

online programme, 'The moral side of murder' (Sandel, 2009), where a Harvard lecturer takes a student audience through a series of ethical decisions. After students had watched the programme we would discuss it in the next lecture. In third and fourth year, ethical decision making is more practice-based and can involve complex social issues. Students understand that although there are codes of ethical practice, there are no straight-forward right or wrong answers. For example, in discussion of whether or not people who use substances should keep their children, students can easily move to a stage of thinking about 'well, surely that depends on the level of substance use', but then they might not take that further into the complexities of substance use in society.

In this case, getting the relationship between theory and practice right for students was emphasised, in order to ensure that ethical and professional principles were understood in relation to student experience of practice contexts. This example indicated challenges of initial theoretical lectures on ideas about ethics, followed by a move to a more embedded approach involving theories about reflective analysis, deliberation and judgement. In a pragmatic sense, profession-specific materials were provided through face-to-face and online lectures to inform students of required codes of practice and competency frameworks; these underpinned evidence-based experiential practice learning and assessment. Embedded approaches were exemplified in the use of Internet video resources on professional dilemmas followed by group discussion, as in the Harvard example (Sandel, 2009). In this example, the group involved second-year students who had not yet undertaken practice experience. As a result, an ethical approach at this point might respond to Perry's (1970) idea of exploring dualism in the students' own perspectives, or multiplicity of responses in relation to simulated practice dilemmas. Third- and fourth-year social work students then represented King and Kitchener's (1994) move from abstracted and contextual stages of ethical understanding, to levels of reasoning and reflective judgment, and Perry's stages of relativism and personal commitment. This case study indicated the developmental nature of ethical learning and the importance of examining theories and principles through situated dilemmas, whether drawn from practice or as simulated scenarios. The respondent considered that as universities create international partnerships with increased student mobility and transnational delivery of online programmes, awareness of ethical approaches within different cultures was becoming more significant. In this respect it was proposed that a wider understanding of world religions and cultures through professional study could benefit inclusive ethical approaches to diversity and equality in society.

In teaching ethics, both case studies gave examples of ways in which Illingworth's (2004) theoretical, pragmatic and embedded approaches to ethical learning are integrated in higher education. The two programmes indicated that complex ideas needed to be delivered by lecturing staff with differing expert interests, in a range of ways that would meet diverse student learning styles. Recognising the situated nature of ethical learning in profession-specific examples, for students in higher education programmes where experiential practice is not a requirement, there are other possibilities for engagement with communities of practice. To illustrate these, four contexts for participative ethical learning are presented next, described as academic, workplace, local and global learning communities.

Four Contexts for Participative Ethical Learning

From Sfard's (1998) proposal of a balance between acquisition and participation as necessary for effective learning, this section proposes that knowledge and skills acquisition, enhanced by broadening experiences of participative learning across different contexts, will allow students to develop their awareness of the purposes of ethical practice as a contribution to social good. In Figure 7.2, four learning communities which can enhance student ethical awareness are shown: the discipline of academic study, workplace-based practice experience, student and community life, and digital learning communities. Reflecting Patrick Geddes's maxim of 'think global, act local' (McDonald, 2004: 12), digital communities are described as having global learning potential, whereas face-to-face interaction in student or community

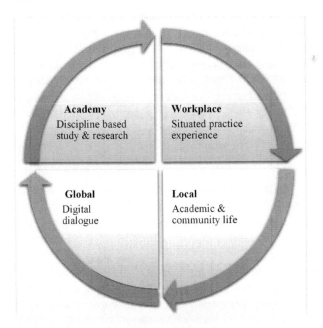

Figure 7.2 Contexts for participative ethical learning.

organisations is described as 'local'. Learning contexts of university and work are termed 'academy and workplace' respectively.

In the 'academic' location, higher education study through processes of academic research and investigation encourages students to develop skills of critical analysis and debate on ethical issues, as participants in local and global communities of learning. In most disciplines, students will undertake collaborative and interdisciplinary learning approaches that offer opportunities to enhance skills of communication, negotiation and debate. Academic research and inquiry follows required ethical standards; for example, informed choice, welfare, privacy, anonymity and confidentiality (Sarantakos, 2013). In the 'workplace' situation, profession-specific programmes of study provide situated opportunities for students to develop ethical awareness in relation to codes of practice, through processes of modelling, coaching, mentoring and supervision within communities of practice (Lave & Wenger, 1991). Similarly, Aristotle's concept of phronēsis involved practice experience, decision-making and teaching others. Where work experience is not integral to a programme of study, other contexts for experiential learning may be introduced, such as international exchanges, or non-university part-time or voluntary work.

In the 'local' position, participation in student life at university can equip students with skills and abilities in fostering equal and inclusive cross-cultural collaboration. Engagement in wider communities of interest which involve participation through volunteering, fund-raising or event organisation might allow students to experience collaboration, ethical decision-making and develop organisational skills and leadership capabilities. As a key factor of Aristotle's development of 'wise practice', opportunities for students to teach others might be generated through peer support programmes, both within and across disciplines. In the 'global' learning location, potential for students to engage with international learning opportunities through interactive communicative technologies continues to expand exponentially. As digital communication plays an increasingly central role in the way that human societies interrelate, grow and change, ethical practices in this context become increasingly essential. Building cross-cultural experience and understanding through online communication across boundaries of geographical context can offer 21st-century learners new horizons of interdisciplinary shared learning, understanding and global citizenship.

The model in Figure 7.2 shows a connected and continuous relationship between each location, to indicate potential for integrated and ongoing learning. In enabling learning across contexts, Bowden et al. suggested that experience should form the primary focus of learning and that the university could facilitate and support, rather than manage, a student-centred approach to learning. The authors proposed that

> [it] is far better to focus on real-life experiences and on what it means to develop such capabilities within them … we advocate a strongly student-centred process and argue that the responsibility for managing it should rest primarily with the student in a context of university support systems.
>
> (Bowden et al., 2000: 11)

An example of facilitating the recording of inter-related ethical learning might be an online evidence-based personal professional portfolio, commonly promoted in higher education for employability and career progression. This is developed throughout the student's academic career and used to demonstrate graduate attributes relating to personal, professional, ethical and intellectual achievements, through academic study, professional practice and participation in local and global community life. A learning framework, as in the example of UTS (2011), can encourage students to demonstrate the relationships between ethical understanding and intellectual knowledge and skills, recognising the significance of academic, work, local and global locations for experiential learning. To develop ethical responsibility as a graduate attribute, it is recognised that learning approaches which foster individual and collaborative communication, deliberation, problem-solving and decision-making can enhance professional awareness and employability (Hayes & Llewellyn, 2010). Similarly, transferable ethical values embedded in graduate attributes can be enhanced by investigative and participative experiences of higher education, not only within the discipline of study but also through active participation in local and global communities of learning, with benefit to the individual graduate, their chosen profession and the societal context of their practice.

Practice Guide

In order to broaden the scope of ethical learning approaches, the next section examines further practical examples of ethics teaching and learning, in a series of critical and creative activities which encourage reflective and participative analysis and debate about ethical dilemmas. Where Illingworth (2004: 9) found that 'theoretical, pragmatic and embedded' teaching practices were most commonly used in teaching ethics across UK universities, 'embedded' learning approaches were described as 'reflective practice, narrative and dramatisation' (ibid: 35). In this section, the latter three embedded approaches are used to present examples of individual and participative ethical learning methods.

Reflective Practice

Reflection is a key concept of 21st-century approaches to professional learning which involves learner engagement in the critical analysis, interpretation and critique of their practice. To ensure a balance between knowledge acquisition and participative experiential learning, reflection offers a means of linking theory to practice and surfacing and challenging influences or assumptions (Rolfe et al., 2001; Moon, 2004). For this chapter, key theories about reflection include Schön's (1983) ideas of reflection on- and in- action; Aristotle's concept of deliberation as reflection for action; Freire's (1970) suggestion of praxis as of reflection and action, and King and Kitchener's (1994) stages of reflective judgement.

Practical techniques for encouraging reflection can involve written accounts, dialogue or group discussion, which might use structured analytical frameworks, values clarification or creative methods such as narrative or dramatisation. Examples of analytical frameworks for reflection include Borton's (1970) reflective questions of 'What? So what? Now what?' (cited in Jasper, 2013: 99–101), or Gibbs's (1988) reflective cycle of process of describing an experience, identifying feelings, evaluating positive or negative aspects, sense-making, concluding and taking action (cited in Jasper, 2013: 80). Johns's (2013: 37) model of structured reflection focuses on five core stages, described as 'preparatory, descriptive, reflective, anticipatory and insight', allowing the practitioner to progress from an initial stage of self-awareness, through analysis of change and improvement, to determining what has been learned from the experience. An analytical framework for ethical decision-making, based on the work of Nash (1981), Forester-Miller and Davis (1995) and Guy (1990), presents a basis for reflective thinking towards action. In this process, decision-making begins with gathering information, considering alternative choices and consequences, followed by implementation and acknowledgement of implications.

- Information – what is known about the situation?
- Influences – what history, background and influences?
- Assumptions – what assumptions could influence decisions?
- Alternatives – what different approaches are possible?
- Consequences – what are short or long term outcomes of each?
- Resolution – what decisions are made?
- Implementation – what action is carried out?
- Implications – what responsibility, evaluation and next steps?

Through consideration of implications, taking responsibility for stages of resolution and action are key parts of the decision-making process. Examples of this stage included questions of 'Could you explain this decision to your manager, or to your family?' or 'How would you support this decision if interviewed by the media, or on TV?' (Nash, 1981: 79–90).

In values clarification, activities with small groups might involve the provision of statements concerning inequalities or moral concerns, where students are asked to position themselves on a line from 'strongly agree' to 'strongly disagree' depending on their views about the issue. After providing more information which might alter opinions, the activity is repeated. At each stage, students are asked why they have selected a particular viewpoint, or why they have changed their opinion. In large-group teaching, an audience-response system can be used in values clarification to encourage participation and reflective dialogue about ethical issues. From structured analytical approaches, the next two sections outline creative methods for reflective analysis and resolution of ethical dilemmas.

Narrative

Reason and Hawkins (1988) suggested that narrative explanation and expression are two key modes of reflecting on and processing experience. The authors proposed narrative storytelling as an emergent paradigm of inquiry which allowed people to connect more effectively with the underlying issues of experience, and as a result see more clearly the influences and meanings which form practice. As a method of examining ethical issues, Illingworth (2004) proposed that narrative can be a crossover between reflective writing and dramatised scenarios. Creative writing techniques of telling a story from the viewpoint of different characters or rewriting an experienced critical incident from a third-person perspective can reveal new understanding and awareness. Narratives as storytelling or poetry can illustrate problems, conflicts, successes and challenges, or can offer ways to look at things from different angles and to explore alternative perspectives. Using metaphors in reflective writing can help to clarify assumptions and values, and identify some of the key restrictions or enablers in a situation.

Illingworth (2004: 51) warned of possible sensitivities for students in writing or sharing personalised narratives, suggesting that this approach needed careful guidance and support, recommending that 'a moderate distance from issues is conducive to a balanced and constructive debate'. To present distance, the author suggested that using books, films or television programmes as source materials could provide objective examples of how people deal with difficult moral dilemmas. In this case, structured discussion and debate about the ethical situations represented can provide opportunities for analysis, clarification and insight concerning the actions and characters involved without direct experiential or emotional involvement.

Dramatisation

As a further example of active participative learning, exploring ethical scenarios through scripted or improvised dramatisation can offer students a supported environment in which to examine complex problems and to develop communication skills for practice. Illingworth (2004) proposed benefits of dramatisation to include opportunities to engage with multiple perspectives; for example, of culture, gender or beliefs; empathising with others who might have different viewpoints to their own; understanding service users' perspectives; practicing decision-making and using skill sets of communication, listening and engagement. In the nursing case study, scripted action was used in assessment of ethical communication skills. Similarly, non-scripted, improvised action with professional or volunteer actors can offer insightful ways to explore scenarios, uncover complexities and develop decision-making capabilities. A small-group session using dramatisation of scenarios might involve improvised action with involvement of staff and/or students, ensuring that student participation is voluntary and that the process begins and ends with discussion of the learning process. Resources might include an outline of the dilemma, with character cards describing each participant and their involvement in the situation. Other methods include small groups of five to six presenting progressive stages in a scenario; or a freeze-frame technique, where groups present a series of 'still photographs' to show a dilemma, consequences and resolution. Perry's (1970) suggested stages of multiplicity and relativism in ethical issues could relate to this approach, where students might debate individual sociocultural views and situated experiences within the activity.

Boal's (2000) concept of Forum Theatre, based on the consciousness-raising and emancipatory ideas of Paolo Freire (1970), focuses on critical analysis and decision-making for action. Boal's proposal was that humans are both spectators and actors, so in Forum Theatre, boundaries between actors and audience are removed. Actors present the influence, action and outcome of a social concern. Members of the audience are invited to stop the presentation at a point where they wish to contest the action, and, by taking the place of the actor (or directing the action), resolve the dilemma in a different way. An example of a Forum Theatre issue might be substance abuse through peer pressure, with members of the audience proposing different actions and solutions. The activity concludes with follow-up discussion about the dilemma, to examine the social context of the issue and to challenge assumptions. Where a range of approaches have evolved from Boal's original format of Forum Theatre, core features include critical reflective analysis on social issues, awareness of potential for change and dialogue as participative transformative praxis.

In these three embedded participative approaches, building on theoretical ethical knowledge and practical skills, ethical approaches as 'ways of being' can be developed (Bowles et al., 2006: 224). The authors use this term to describe a capacity to exercise virtues such as integrity, discretion, tolerance, empathy, and being open-minded and reflective. Embedded, participative approaches offer opportunities for students to further develop capacity for self-awareness and reflective deliberation, following Hugman's (2005: 162) proposal that ethics education supports graduates in becoming 'mindful, reflective and insightful'.

Conclusion

This chapter has argued that as graduates prepare to become professional practitioners in an era of complex and challenging technological advancement and globalisation, ethical education has increasing significance in fostering graduates as 'agents of social good' (Bowden et al., 2000). As technologies expand the creation, analysis and accessibility of knowledge, a corresponding increase in learning the skills and insights of wise practice becomes necessary to ensure that graduates can apply the right knowledge, in the right way, at the right time.

The processes for ethical learning, including Aristotle's idea of phronēsis, formed through experience, deliberation, artistry, mastery and teaching others, suggest a continuous learning approach that not only underpins experiential qualifying learning for students, but also describes a framework for career-long ethical learning in professions. The three theoretical models of Perry (1970), Kohlberg (1986) and King and Kitchener (1994) illustrate the progressive nature of ethical learning, indicating moral growth from dualism to multiplicity, relativity and reflective judgment. Examples of these learning processes and of Illingworth's (2004) theoretical, pragmatic and embedded approaches to ethics education underpin the two case studies drawn from Scottish nursing and social work programmes. In these two cases, ethical theories and professional codes of practice were first introduced in lectures and as online materials. Structured discussion about practice-related dilemmas and problem-based learning activities then provided opportunities for students to develop skills of communication, critical analytical reflection, self-awareness, reasoning and reflexivity.

Examples of local and global participation in academic study and workplace experience are potential locations for wider awareness of ethical issues. Recommendations for expanding interdisciplinary, international and digital learning opportunities have the potential to further enhance awareness and understanding of cultural diversities. As practical approaches for the development of ethics education in the curriculum, Illingworth's (2004: 35) three embedded methods of ethical learning, reflective practice, narrative and dramatisation provide an example examples of activities which can enhance ethical self-awareness and insight. To conclude, if, as Hugman (2005) suggested, levels of ethical learning reflect the importance placed on moral practice in professions, then it is proposed that all professions share a responsibility to ensure that ethical graduates are prepared for their future roles in shaping and transforming well-being, social justice and inclusive citizenship in global societies.

References

Banks, S. (ed) (2014) *Ethics: Critical and Radical Debates in Social Work*. Bristol: Policy Press.

Barrie, S. (2004) 'A research-based approach to generic graduate attributes policy'. *Higher Education Research & Developmen*. 23 (3): 261–275.

Beauchamp, T. & Childress, F. (2001) *Principles of Biomedical Ethics* (5th Ed). Oxford: Oxford University Press.

Boal, A. (2000) *Theatre of the Oppressed*. London: Pluto Press.

Borton, T. (1970) 'Borton's developmental framework'. In Jasper, M. (2013) *Beginning Reflective Practice* (2nd Ed). Andover: Cengage Learning EMEA. pp 99–104.

Bourdieu, P. (1986) 'The forms of capital'. In Richardson, J. G. (Ed.) *Handbook of Theory and Research for the Sociology of Education*. New York: Greenwood Press. 241–258.

Bowden, J., Hart, G., King, B., Trigwell, K. & Watts, O. (2000) *Generic Capabilities of ATN University Graduates*. Canberra: Australian Government Department of Education, Training and Youth Affairs.

Bowles, W., Collingridge, M., Curry, S. & Valentine, B. (2006) *Ethical Practice in Social Work: An Applied Aproach*. Maidenhead: Open University Press.

Bronfenbrenner, U. (1994) 'Ecological models of human development'. In *International Encyclopaedia of Education Vol. 3* (2nd Ed). Oxford: Elsevier.

Cahn, S. (1990) *Classics of Western Philosophy* (3rd Ed). Cambridge: Hackett Publishing Company.

Carr, D. (2000) *Professionalism and Ethics in Teaching*. Abingdon: Routledge.

Committee on Standards in Public Life (2015) *Ethical Standards for Providers of Public Services - Guidance*. London: HMSO. [Accessed 21.2.16].

Cough, P. (2002) *Narratives and Fictions in Educational Research*. Buckingham: Open University Press.

Evetts, J. (2013) 'Professionalism: Value and ideology'. *Current Sociology* 61 (5–6): 778–796.

Flexner, A. (1915) *Is Social Work a Profession?* New York: The New York School of Philanthropy.

Flyvbjerg, B. (2001) *Making Social Science Matter: Why Social Inquiry Fails and How It Can Succeed Again*. New York: Cambridge University Press.

Forester-Miller, H., & Davis, T. (1996) *A Practitioner's Guide to Ethical Decision Making*. Alexandria, VA: American Counselling Association (ACA).

Foucault, M. (1984) 'On the genealogy of ethics: an overview of work in progress'. In Rabinow, P. (Ed) *The Foucault Reader*. New York: Pantheon Books. 340–372.

Freire, P. (1970) *Pedagogy of the Oppressed*. New York: Continuum.

Gibbs, G. (1988) 'Gibb's reflective cycle'. In Jasper, M. (2013) *Beginning Reflective Practice* (2nd Ed). Andover: Cengage Learning EMEA. pp 79-80.

Guy, M. (1990) *Ethical Decision Making in Everyday Work Situations*. New York: Quorum Books.

Habermas, J. (1971) *Knowledge and Human Interests*. London: Heinemann.

Hayes, S. & Llewellyn, A. (2010) *Assessment, Planning, Implementation and Evaluation in Health and Social Care*. Exeter: Reflect Press.

Hilton, S. & Slotnick, H. (2005) 'Proto-professionalism: how professionalism occurs across the continuum of medical education'. *Medical Education* 39: 58–65.

Hugman, R. (2005) *New Approaches in Ethics for the Caring Professions*. London: Palgrave Macmillan.

Illingworth, S. (Ed) (2004) *Approaches to Ethics in Higher Education Learning and Teaching in Ethics across the Curriculum*. Leeds: University of Leeds, PRS-LTSN. [Accessed 10.7.16].

Jasper, M. (2013) *Beginning Reflective Practice* (2nd Ed). Andover: Cengage Learning EMEA.

Johns, C. (2013) *Becoming a Reflective Practitioner* (4th Ed). Chichester: Wiley-Blackwell.

King, P. M. & Kitchener, K.S. (1994) *Developing Reflective Judgement: Understanding and Promoting Intellectual Growth and Critical Thinking in Adolescents and Adults*. San Francisco: Jossey Bass Wiley.

Kohlberg, L. (1986) *The Philosophy of Moral Development*. San Francisco: Harper & Row.

Kolb, D. (1984) *Experiential Learning: Experience as the Source of Learning and Development*. Englewood Cliffs, NJ: Prentice Hall.

Lave, J. & Wenger, E. (1991) *Situated Learning: Legitimate Peripheral Participation*. Cambridge: Cambridge University Press.

Maslow, A. H. (1943) 'A theory of human motivation'. *Psychological Review* 50: 370–396.

McDonald, M. (2004) *Think Global, Act Local: The Life and Legacy of Patrick Geddes*. Edinburgh: Luath Press.

Monrouxe, L., Rees, C. & Hu, W. (2011) 'Differences in medical students' explicit discourses of professionalism: acting, representing becoming'. *Medical Education* 45: 585–602.

Moon, J. (2004) *A Handbook of Reflective and Experiential Learning: Theory and Practice Reflection in Learning & Professional Development: Theory and Practice*. London: Taylor & Francis.

Nash, L. (1981) 'Ethics without the sermon'. *Harvard Business Review* 59: 79–90.

Nicol, D. (2010) *The foundation for graduate attributes: developing self-regulation through self and peer assessment*. Glasgow: QAA Scotland.

O'Neill, O. (2002) *A Question of Trust*. London: BBC. Reith Lectures (3).

Perry, W. (1970) *Forms of Intellectual and Ethical Development in the College Years: A Scheme*. Troy, MO: Holt, Rinehart & Winston.

QAA (Quality Assurance Agency) Scotland (2011) *Graduates for the 21st Century: Integrating the Enhancement Themes – Outcomes and Achievements*. Glasgow: QAA Scotland.

Reason, P. & Hawkins, P. (1988) *Human Inquiry in Action*. London: Sage.

Rolfe, G., Freshwater, D. & Jasper, M. (2001) *Critical Reflection for Nursing and the Helping Professions*. Basingstoke: Palgrave Macmillan.

Sandel, M. (2009) *Justice: What's the right thing to do? Episode 1: The moral side of murder*. WGBH Boston/Harvard University. Online video course [accessed 21.4.16].

Sarantakos, S. (2013) *Social Research* (4th Ed). Basingstoke: Palgrave Macmillan.

Schön, D. (1983) *The Reflective Practitioner: How Professionals Think in Action*. Aldershot: Ashgate Publishing Ltd.

Schön, D. (1987) *Educating the Reflective Practitioner*. San Francisco/Oxford: Jossey-Bass.

Sfard, A. (1998) 'On two metaphors for learning and the dangers of choosing just one'. *Educational Researcher* 27 (2): 4–13.

Sullivan, W. (1995) *Work and Integrity: The Crisis and Promise of Professionalism in North America*. New York: Harper Collins.

UTS (University of Technology Sydney) (2011) *UTS Model of Learning*. https://www.uts .edu.au/research-and-teaching/teaching-and-learning/uts-model-learning/uts-model-learning (Accessed 12.7.16)

Vardy, P. & Grosch, P. (1999) *The Puzzle of Ethics*. London: Fount/HarperCollins.

Chapter 8

The Professional Graduate 27/6/17

Mike Ramsay and Elizabeth Monk

Introduction: Defining the Professional Graduate

The professional graduate may be characterised as one who is qualified, by virtue of their degree level education, to enter a given profession or field; in other words, to have studied within a specific professional discipline (Wheelahan, 2003). Such degrees may be described as vocational in nature and often, as in the case of health-care, teaching or legal professionals, confer a license to practice. We contend that a definition of 'professional' will use more than one lens but will reference the possession of sets of core graduate attributes, which, is another way of defining 'graduateness' (Macdonald Ross, 1996). First, we explore the construct of the pro-fessional graduate then, using two divergent, professional exemplars, we illumi-nate commonalities and variations in the construction of the professional graduate. Emergent here is the concept of graduateness, which is increasingly applied to graduate attributes, values and attitudes that one may ascribe to the dispositional qualities of the graduate.

Graduateness

In recent years, Higher Education (HE) initiatives across the world have highlighted the need for all graduates to be employment ready, demonstrating not only subject specific knowledge and skills, but also the generic skills required for work. In 1997, The National Committee of Inquiry into Higher Education (NCIHE) proposed principles for general education in the United Kingdom (UK) that resulted in change, including an awareness that learning outcomes should reflect employer requirements, including general or transferable skills (NCIHE and Dearing, 1997). Several studies were undertaken following the Dearing Report, determining skills that employers expect from graduates (Williams and Owens, 1997; Fallow and Steven, 2001). These studies identified that graduates of HE programmes should exhibit generic skills that will enable them to acquire and retain employment; in other words a requirement of graduateness and consistent with Macdonald Ross's (1996) notion of graduates possessing core attribute-sets.

Graduateness is a term which has become more prevalent in academic writing and in the HE phraseology in recent years, although its origins may be from the writings of John Newman in 1852 in his discourse on "The Idea of a University":

> ... to see things as they are, to go right to the point, to disentangle a skein of thought, to post with credit and to master any subject with facility. (Newman, 1986: 135, originally 1852, cited by Topping and Taylor, 2010)

This quote reflects the skills of graduates as viewed at the time, but involves many attributes one would associate with having been acquired from a journey through degree study. There is decisive thinking, analysis of competing ideas and an idea of capability or competency suggested; interestingly with the notion of transferability of these skills with reference to mastering "any subject". In this, Newman is advancing a notion of the personal development via acquisition of attributes or skills that accompanies degree study and attainment.

'Graduateness' may be variously defined; however, it currently does not appear in the *Oxford English Dictionary*. It can be found in an online dictionary and is on Wiktionary defined as, "The generic qualities expected of any graduate" (Wiktionary.org, 2013). This lack of status, for what is a term with increasing use in higher education is problematic, not least because the term has a body of academic literature devoted to it. We contend that it should have both enquiry and a subsequent case built for either its fuller acceptance in the language or its reframing or removal from use within higher education. This view is supported in the literature whereby some authors place the word in quotation marks (e.g., Wheelahan, 2003; Smith, 2004; Bernstein et al., 2012), while others do not (e.g., Walker, 1998; Burke and Harris, 2000; Macdonald Ross, 2010).

Glover et al. (2002) lay out the history of the term graduateness and outline both the common themes and competing views around the term. They focus on a definition of "the effect on knowledge, skills and attitudes, of having undertaken an undergraduate degree" (ibid.: 294). They continue by acknowledging the varied interpretation of the term by stakeholders interested in the concept. This definition is important as it conveys a generality of the outcome of successful degree-level study, without bearing down upon the potential detail contained therein. Smith (2004) identifies the difficulties in defining the qualities of graduateness and the value that graduates give to society. He continues by noting the narrow parameters of utility of the graduate as opposed to any other perceived benefit (Smith, 2004). Keith (2010) melds two views by citing both Macdonald Ross (1996) and Wheelahan (2003) who talked of graduate skills and study in a discipline, respectively. Steur et al. (2012) suggest that those concluding undergraduate studies (in any discipline) are fundamentally changed by their learning experiences and marks them from others who have not shared this developmental journey. Walker (1998) refers generically (without describing his notions as a definition) to capable graduates as possessing enough knowledge and skills to function capably, know how to use their skills and yet are also skilled in applying their knowledge. Walker extends this by suggesting that graduate level skilled performance is more than possessing or using a set of specific skills, but is also about setting these within a context of "social, intellectual and moral implications of actions" (Walker, 1998: 2). He continues by cautioning that focusing solely upon key skills-sets (without context) is the antithesis of graduateness, as it relegates learning to being merely occupationally task-oriented (Walker, 1998). Jones (2001) supports this need for discipline context and argues that the socialisation of practice, within disciplines, shapes graduates' understanding of the so-called generic skills.

The application or centrality of these generic skills in how graduateness is manifest is less well agreed upon. For example, Steur et al. (2012) offer the view that graduateness models that are conflated with employability alone risk omitting an accurate assay of the graduate's intellectual capabilities. They go further by cautioning that many such papers deal with graduates' work-readiness. Counter to this is Okay-Somerville and Scholarios (2013), who state that graduateness is employability; however, this view does not say much about how this is demonstrative of professional values or professionalism.

The acquisition of knowledge and skills or competencies are widely agreed upon as facets of graduateness (Walker, 1998; Smith, 2004; Keith, 2010; Steur et al., 2012). Some see the question of generic skills as the hallmarks of graduateness. For example, Wheelahan (2003: 3) observes the advent of generic skills and knowing as being termed "attributes". Equally, Smith (2004: 127) notes the danger of focussing solely upon the "usefulness" of graduate level study and of graduates, at the potential cost to higher ideals of education around autonomy, generation and reappraisal of contemporary ideas and producing knowledge. Instead he cautions that social value is focussed upon graduates being like value-for-money outcomes of education with packets of skills and a readiness to function in work – a financially driven imperative – rather than seeking other esoteric intellectual capabilities. Star and Hammer (2008) note the potential erosion of the higher purpose of degree study and suggest a generic skills approach is to maximise graduate employability. Steur et al. (2012) largely agree with this erosion stance and have created a model of graduateness incorporating intellectual, social and moral development of students' constituents of understanding and a visible attribute-set of the concept.

Wheelahan (2003) notes the particular strength of the links with graduateness in the UK, citing the Higher Education Quality Enhancement Group (HEQC) (1995) report as germinal to a wider academic interest in the term and notion of graduateness and suggests that internationally interest is growing. This highlights a global spread of interest in graduateness and that this strong link with the UK, whilst still apparent in literature, is now replicated elsewhere. North American literature using the term 'graduateness' is nearly non-existent; there are, however, many sources from there where the presence and value of graduate attributes are discussed. A discourse of graduateness can be found in a wide body of professional literature in Europe, Australia, New Zealand and Asia. This body of writing contains explorations of graduateness in a wide range of differing professions within healthcare, business and engineering. This shows something of the width of the concept and of the interpretation of its meaning.

Okay-Somerville and Scholarios (2013) add a new term to the literature in "graduatization" as they explore the attributes of graduates in newly emergent professions that have only recently begun to provide graduate-level preparation. They term graduateness as "employability skills" (ibid.: 557). Interesting here is that they conflate graduateness solely with skills an employer may desire in graduate employees, a view which may run counter to the earlier expressed caution from Steur et al. (2012). Other authors link the attributes with employability, but do not define graduateness solely on that basis alone. Another pertinent issue to emerge from within the notion of 'graduatization' is the apparent acknowledgment of the presence of the developmental process, arguably culminating in graduateness and to, following their argument, employability (Okay-Somerville and Scholarios, 2013). We advance a notion here of the graduate possessing a cluster of skills, values, attitudes and competencies that they can use to enact in the working role. This capabilities-set and the requirement for them to be diligent, responsible and accountable (often to a registration body) arguably establishes the hallmarks of employability, but more, demonstrates the credentials of the professional graduate. Barrie (2006) notes the lack of any theory underpinning the determination of these lists of generic skills which he defines as,

> The skills, knowledge, and abilities of university graduates, beyond disciplinary content knowledge, which are applicable in a range of contexts and are required as the result of completing any undergraduate degree.
>
> (Barrie, 2006: 217)

He further notes the proliferation of terminology for what he terms "graduate attributes," but which are also referred to as soft skills, transferable or employable skills, as well as competencies or capabilities, and even key outcomes. More recently the idea of professionalism and emotional intelligence can also be added to this debate over terminology.

Professionalism

Professionalism has been described in sociological terms by identifying groups and individuals with certain professional traits and activities (Copnell, 2010). There is some obvious overlap with situated learning and Lave and Wenger's (1991) definition of communities-of-practice, where members share a common interest, or profession and where the skills are learnt through watching more experienced members. Saks (2012) reviews the taxonomic view of professions and argues that the view that professions could be defined in terms of the characteristics that they possess may be imperfect, and instead that professionalism may be defined by the way that

> occupational groups gain and/or maintain professional standing based on the creation of legal boundaries that mark out the position of specific occupational groups – be they in accountancy and architecture or law and medicine.
>
> (Saks, 2012: 4)

Knowledge and expertise cannot be discounted within this description as this is one mechanism by which these communities of practice are formed. A formal dictionary definition of professionalism states "the conduct, aims, or qualities that characterize or mark a profession or a professional person" (Merriam-Webster, 2016) with profession in turn defined as "a calling requiring specialized knowledge and often long and intensive academic preparation" (Merriam-Webster, 2016). However, when reviewing disciplines' own codes of professionalism the focus is more on moral and ethical behaviour. In medicine, for example, professionalism may be viewed as a morally virtuous endeavour (Andruszkow et al., 2014).

Professionalism is therefore complex in nature and definition (Burford et al., 2014) and arguably nuanced for families of professions, such as healthcare. A number of individual attributes have been suggested as aspects of professionalism, including accountability, integrity, personal mastery/self-control, trustworthiness and interpersonal skills (Decker, 1999). Here, it is possible to see a resonance with Newman's (1986, cited by Topping and Taylor, 2010) contention, which also includes problem-solving, capability and discipline mastery: attributes applicable to a wide range of professional groups and roles.

These are the types of attributes found within codes of conduct for professions. Codes of conduct contribute to a sense of professionalism. These typically include conduct aspects around service, educational, ethical and personal domains. For example, *The Code: Professional Standards and Behaviour for Nurses and Midwives* (Nursing and Midwifery Council [NMC], 2015) identifies four principles: prioritise people, practice effectively, preserve safety and promote professionalism and trust. This code builds on its predecessor and reflects both the public and profession's expectations. Similarly in accounting, international standards have been developed to ensure that all members of professional accounting bodies have attained the same core competences and capabilities, which include an ethical and moral awareness. Professionalism is, therefore, a societal expectation and professional service/ behaviour ideal, framed around moral, ethical and service conduct aspects of practice. Professional codes are only one route to professionalism, as students are exposed to a variety of other influences including education and wider individual and social factors (Burford et al., 2014). This interplay appears to be a source of professionalism's complexity. Jones (2001) notes that the needs of the employer and the profession that the graduate will enter also affects the attributes needed, and that these need to be taught in a way that embraces both their scholarly nature and their place in professional practice.

Professionalism – towards a definition?

Our understanding of professionalism as a graduate attribute is that it incorporates many of the attributes associated with the nebulous term 'graduateness', but that it also incorporates conduct, capability and ethical expectations from wider society which go beyond attributes and includes sets of attitudes and values.

A Case of Two Professions

This relationship between graduateness and professionalism may be particularly relevant in the UK to subjects that are a new academic discipline, such as nursing, or where the academic degree specialism is not actually a requirement of the job, such as accounting. Whilst this is not the case in all countries, this academic status suggests that these can serve as an interesting focus for a closer analysis of what graduateness might be in two differing professions, and in particular, what attributes are linked to the concept of professionalism in these two fields.

Nursing Vignette

Nursing is a discipline which has undergone a relatively recent process of professionalisation, compared with medicine. Professionalism is traditionally defined sociologically, by traits or professional activity (Copnell, 2010). Such factors typically include possession of a unique body of discipline knowledge, specific (often university-based) educational arrangements to enter the field, regulatory bodies to govern/uphold the reputation of the profession, to oversee education and practice standards and the conferring/registration of licenses to practice. As such, the educational preparation and body of knowledge elements have only become widely realised in recent decades.

In the formative years, as the role developed as a career, nursing was preoccupied with gender and class politics, obedience, personal morality and caring tasks (Burnard and Chapman, 1990). Trainees were assessed through observation, culturally socialised and examined. These may be viewed as influences to a sense of service and duty and even as precursors to a more professional realm.

Nursing, as a discipline, has an educational history that shows a convoluted journey towards the graduate profession and this is increasingly becoming worldwide. Modern nursing, as a professional role, emanated from historical religious and lay origins in the mid-19th century. Florence Nightingale is a central figure in the early journey to professionalising nursing (Burnard and Chapman, 1990). She created a professionally qualified lady practitioner, one inferior to medicine and premised around personal morality and vocation and an obedient, assisting role, therein sowing the first seeds of academic learning in the field (ibid.).

Nightingale established a two-tier approach with nurses trained as above, but with the addition of an upper echelon of "lady-pupils" who would qualify for "superior situations" (Burnard and Chapman, 1990: 4). Twenty years after this innovation, many of these pupils were matrons around the UK (Burnard and Chapman, 1990). Here we see the early establishment of a hierarchy of qualified nursing education, albeit premised on a Victorian ethos of virtue, gender, class and wealth as opposed to ability and values.

Nightingale's idea was to help patients physically and spiritually and to act as an able medical assistant to the doctor's curing function. Initially minimalist education attributes were supervened by the demand for virtuous morality and these (female) nurses were at the side of the (typically male) doctor and acted upon their instruction (Burnard and Chapman, 1990; Rafferty, 1996). Throughout the 20th century, however, a refinement and modernisation of these initial ideals took place in westernised economies that eventually saw the advent of degree-level studies, professional registration and the development of a unique body of knowledge: the building blocks of professionalism.

McCormick (1997) paints a somewhat analogous picture of the developing role of the nurse in the United States, but develops this further with the highly academic, specialist and technicist role being advanced much more quickly from the middle of the twentieth century. This appears to have led to a much more fierce professional identity and autonomy at a much earlier point in North America. Saliently, degree-level baccalaureate preparation was introduced and heralded the harnessing of the talents of Masters' graduates in great numbers, many years before other countries. The result was a raft of high-range nursing theory emanating from the US (Watson, 1985). Tiers of nursing also characterise the profession in the US with care and status division evident along academic lines (Watson, 1985; McCormick, 1997). The associate level of professionally qualified nurses grew out of a nursing shortage following World War II and the emergence of community colleges in the US (Vinson, 2000).

The development of a baccalaureate programme is attributed to creating a new type of knowledgeable, clinically capable, research and academically able nurse. A nurse who was able to care and function in a professionally autonomous fashion that was in advance of what had been traditionally seen in nurses in the UK: nurses demonstrating many attributes of their graduate capability. This level of autonomy and innovation in the US has shown that this type of academically able nurse can change the way nursing happens; how it is viewed and thought of and how its own future unfolds (Girot, 2000). This situation is arguably the outcome of graduateness being brought to bear en masse. Studies are now being published which are identifying some of the nature of the value of the graduate nurses in terms of minimising clinical risk and adverse events, across developed countries (Aiken et al., 2003).

The developing professional lens led to the growing academic aspects of nurse education in, first North America, then the United Kingdom and beyond. Increasing levels of academically prepared and clinically capable nurses has resulted in an interest in what such nurses offer to the profession, combined health care, and to patients. The professional nursing graduate is therefore a product of an international professionalisation and 'graduatization' agenda of their discipline over the past one hundred years.

Concluding view of the professional nursing graduate

Distinctive nursing tiers may still be seen in some countries, such as between those practising who are diplomates and others who are graduates in the UK or between licentiate and baccalaureates in the United States.

A specific model of nursing graduateness has been proposed by Lyte (2007) who suggests that nursing (as a profession in the UK where degree level preparation is comparatively recent) has had to consider the attributes that all graduates possess and those that are perhaps unique to the profession. The notion of employability as a key generic marker of the graduate has also had to be considered, within an ever more degree-rich nursing workforce and as society ascribes increasing currency to knowledge base (Lyte, 2007). Lyte considers transferable skills (potentially common in all graduates) in a framework reflecting the demands and uniqueness of nursing, placing particular emphasis on academic and operational competence giving rise to enhanced professional, service and caring commitment and to being interprofessionally and lifelong learning capable. These, in turn, are influenced by a strengthened values and attitudes base, such as *empathy*, for example (ibid.).

In summary, nursing graduateness may be encapsulated as having emerged much more recently than in other professions. The nursing graduate shares core characteristics with other graduates, especially with those in allied professions, but profession-specific learning, professionalisation and learning influence them to demonstrate features that mark their performance and disposition. These features coalesce to create what one may characterise as the contemporary nursing graduate: one who epitomises the professional.

Embedding professionalism within nursing curricula

Professional values are increasingly becoming embedded within nursing curricula. This is done formally in terms of theoretical elements of teaching and learning and, more vicariously, via professional role-modelling on clinical placements. The former has the advantage of being able to tap into contemporary thinking like the Nursing and Midwifery Council Code of Conduct (Nursing and Midwifery Council [NMC], 2015) for reflection and latest evidence, though may be criticised as lacking practice context. The latter is beneficial where the role-modelling is excellent, but is variable where the practitioner is not functioning so well.

Traditionally, the vicarious route was the more common approach. As nursing has become a graduate profession, the theoretical learning aspect has developed more to produce the dual approach commonly seen today.

As reflection is central to revalidation in UK nursing, portfolios of evidence can be utilised to rehearse the reflexive skills necessary around professional conduct and performance. These also help students develop links between theoretical and clinical learning and can help students illuminate their developmental professional journeys. This can highlight theoretical understandings, clinical skills development and professional attribute acquisition.

Accounting Vignette

Accounting is a professional subject bound by recognised worldwide qualifications. The International Federation of Accountants (IFAC) was established in 1977 and states on its website that it is "the global organization for the accountancy profession dedicated to serving the public interest by strengthening the profession" (IFAC, 2016a). One of its aims is

[d]eveloping high-quality international standards in auditing and assurance, public sector accounting, ethics, and education for professional accountants and supporting their adoption and use. (IFAC, 2016b)

National professional accountancy bodies gain recognition from being members of IFAC, and currently there are over 175 members in more than 130 countries, which represent around 3 million accountants, in public practice, education, government service, industry and commerce. The International Accounting Education Standards Board (IAESB), which is one of one of IFAC's committees, has issued eight International Education Standards (IESs) for professional accountants which cover both the Initial Professional Development (IPD) and Continuing Professional Development (CPD) of accountants who are either training to become, or who are already, members of IFAC member bodies, respectively. IESs require competence to be achieved and appropriately assessed in professional knowledge; professional skills; and professional values, ethics and attitudes. It is clear that IFAC, and the national professional bodies who are members are focused on ensuring the professionalism of their members, and that graduate education is seen as one way to achieve this. However, unlike nursing and law, there is no requirement to study accounting at university in order to qualify for the profession. Most professional bodies across the world do require an undergraduate degree (or equivalent) before candidates can progress to professional examinations and training (Australia, CPA and ICAA; India, ICAI and ICWAI; Saudi Arabia, SOCPA; Uganda, ICPAU; and UK – ICAS, ICAEW, CIPFA and CIMA), but only SOCPA (Saudi Arabia) and CPA (Australia) require a specific accounting degree. Some professional bodies do not require this (UK, ACCA and Australia, NAI), and in the UK, ICAS also have non-degree entry routes for a minority (4%) of its trainees.

The attributes of professional accountants are fundamental to them being able to apply accounting rules and to monitor their implementation (Humphrey, 2011). However, the quality and content of professional accounting training programmes has been criticised over the years, particularly as professional training stresses the technical aspects and fails to deliver on skills, ethics, accountability, transparency and good corporate governance (e.g., see Howieson, 2003; Jackling and De Lange, 2009). The professional accountancy bodies have also issued several warnings that university teaching may not be reaching either the needs of the students, or those of employers (see, e.g., AICPA, 1978; Accounting Education Change Commission, 1990, 1992; Behn et al., 2012), again highlighting a lack of generic skills in under-graduate accounting degree programmes. This view is echoed by academics, who note also the need to take account of the global harmonisation of accounting and auditing standards and thus the need for the education in different countries to ensure that professionally qualified accountants, from whichever jurisdictions, have attained a comparative level of knowledge and attributes; both specific and generic

(Rezaee and Burton, 1997; Hassall et al., 2005; Crawford et al., 2014). To this end, International Education Standards (IESs) have been developed to set out a clear descriptor of the professional knowledge topics; intellectual skills; and values, ethics and attitudes that IFAC requires for a professional accountant to possess in order to gain entry to an accredited professional body. The professional knowledge topics in IES 2, whilst mainly subject specific, also include general business awareness and IT competence which may be seen as more generic in nature. IES 3 identifies the attributes seen as necessary to function as a professional accountant. These attributes are identified under five subheadings – intellectual skills; technical and functional skills; personal skills; interpersonal and communication skills; and organisational and business management skills – and are conceived of as generic, transferable competences that are acquired during the course of a broad general education. IES 4 lists the more conceptual abilities covering issues such as social responsibility, independence, scepticism, accountability, governance and whistleblowing.

It should be noted that these capabilities are seen as a requirement for those who have already become professional accountants, and thus some of these capabilities may be acquired in the workplace. However, as noted above, there is within these standards an assumption that a professional accountant has a graduate level qualification and that these capabilities can be attributed to that degree process (IFAC, 2009, IES 2 para.4). Competences that are acquired, or should be acquired, during a programme of undergraduate education can be broadly split between subject specific and generic attributes or capabilities. Evidence of this split can be seen in the Quality Assurance Agency (QAA) benchmark statement for Accounting and other subject disciplines in the UK (QAA, 2007). With regard to generic attributes, these have also been described as skills or capabilities that are transferable; that is, they can be transferred from one job or career to another and that are required for employability. Barrie (2006) suggests that 'skill' implies a measurable outcome and that a more appropriate term is 'attribute', but this terminology has yet to be embedded in the accounting education literature. Other terms used to describe such attributes in the accounting education literature and educational or professional pronouncements include 'soft', 'key' or 'core' skills (QAA, 2007; Dacko, 2006; Yorke, 2006), as well as 'capabilities' and 'competencies' (IFAC, 2016a). HE course outlines and programme documentation reflect the global acknowledgement that HE should produce students who have mastered both a specific discipline and also

> A set of achievements – skills, understandings and personal attributes – that makes graduates more likely to gain employment and be successful in their chosen occupations, which benefits themselves, the workforce, the community and the economy.
>
> (Yorke, 2006: 8)

Thus there is an issue with terminology within accounting education.

To succeed as assurance and advisory professionals in various areas of public practice, professional accountants and auditors need to develop expertise in areas such as analytical reasoning, communication, negotiating, management, marketing, interpersonal and general business skills (ICAEW, 1996). Howieson (2003) argues that professional accountants must demonstrate a broad business understanding to ensure that they are competitive and can quickly adapt to changes in the market place, stating,

> Accountants ... need to have specialist knowledge in a specific industry but they will also have to possess a range of generalist ('generic') skills which enable them to apply their specialist knowledge within the 'big picture' context of a client's/employer's organisations and strategy.
>
> (Howieson, 2003: 80)

A review by Crawford et al. (2011) of the professional skills listed in IES 3 (IFAC, 2009) shows that the majority are generic, with the subject specific capabilities more commonly included under the technical and functional professional knowledge heading of IES 2. Table 8.1 tabulates the competences in the QAA Accounting benchmark statements, with those of IES 3 and IES 4. These same attributes dominate the accounting education literature although they are grouped differently by different authors (see, e.g., Gammie et al., 2002; Dacko, 2006), and the accounting professions (Accounting Management Solutions, 2007: AICPA, 1978). Thus, the agreed competencies cover a variety of 'employability' or non-technical skills: decision-making skills; analytical skills; problem-solving skills such as lateral thinking and creativity (a–c); communication skills (oral and written); interpersonal skills including teamwork and the ability to work on one's own (o–u); organisational skills such as planning, time-keeping, responsibility and strategic thinking (v–y). There are also clearly overlaps between the literature's identification and categorisations of generic skills with IESs and the QAA Accounting benchmark statement.

These attributes are seen as part of the graduateness of students both by employers who want universities to teach these and by academics who deem them to be important for graduates to possess, although the employers were more likely to expect a graduate to possess analytical skills, presentation skills and written communication skills (Crawford et al., 2010).

Accountancy faculty in universities perhaps tend to focus on delivering the knowledge-based topics which can be directly linked to the technical needs of the profession rather than developing a more rounded graduate. Calls for universities to incorporate employability skills are well documented (Cramner, 2006; Fallows and Steven, 2000; Stoner and Milner, 2010), and the more generic professional skills of IES 3 are now also an integral part of the curricula in most universities around the globe. However, there is also discussion in the literature that argues that the generic attributes need disciplinary context (Jones, 2001) and that the ethics, values and attributes of IES 4, which represent the more intangible aspects of professionalism, appear to be relatively neglected in curricula (Jackling and De Lange, 2009)

Table 8.1 Graduate level attributes identified by professional and higher education institutions

Cognitive Abilities and Generic Skills (Accounting benchmark statement, QAA, 2007)	Professional Skills and General Education (IES3, IFAC 2009)	Professional Values, Ethics and Attitudes (IES 4, IFAC 2009)
(a-c) the ability to locate, extract and analyse data from multiple sources; (b,c) critical evaluation of arguments and evidence; (b,c) the ability to analyse and draw reasoned conclusions; (d) numeracy skills, including manipulating data and appreciating statistical concepts at an appropriate level; (j) capacities for independent and self-managed learning; (o,p) an ability to work in groups, and other interpersonal skills, including oral as well as written presentation skills (t) communication skills including the ability to present quantitative and qualitative information, together with analysis, argument and commentary.	**Intellectual skills** (a) the ability to locate, obtain, organise and understand information from human, print and electronic sources; (b) the capacity for inquiry, research, logical and analytical thinking, powers of reasoning, and critical analysis; and (c) the ability to identify and solve unstructured problems which may be in unfamiliar settings. **Technical and functional skills** (d) numeracy, mathematical and statistical applications and IT proficiency; (e) decision modelling and risk analysis; (f) measurement; (g) reporting; and (h) compliance with legislative and regulatory requirements **Personal skills** (i) self-management; (j) initiative, influence and self-learning; (k) prioritise and organise work to meet tight deadlines; (l) anticipate and adapt to change; (m) consider professional values ethics and attitudes in decision making; and (n) professional skepticism.	(k) timeliness (m) ethical dilemma resolution (n) scepticism (z) conflict resolution; (aa) independence; (bb) reliability.

Interpersonal and communication skills

(o) work with others in a consultative process, to withstand and resolve conflict;

(p) work in teams;

(q) interact with culturally and intellectually diverse people;

(r) negotiate acceptable solutions and agreements in professional situations;

(s) work effectively in a cross-cultural setting;

(t) present, discuss, report and defend views effectively through formal, informal, written and spoken communication; and

(u) listen and read effectively, including a sensitivity to cultural and language differences.

Organisational and business management skills

(v) strategic planning, project management, management of people and resources, and decision making;

(w) organise and delegate tasks, to motivate and to develop people;

(x) leadership; and

(y) professional judgement and discernment.

Source: Adpated from Crawford, L., Helliar, C., and Monk, E.A. (2011). p. 119.

Embedding professionalism in accounting curricula

As noted above, within the accounting education literature it appears that professionalism has become synonymous with accountability and ethics. There are a number of studies, discussing how best to embed the teaching of ethics, which often focus more on teaching method, suggesting that some element of real world experience is necessary: often through the means of case study; group work and role play (see, e.g., McPhail, 2001). Smith (2012) notes the universality of some values of ethical education such as honesty, justice and the good of society. Kermis and Kermis (2014) suggest a programme to embed what they call professional presence which focuses on professional development and career planning, alongside time management, with guest speakers to contextualise and the opportunity for students to put into practice some of the more generically employable skills they have learnt. The focus is very much on career development and job readiness. This understanding of how students need to present themselves when they join the profession seems to be key. Guest lectures who can articulate how to embody professionalism may be one way to help develop this, but educators themselves can help to instil this attitude in their students by ensuring that all modules expose students to ethical issues and professional behaviour. Stand-alone modules aimed at teaching ethics or emotional intelligence run the risk of marginalizing this and in effect preaching to the converted (Rachse et al., 2013). Bosco et al. (2010) in their study found that business students were more likely to adopt higher moral standards when ethics was not a topic on the syllabus, but was discussed within the module. Ethics as a separate topic might mean the topic is not contextualised and thus is less relevant to the students, whereas a more integrated approach, where all aspects of the module can be discussed with reference to professional values, attitudes and ethics, would seem to be a more reliable way to improve the professionalism and moral compass of students.

Conclusion: Analysis of Vignettes

There is acknowledgement that several discipline-specific attributes exist that characterise the nature of professional graduates in nursing and accountancy. For example, empathy and clinical competence are greatly important for nurses and technical competencies and business awareness are important for accountants. We seek here, however, to illuminate the shared attributes that denote professionalism in graduates of the two disciplines. Whilst these attributes are shared, they are operated contextually and professionally in differing ways and levels in pursuit of patient/client benefit, satisfaction and confidence.

The shared professional attributes (shown here in Figure 8.1) are drawn from a variety of literature and are represented by those framed in blue as being skills-based, those in red being concerned with values and attitudes and those in purple showing those which have elements of both skills and attitudinal components.

These attributes could arguably be chanced upon experientially by practitioners. Their coherent acquisition and purposeful instilling into the practice and

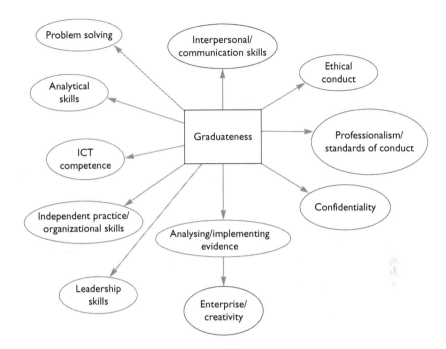

Figure 8.1 A model of shared professional attributes.

personal disposition of the graduates, however, is one of the designed outcomes of undergraduate education in the two fields. This shows the deliberate creation of new professionals, as part of the graduate learning experience, in both theoretical and cultural exposure in practice placements of these differing professions.

References

Accounting Education Change Commission (1990) Objectives of education for accountants: Position statement number one. *Issues in Accounting Education,* 5 (1): 307–312.

Accounting Education Change Commission (1992) The first course in accounting: Position statement number two. *Issues in Accounting Education,* 7 (2): 249–251.

AICPA (1978) *American Institute of Certified Public Accountants, Commission on Auditors' Responsibilities, Report, Conclusions and Recommendations.* Durham, NC: AICPA.

Aiken, L. H., Clarke, S. P., Cheung R. B., Sloane O. M. and Silber, J. H. (2003) 'Education levels of hospital nurses and surgical patient mortality'. *Journal of the American Medical Association,* 290 (12): 1617–1623.

Andruszkow, H., Hildenbrand, F. Pfeiffer, R., Horst, K. and Pape, H-C. (2014) 'Professionalism in health care'. In: Stahel, P.F. and Mauffrey, C. (Eds.), 2014. *Patient Safety in Surgery.* London: Springer-Verlag, pp. 123–128.

Barrie, S. C. (2006). 'Understanding what we mean by the generic attributes of graduates'. *Higher Education,* 51 (2): 215–241.

Behn, B. K., Ezzell, W. F., Murphy, L. A., Rayburn, J. D., Stith, M. T. and Strawser, J. R. (2012) The Pathways Commission on Accounting Higher Education: Charting a national strategy for the next generation of accountants. *Issues in Accounting Education*, 27 (3): 595–600.

Bernstein, C., Ettema, D., Suzuki, H., Fujii, S., Fujii, S. and Osman R. (2012) *"Graduateness": a contested idea*. International Congress of Psychology (conference proceedings) July 21, 2012.

Bosco, S. M., Melchar, D. E., Beauvais, L. L. and Desplaces, D. E. (2010) 'Teaching business ethics: The effectiveness of common pedagogical practices in developing students' moral judgment competence'. *Ethics and Education*, 5 (3): 263–280.

Burford, B., Morrow, G., Rothwell, C., Carter, M. and Illing, J. (2014) 'Professionalism education should reflect reality: findings from three health professions'. *Medical Education*, 48, 361–374.

Burke, L. M. and Harris, D. (2000) 'Education purchasers' views of nursing as an all-graduate profession'. *Nurse Education Today*, 20: 620–628.

Burnard, P. and Chapman, C. (1990) *Nurse Education: the way forward*. London: Scutari Press.

Copnell, G. (2010) 'Modernising allied health professions careers: attacking the foundations of the professions?' *Journal of Interprofessional Care*, 24 (1): 63–69.

Cranmer, S. (2006). 'Enhancing graduate employability: best intentions and mixed outcomes'. *Studies in Higher Education*, 31 (2): 169–184.

Crawford, L., Helliar, C., Monk, E., Mina, M., Teodori, C., Veneziani, M. and Falgi, K. (2010) 'IES compliance and the knowledge, skills and values of IES 2, 3 and 4'. *IAAER/ACCA Research Project*.

Crawford, L., Helliar, C. and Monk, E. A. (2011) 'Generic skills in audit education'. *Accounting Education: an international journal*, 20 (2): 115-131.

Crawford, L., Helliar, C., Monk, E. and Veneziani, M. (2014) 'International Accounting Education Standards Board: Organisational legitimacy within the field of professional accountancy education'. *Accounting Forum*, 38 (1): 67–89. Elsevier.

Dacko, S. (2006) 'Developing the top five skills within an MBA programme: implications for management educators'. *The International Journal of Management Education*, 5 (2): 21–31.

Decker, P. J. (1999) 'The hidden competencies of healthcare: why self-esteem, accountability and professionalism may affect hospital consumer satisfaction scores'. *Research and Perspectives on Healthcare*, Winter, 77 (1): 14–26.

Fallows, S., and Steven, C. (2000) 'Building employability skills into the higher education curriculum: a university-wide initiative'. *Education + training*, 42 (2), 75–83.

Gammie, B., Gammie, E. and Cargill, E. (2002) 'Personal skills development in the accounting curriculum'. *Accounting Education*, 11(1): 63–78.

Girot, E. A. (2000) 'Graduate nurses: critical thinkers or better decision makers?' *Journal of Advanced Nursing*, 31 (2): 288–297.

Glover, D., Law, S. and Youngman, A. (2002) 'Graduateness and employability: student perceptions of the personal outcomes of university education'. *Research in Post-Compulsory Education*, 7 (3): 293–306.

Hassall, T., Joyce, J., Montaño, J. L. A. and Anes, J. A. D. (2005, December) 'Priorities for the development of vocational skills in management accountants: A European perspective'. *Accounting Forum*, 29 (4): 379–394.

HEQC (Higher Education Quality Council: Quality Enhancement Group). (1996) *What Are Graduates? Clarifying the attributes of 'graduateness': a discussion paper*. Available at: http://www.lgu.ac.uk/deliberations/graduates/starter. Accessed 20/08/ 2013.

Howieson, B. (2003) 'Accounting practice in the new millennium: is accounting education ready to meet the challenge?'. *The British Accounting Review*, 35 (2): 69–103.

Humphrey, C., Kausar, A., Loft, A., and Woods, M. (2011) 'Regulating audit beyond the crisis: A critical discussion of the EU Green Paper'. *European Accounting Review*, 20 (3): 431–457.

IFAC (International Federation of Accountants) (2016a) http://www.ifac.org/about-ifac.

IFAC (International Federation of Accountants) (2016b) http://www.ifac.org/about-ifac/organization-overview.

Institute of Chartered Accountants of England and Wales (ICAEW), Education and Training Committee (1996) *Added Value Professionals: Chartered Accountants in 2005*. London: ICAEW.

International Federation of Accountants (IFAC) (2009) *Handbook of International Education Pronouncements*, 2009 edition. Available at: http://www.ifac.org/sites/default/files/publications/files/handbookof-international-e.pdf.

Jackling, B. and De Lange, P. (2009) 'Do accounting graduates' skills meet the expectations of employers? A matter of convergence or divergence'. *Accounting Education: an international journal*, 18 (4–5): 369–385.

Jones, A. (2001) 'Generic attributes in accounting: the significance of the disciplinary context'. *Accounting Education: an international journal*, 19 (1–2): 5–21.

Keith, J. (2010) *What is graduateness?* Available at: http://sites.google.com/site/graduateness/. Accessed 05/08/2016.

Kermis, G. F. and Kermis, M. D. (2014) 'Financial reporting regulations, ethics and accounting education'. *Journal of Academic and Business Ethics*, 8 (1): 1–14.

Lave, J. and Wenger, E. (1991) *Situated Learning: Legitimate peripheral participation*. Cambridge: Cambridge University Press.

Lyte, G.M.C. (2007) *Graduateness in nursing: a case study of undergraduate nursing students' development and employability*. University of Manchester (Unpublished thesis). Available via: http://www.ethos.bl.uk. Downloaded 05/01/2014.

Macdonald Ross, G. (1996) 'Quality and enhancement: "graduateness"'. *Learning and Teaching Support Network York*: Education Subject Centre.

Macdonald Ross, G. (2010) *Graduateness*. Available at: http://www.heacademy.ac.uk/assets/documents/subjects/prs/PrsDocuments/370.pdf. Accessed 23/10/2013.

McCormick, K. A. (1997) 'Nursing in the 21st Century – guideposts in an information age'. In: Ferguson, V.D. (Ed.) (1997) *Educating the 21st-Century Nurse: challenges and opportunities*. New York NY: NLN Press

McPhail, K. (2001) 'The other objective of ethics education: Re-humanising the accounting profession – a study of ethics education in law, engineering, medicine and accountancy'. *Journal of Business Ethics*, 34 (3–4): 279–298.

Merriam-Webster. (2016) http://www.merriam-webster.com/dictionary/professional.

NCIHE (National Committee of Inquiry into Higher Education) and Dearing, S. R. (1997) *Higher Education in the Learning Society: Reports of the National Committee*. NCIHE.

Okay-Somerville, B. and Scholarios, D. (2013) Shades of grey: understanding job quality in emerging graduate' *Human Relations*, 66 (4): 555–585.

Quality Assurance Agency (QAA) (2007). Subject specific benchmark statement: Accounting. Available at: http://www.qaa.ac.uk/en/Publications/Documents/Subject-benchmark-statement-Accounting.pdf.

Rafferty, A. M. (1996). *The Politics of Nursing Knowledge*. London: Psychology Press.

Rasche, A., Gilbert, D. U. and Schedel, I. (2013) 'Cross-disciplinary ethics education in MBA programs: rhetoric or reality?' *Academy of Management Learning & Education*, 12 (1): 71–85.

Rezaee, Z. and Burton, E. J. (1997) 'Forensic accounting education: insights from academicians and certified fraud examiner practitioners'. *Managerial Auditing Journal*, 12 (9): 479–489.

Saks, M. (2012) 'Defining a profession: The role of knowledge and expertise'. *Professions and Professionalism*, 2 (1): 1–10.

Smith, A. (2004) 'How to define a graduate'. *Critical Quarterly*, 46 (4): 126–130.

Smith, K. (2012) 'Lessons learnt from literature on the diffusion of innovative learning and teaching practices in higher education'. *Innovations in Education and Teaching International*, 49 (2), 173–182.

Star, C. and Hammer, S. (2008) Teaching generic skills: eroding the higher purpose of universities, or an opportunity for renewal? *Oxford Review of Education*, 34, 2, 237–251.

Steur, J. M., Jansen, E.P.W.A. and Hoffman, W.H.A. (2012) 'Graduateness: An empirical examination of the formative function of university education'. *Higher Education*, 64: 861–874.

Stoner, G. and Milner, M. (2010) 'Embedding generic employability skills in an accounting degree: development and impediments'. *Accounting Education: an international journal*, 19 (1–2): 123–138.

Topping, A. and Taylor, J. (2010) 'A Nurse Education Workforce Fit for Purpose?' In: 2010 *GANES 2nd International Conference for Nurse Educators*, December 2010, Washington, DC, USA. (Unpublished). Available at: http://eprints.hud.ac.uk/10982/1/GANES_Topping_%26_Taylor.pdf. Accessed 31/10/2013.

Vinson, J. A. (2000) 'Nursing's epistemology revisited in relation to professional education competencies'. *Journal of Professional Nursing*, 16 (1) 39–46.

Walker, L. (1998) *Key Skills and Graduateness*. Available at: http://www.heacademy.ac.uk/assets/documents/resources/heca/heca_ks11.pdf. Accessed 05/10/2013.

Watson, J. (1985) *Nursing: the philosophy and science of caring*. Niwot, CO: University Press of Colorado.

Wheelahan, L. (2003) *Recognition of prior learning and the problem of graduateness*. Available at: http://www.avetra.org.au/abstracts_and_papers_2003/refereed/Wheelahan.pdf. Accessed 26/10/2013.

Wiktionary.org (2013) Available at: http://en.wiktionary.org/wiki/graduateness. Accessed 11/10/2013.

Williams, H. and Owen, G. (1997). *Recruitment and Utilisation of Graduates by Small and Medium Sized Enterprises*. London: DfEE.

Yorke, M. (2006) 'Employability in higher education: what it is – what it is not'. *Learning and Employability Series*, 1: 1–21.

Chapter 9

The Digitally-Literate Graduate

27/6/17

Andy Jackson

Introduction

In conversations with employers as part of discussions within my own university, it's often the case that, when asked what they want from a graduate, they focus primarily on the professional or vocational skillset required to do a particular job, usually evidenced by their possession of a certificate or other proof of graduation. Ask them, however, what makes a *good* graduate (i.e., an employable one) and they may point towards more abstract evidence of success, quoting less definable, less *measurable* skills or behaviours: independence, curiosity, resourcefulness, criticality. In the higher education (HE) sector, these skills have often been considered secondary to vocational or subject-oriented skills and are generally not as coherently or consistently taught within the curriculum; indeed, it can be argued that such skills can't be 'taught' at all, and are either inherent or absent. Recent surveys (summarised in Goldstein's 2016 SCONUL report) show that employers are starting to favour generic competences over subject-specific skills. *Digital Literacy*, the focus of this chapter, is an umbrella for these skills and behaviours, and many more besides. The concept of the 'digitally literate graduate' has gone from being something associated with only the cream of the graduate crop, to being something which employers now expect to come as standard.

Development of Digital Literacy

Digital Literacy was described with elegant succinctness by Jisc (2015) as being "the capabilities which fit someone for living, learning and working in a digital society". As a concept, it grew out of a variety of other literacies which began to emerge in the internet age, defined by Martin (2008) as including the following.

- Computer, IT or ICT Literacy
- Technological Literacy
- Information Literacy
- Media Literacy
- Visual Literacy

- Communication Literacy
- Digital Literacy

Attempts to give clearer boundaries to these different literacies by policymakers and pedagogists has been challenging, and the great conversations that have taken place across the last decade have failed to give these areas the necessary exclusivity. Through these wide-ranging discussions, Digital Literacy has emerged from this list as a more inclusive term; it being synonymous with an identified gathering of skills and behaviours. A variety of recognised organisations have been developing frameworks in an attempt to give some structure to the concept and to encourage the integration of digital literacies teaching into curricula across all disciplines. The term 'Digital Literacy' is sometimes used interchangeably with proposed alternatives, including 'learning literacy' and 'transliteracy', but the need to develop these alternatives reflects the difficulties experienced in pinning down what essentially remains an abstract term. 'Digital Literacy' persists, however, as the term with the greatest currency.

One of the key issues preventing a swifter and more coherent integration of Digital Literacy into the curriculum has been the perceived divide between the students who, it is assumed, have greater familiarity and facility with digital technologies, and teaching staff who, on the whole, feel less 'connected'. The concept of the 'digital native' and the 'digital immigrant' was identified by Prensky as early as 2001, but the broad insights of Prensky's original work, largely focusing on the age of the individual and the technology extant at times in their lives, have since been challenged. Commentators such as Bennett, Maton and Kervin (2008) argue that Prensky's treatise was too simplistic, and that 'Generation Y' or Millennials (as Digital Natives are also sometimes called) are not so easily pigeonholed. To do so, "fail[s] to recognise cognitive differences in young people of different ages, and variation within age groups" (Bennett, Maton and Kervin, 2008: 779). Further comments from Siva Vaidhyanathan, author of influential 2011 book *The Googlization of Everything*, quoted in *The Economist*, echo this when he argues:

> This is essentially a wrong-headed argument that assumes that our kids have some special path to the witchcraft of 'digital awareness' and that they understand something that we, teachers, don't – and we have to catch up with them.
> (*The Economist*, 2010)

The key disconnection, therefore, is possibly not uniquely between those 'born digital' and those predating this era, but is maybe more between the digital world as a whole and those who populate it. Thaxter and Koseoglu writing on Edcontexts .org (2015) see the disconnection between the technology and its users as being more than just a matter of age and experience when they write:

> No matter how hard we try, we still may not be aware of the bigger picture of how digital technologies can enable learning in so many different ways.

We seem to be running flat out to keep up with emerging technologies whilst desperately trying to respond to the growing consensus that traditional learning theories are either obsolete or, at the very least, need adapting to meet the evolving needs of the 21st century learner.

(Thaxter and Koseoglu, 2015)

This is a scenario many readers of this chapter will recognise, and the 'bigger picture' referred to is constantly changing and hence unlikely to reveal itself with any clarity in the foreseeable future. It is argued, therefore, that we need to concentrate less on digital *applications*, that is, the technologies, transient as they are, and instead on digital *behaviours,* that is, the more enduring intellectual characteristics of the learner. This may help overcome the challenges of a changing digital landscape, and instead equip the learner with a degree of digital self-sufficiency. We can achieve this by setting out frameworks for Digital Literacy development in our institutions and thus give digital skills their necessary place alongside functional, discipline-oriented skills, as an acknowledged graduate attribute.

Digital Literacy frameworks

In the early part of the 21st century there have been ambitious attempts to create coherent, unifying structures running through the various stages of education and development. Arguably the most successful of these in terms of completeness was the National Information Literacy Framework Scotland (Crawford and Irving, 2007), in which the authors sought to establish that attaining a state of Digital Literacy is a product of years of development across primary, secondary and tertiary education. Their work resulted in a 'spine' of competences and behaviours across the various levels of education and on into workplace learning, although it should be noted that this was purely in the *information literacy* field. While this work has been influential, the nature of the subject means that any initiatives arising are hampered by the speed at which the landscape is transformed.

Looking more broadly, there are a number of *Digital Literacy* frameworks which have been developed over the last few years, with the intention being that they unify frameworks covering the disparate 'literacies'. Some emanate from individual higher education institutions (HEIs) such as the Open University framework (Open University, 2012a) and Cardiff University's Digidol initiative (Cardiff University, n.d.) whereas others have been developed by national advisory bodies such as SCONUL's 7 *Pillars of Information Literacy* model, which can be viewed through a variety of specialist 'lenses', including Digital Literacy (SCONUL, 2016) and employability (Goldstein, 2016) and the US Digital Literacy initiative (2015). The European Commission also developed a framework of digital competences in 2013 entitled DIGCOMP which goes into detail about the nature of these competences at several levels of expertise (European Commission, 2013). Shortly before going to press, the European Commission built on this with the announcement of a 'New Skills Agenda for Europe' (European Commission, 2016), which included the

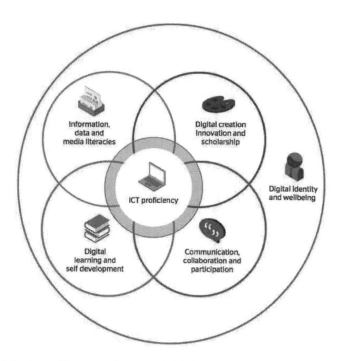

Figure 9.1 Jisc Digital Literacies Framework, 2015.

development of a 'Digital Skills and Jobs Coalition'. It remains to be seen how this will develop and shape the digital skills landscape in Europe over the next few years.

Primary among these frameworks is the Jisc Digital Literacies Framework (Jisc, 2015) which has been regarded by Digital Literacy practitioners globally as a benchmark. The most recent version of the framework contains the conceptual diagram below (Figure 9.1).

A detailed range of skills and behaviours identified by the Jisc framework as being central to the development of the digitally literate graduate include the following from the Futurelab report (Hague and Payton, 2010: 19).

- Creativity
  - Using digital technologies to create or co-create new learning or understanding
- Critical thinking and evaluation
  - Applying critical analysis and evaluative skills coherently and explicitly to tackle both work-related and social issues or problems
- Cultural and social understanding
  - Appreciation of the diversity of the global community and an understanding of the ways that such diversity affects the workplace, the marketplace and the social environment

- Collaboration
  - The use of digital tools and techniques to collaborate with colleagues or partners to achieve learning or employment-related aims
- The ability to find and select information
  - Resourcefulness and intellectual curiosity allied to well-developed systematic information retrieval techniques
- Effective communication
  - Using digital technologies and personal communication skills in an appropriate and effective manner across a range of media
- E-safety
  - The ability to function safely, securely and legally within a digital environment
- Functional skills
  - The use of digital technologies to operate in a professional capacity in a particular field or profession

Sharpe and Beetham (2010) looked at the development of digital literacies in a more learner-centred way, presenting a 'pyramid' model for personal development in a digital literacies context (Figure 9.2), moving from: 'I have…' (an awareness of the resources available to the learner), to 'I can…' (an understanding of the skills the learner possesses) to 'I do…' (the adoption of a set of appropriate behaviours and qualities which make them effective learners), and finally to 'I am…' (the learner's ability to manage their own skills and behaviours and address any gaps in them by taking responsibility for their learning).

It is this more expanded description which points to the direction which curricula must take if they are to deliver digitally literate graduates. We must attempt to develop not only engaging teaching and learning activities which foster the development of the digital graduate, but also appropriate assessments which successfully bring together subject content with digital tools and applications in a coherent way.

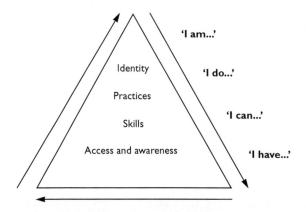

Figure 9.2 Sharpe and Beetham 'pyramid model of digital literacy development'.

Digital Literacy as a Graduate Attribute

Digital Literacy is still a relatively young concept and, as such, its incorporation into institutional graduate attributes is inconsistent. However, it is likely that above all other attributes, this is one which employers have every reason to expect in the 21st-century graduate. Perceptions that today's graduate comes as a fully formed digitally-literate package are often misplaced, and there is a considerable body of work suggesting a skills gap is emerging between the capabilities of graduates and the requirements of the workplace.

- A 2013 survey of employers and Universities in relation to science, technology, engineering and maths (STEM) subjects revealed that "59% of businesses and 79% of Universities surveyed believe there aren't enough skilled candidates leaving education to meet industry's employment requirements" (Farmer, 2013).
- A 2014 survey by the McKinsey Center for Government revealed significant shortfalls in graduate and employability skills across Europe (McKinsey Center for Government, 2014).
- A 2015 poll of managers in the finance sector revealed that 75% of UK school leavers lack essential job skills (Chartered Institute of Management Accountants, 2015).
- Contrary views are expressed by Steven C. Ward of the London School of Economics in a 2015 blog posting entitled 'There is no skills-gap: it is employers who have not kept up with the improved skills of graduates' (Ward, 2015), in which he argues that the socio-political context of the job market is varied and fluctuating, and that it is too simple to focus on a skills gap that affects every graduate and every employer in the same way. He goes on to state, "In this 'skills = jobs' formula, University students should be less concerned with understanding the way the world works and more focused on the ways of the world of work".

The published graduate attributes for many HEIs speak figuratively of some of the same family of skills that Digital Literacy encompasses, but often in a more abstract and less direct manner. It may therefore be questioned why it is necessary to make the concept of Digital Literacy explicit as a graduate attribute if it is implicit in the more commonly used attributes. However, many employers have stated that they are actively looking for a defined range of digital competences, fluency and innovation in their graduate workforce (Bloomberg, 2015; National Association of Colleges and Employers, 2014).

An additional area where work is being done to prepare students for employment is in the recent trend towards developing institutional 'graduate awards' schemes. These are usually portfolio-based, with students selecting a range of skills-based training sessions from a repertoire of extracurricular opportunities. Such programmes are usually driven by the university Careers Service (or equivalent), with buy-in from the whole organisation being a crucial enabler for success. Many programmes contain a selection of Digital Literacy–focused training opportunities, usually aiming to prepare students for the workplace. Programmes generally lead to some form of certification which is recognised by employers as being supplementary to the more formal subject-based qualification. Observation within my own institution leads me to speculate that the recipients of such awards are often those who take the most interest in career planning at an early stage. A useful resource providing information on the organisation and delivery of such programmes is provided by the Association of Graduate Careers Advisory Services under the direction of the UK Quality Assurance Agency (Quality Assurance Agency, n.d.). To aid the development of such awards as a form of shared currency among graduates, some educational institutions at both further and higher level (notably Borders College, the Open University and the University of Sussex in the UK) are developing digital 'open badges' which can be attached to portfolios and online career profile tools such as LinkedIn.

HE Institutions identifying Digital Literacy as a Graduate Attribute

It is currently the case that in Institutions which have developed and published their graduate attributes, Digital Literacy is only now starting to appear in explicit terms. Examples of UK HE institutions currently listing Digital Literacy as a Graduate Attribute include the following:

- Bath Spa University, who state that "Our graduates will be…Digitally literate: able to work at the interface of creativity and technology" (Bath Spa University, 2015).
- Oxford Brookes University, who provide attributes relating to Digital Literacy at Foundation degree level, Graduate level and Postgraduate level, consisting of two broad areas (Oxford Brookes University, 2016):
    - "The functional access, skills and practices necessary to become a confident, agile adopter of a range of technologies for personal, academic and professional use".
    - "To be able to use appropriate technology to search for high-quality information; critically to evaluate and engage with the information obtained; reflect on and record learning, and professional and personal development; and engage productively in relevant online communities" (Oxford Brookes University, n.d.).
- Leeds Beckett University, who state in their innovative *Little Book of Graduate Attributes* that their graduates will "be Digitally Literate (able to confidently and critically identify and use information and digital technologies to enhance academic, personal, and professional development)" (Leeds Beckett University, 2015).

- The Open University has produced detailed guidance on both digital and information literacy and employability, evidenced by their mapping of skills against employability attributes as defined by the Confederation of British Industry (Open University, 2012b).
- Glasgow University, in association with its own Student Representative Council has set out a Graduate Skills matrix in a clear and attractive manner. It is backed with short student-centred testimonials on the relevance of transferable skills (University of Glasgow, 2013).

Predating much of this work, the University of Sydney was an early pioneer in linking graduate attributes to transferable skills, and was one of the first HEIs to identify the importance of Information Literacy (as opposed to Digital Literacy), featuring it as one of their five headline 'clusters of abilities'. They declared that "Graduates of the University will be able to use information effectively in a range of contexts" (University of Sydney, n.d.) – a short statement but one which runs through each layer of their graduate attribute framework. This emphasis is largely due to the seminal work of Simon Barrie on graduate attributes in the early years of this century (Barrie, 2004).

Digital Literacy Skills in the Workplace

A good basis for reading about this topic can be found in Charlie Inskip's literature review 'Information literacy is for life, not just for a good degree' (Inskip, 2014) and in an annotated bibliography on *Information Literacy in the Workplace* by Williams, Cooper and Wavell (2014). A number of organisations and companies have investigated the need for good Digital Skills in the workplace. Lloyd's Bank published a study in 2014 entitled 'Benchmarking the digital maturity of small and medium-sized enterprises and charities in the UK', where it is revealed that small- and medium-sized enterprises (SMEs) have succeeded in boosting their use and understanding of the digital environment, and that 77% of SMEs in the UK now have the right digital skills to function effectively. Whilst this seems to indicate a measure of success, it still equated to around 1.85 million organisations with a very low level of digital understanding and capability. The report further defines this by stating that "many make no use of the internet at all and do not have any web or social media presence" (Lloyds Bank, 2014: 7). Potentially, many UK organisations will face a great threat over the coming years as the public learn to engage more fully with the digital economy. Those organisations which do enter the digital sector will require the attendant skills to be in place within their workforce. It is becoming clear that it will fall to the education sector to provide the necessary training. The need for a digitally literate workforce could hardly be more acute.

The House of Lords' 2015 report on Digital Skills, entitled *Make or Break: The UK's Digital Future* (House of Lords Select Committee on Digital Skills, 2015a) is informed by comments from employers and leaders of educational or employability projects. Angela Morrison from Direct Line Group Insurers states that she would "like to see technical skills being equivalent to reading, writing and arithmetic in schools" (House of Lords Select Committee on Digital Skills, 2015b). Clare Sutcliffe from Code Club, an after-school initiative aimed at improving technical/ICT skills in 9- to 11-year-olds says it is about "strengthening or giving more responsibility to industry for passing on information about the skills that they require but also actually delivering training as well" (ibid.). A spokesperson from Virgin Media commented that "digitally mature small businesses were three times more likely to grow than immature ones" (House of Lords Select Committee on Digital Skills, 2015c), while, according to UK industry advisors McKinsey and Company (2011), SMEs "who made full use of the internet, and associated activities such as e-commerce, enjoyed particular benefits…grow faster, export more and create more jobs".

Digital Literacy is also addressed by the USA's *Workforce Innovation and Opportunity Act* (US Congress, 2014), a commentary on which by the American Library Association states that this includes "a definition of "workforce preparation activities" that specifically includes Digital Literacy skills" (American Library Association, 2015). A recent survey of UK employers commissioned by the BCS, the Chartered Institute for IT, established that 81% of employers surveyed said that they "regard digital skills to be an important requirement when employing people" (BCS, 2014). Scotland has developed a strong stance on Digital Literacy as part of the curriculum, and it is afforded a strong role in the Curriculum for Excellence initiative. In 2015 Scotland also announced a public consultation on a Digital Learning and Teaching Strategy for Scotland, which points at a renewed interest in the concept as part of the fabric of education and culture (Education for Scotland, 2015).

Planning for Future Developments

Given the highly fluid and progressive nature of the digital environment, it can be difficult for employers to make long-term plans for their use of technology and for shifts and trends in the marketplace and amongst their clients and customers. In recent years, for instance, there has been a shrinking in the market for dedicated MP3 players, DVD players, digital cameras, fixed/landline telephones and even the standard wristwatch, which only tells the time, is being replaced by multifunction smartwatch devices incorporating biometric or GPS technology and in some cases even Internet access.

By the act of writing, this chapter is now fixed at a particular time in the evolution of technologies. It has not always been possible to predict the rise of certain technologies, or the demise of others; indeed, the ability to do so with accuracy could make a person rich if he or she were speculating on the share market with that level of insight. The fallout from this is that workforce planning will become more challenging. The skills gap between the needs of a fast-moving market and the attributes of graduates who step off the conveyor belt with a range of ICT skills which are already at risk of being superseded will remain. One attempt to speculate knowledgeably on workforce skills planning appeared in 2010 with the publication of *Horizon scanning and scenario building: scenarios for skills 2020 – a report for the national strategic skills audit for England 2010* (UK Commission for Employment and Skills, 2010) which "[e]xamines issues and trends in the UK and globally which may impact on the employment situation and skill requirements in the UK over the long-term", under the ambitious headings *World Markets, National Enterprise* and *Global Sustainability.*

Some organisations attempt to scan the IT and skills horizon for signs of emerging technologies or trends in usage or behaviour. Chief among these is the New Media Consortium (NMC) which, since 2004, has produced their annual *Horizon Report* attempting to provide intelligence and insight to support HE in their attempts to prepare graduates for changes in the digital landscape, at least for a few years beyond their graduation. The NMC currently produces four separate reports aimed at different sectors: Higher Education, Libraries, Museums and the 'K-12' years. The intention was not to imagine the unimaginable, Cassandra-style, but to separate speculative developments in technology from ones which had a genuine chance of success, based on analysis of the education and employment markets. The reports were divided into technologies likely to gain a foothold in one year or less, in two to three years, or in four to five years. The very first *Horizon Report* correctly predicted learning objects and context-aware computing, while the 2005 report foresaw with accuracy the arrival of ubiquitous Wi-Fi and social networks (using the term 'knowledge webs', which has since fallen into disuse). In recent years it has correctly predicted the rise of cloud computing, eBooks and massive open online courses (MOOCs) among other things. Other speculations have been less accurate; educational gaming and virtual worlds enjoyed brief successes but these were not sustained. However, they have not disappeared completely and could still make a resurgence. Some predictions are carried forward over several years, and many have longer (or shorter) gestation periods than originally predicted.

At the time of writing, the 2016 Higher Education edition (The New Media Consortium, 2016) is predicting, among others, the following;

- Redesigning of the learning space
- Growing focus on measuring of learning
- Blending of informal and formal learning
- Learning analytics and adaptive learning
- Augmented and virtual reality
- **Improving Digital Literacy**

The inclusion of Digital Literacy (which appears for a second consecutive year) is an indication that the same concerns expressed in this chapter are being expressed by proven observatories of digital trends such as the *Horizon Report*, which states:

> This new category of competence is affecting how colleges and Universities address literacy issues in their curriculum objectives and teacher training programs.
>
> (The New Media Consortium, 2016: 24)

and also that "Through the creation of frameworks, higher education leaders are helping students and faculty learn skills for working in a digital society".

Case Studies for Digital Literacies Supporting Employability

This section highlights some of the investigatory work and research that has gone into the links between digital skills and employability, and focuses on the UK context.

Institutional activities

This section summarises a number of UK-based case studies in digital skills and employability. Each case study is drawn from activities reported in the SCONUL Employability project (SCONUL, 2015a).

At City University London, the Library Service undertook a project to assist students in developing skills relevant to employment, making connections between resources provided by the Library and by the Careers Service and also those with a skills development or outreach focus. The project involved the development of an online guide drawing on not just the traditional text-based literature for careers guidance and employability but also on recommended resources from students through the loose process of 'crowdsourcing' (i.e., drawing on the knowledge and experience of participants, usually via the Internet). This part of the process was most helpful in revealing the need for useful resources for company information, and also in the identification of social media outlets for careers, jobs and general employability skills. The project is reported on by Diane Bell and Alex Asman (SCONUL, 2015b).

The University of East Anglia has been engaged in a project whose purpose has been described by Emma Coonan as to "design an online course to help students develop and reflect on their digital literacies in three overlapping contexts: the personal, the academic, and the workplace" (The Mongoose Librarian, 2015). The University of East Anglia have, as previously indicated, identified Digital Literacy as one of their Graduate Attributes, and this project has been set up to feed into the process of developing this attribute. In developing this 'Digital Scholar' online course, Coonan attempted to divert the focus away from the purely didactic experience offered by so many online courses, preferring to encourage students to prepare for their future employability by deploying some of the skills made explicit in their Digital Literacy frameworks: creativity, collaboration and digital publishing, among others. The programme was offered openly in a MOOC-like style, and Coonan states that "the focus throughout is on promoting participants' awareness of online issues, practices and choices as well as tools and apps" (ibid.).

The University of Portsmouth Library developed a session for student employees working in the Library. The session allowed students to consider their experiences and the skills they had developed in their working role and how those could be subsequently developed as transferable and employability skills. Both the process and the end-product of the session involved the use of digital skills, in that they encouraged reflection, creativity and critical skills to effect improvements in curriculum vitae, portfolios and job applications (SCONUL, 2015c).

Learning Services at Edge Hill University have introduced a set of activities leading to the creation of what they term 'Your Digital Tattoo', stemming from a need for students to have the ability to use the Web to present themselves in a positive light to potential future employers. The original concept of the 'Digital Tattoo' comes from work done by the University of British Columbia in this area (University of British Columbia, n.d.). A key factor in this process is the early recognition of the need to protect the confidentiality and reputation of the individual when developing a web presence, particularly when using social media to represent themselves. This is particularly important for students entering a vocational, standards-driven sector of the job market such as teaching, nursing or social work. Students are asked to search for information about themselves, reflect on what it says about them, and then draw-up a list of achievements, interests and personal qualities which they would *like* to have known about themselves, and then use a professional networking/profiling tool such as LinkedIn to develop a more appropriate profile. Advice from professional bodies on the use of social media for those professionals is also presented (SCONUL, 2015d).

At Manchester Metropolitan University (MMU), the Library helped to develop two workshop sessions in conjunction with their Careers and Employability Service. These sessions were tailored to feed into the 'MMU Futures Award', an example of an Institutional portfolio-based extracurricular certificate intended to boost graduate visibility and demonstrate a commitment to excellence. The first session covered the necessary systematic search skills to assist with finding company and employer information and identifying market trends and competition amongst companies and products. The second session covered the development and maintenance of an online presence, managing social media profiles and using innovative personal branding (SCONUL, 2015e).

Leeds Beckett University, who, as stated earlier in this chapter, have incorporated Digital Literacy as an institutional graduate attribute, have put in place a range of learning opportunities for students to make connections between the skills and behaviours they develop in their studies with those required in the future workplace (SCONUL, 2015f). Library staff offered a range of sessions targeted at specific professional and vocational pathways, including the following:

- Assessing workplace Digital Literacy requirements in the creative industries
- Accessing free legal information resources (most legal databases are beyond the affordability of the private individual seeking employment)
- Professional networking for business graduates
- Employability, digital skills and evidence-based practice in the health professions
- Social media presence
- ICT skills refreshers

A number of Institutions in the UK are also exploring the use of 'digital student ambassadors' to raise awareness of the need for fellow students to understand and engage with the digital landscape in their Institutions and the context of their potential future employers. London Metropolitan University are a good example of this initiative, stating that they want their students to have

> an awareness of [their] own digital profile and how [they] present [themselves] online [and also] a knowledge of the digital skills that are important to [them] in [their] subject area and for [their] future career.
>
> (London Metropolitan University, n.d.)

The London School of Economics is also pursuing this line of engagement with students. Eugene McGeown, one of the senior ambassadors involved in the project, states of his involvement that "[n]ot only will you learn a great range of skills that will aid you in your studies, these skills will also help differentiate you in the eyes of an employer" (London School of Economics, 2015).

Conclusion

The mass of literature on this topic is largely uncoordinated, with no national bodies or international collaborations having unequivocal and overarching responsibility for Digital Literacy either in the HE context or in the workplace. In the main, it is Library and Information professionals who are taking a lead on promoting and co-ordinating Digital Literacy in HE and attempting to work with professional bodies, some of whom have recognised the need to articulate Digital Literacy in the documentation of their professional standards. As a consequence of this lack of leadership, it is argued that the most appropriate way forward at present is to share good practice through the organisations who have a stake in this area, including Jisc, The Higher Education Academy (HEA), the Universities and Colleges Information Systems Association (UCISA), individual HEIs, the Confederation of British Industry (CBI), professional and accrediting bodies and other collaborative groups within the employment sector.

The tasks that such bodies are encouraged to focus on include some or all of the following;

- Improved clarity of meaning of the term 'Digital Literacy' and its associated vocabulary.
- Dissemination of good practice in Digital Literacy training in both HE and employment sectors.
- Digital Literacy skills to be more coherently addressed at curriculum level with the adoption of Institutional standards or frameworks which set out measurable, realistic competences.
- Digital Literacy to be explicitly cited as a graduate attribute by HEIs.

- Digital Literacy to be explicitly cited as a professional attribute by professional and accrediting bodies.
- Better dialogue across the HE–employment divide to ensure programmes of study allow graduates to meet current and anticipated workforce skills requirements. This might be achieved through the development of institutional Digital Literacy frameworks in conjunction with employers as detailed in the Practice Guide section which follows.

Practice Guide

This section provides a suggested implementation plan for developing Digital Literacy as a graduate attribute. It offers a greater level of detail to assist with the necessary translation of an aspirational statement on the 'digitally literate graduate' into a strategy for practical development.

Implementing a Digital Literacy framework for employability across disciplines

There are many ways this can be accomplished, with each institution needing to consider the context of their students and the organisational structures in place. The crucial stage, however, is in the development of appropriate intended learning outcomes which give full expression to the need for adequate digital skills and behaviours among the functional skills and behaviours which each programme of study is necessarily required to develop, and are thus embedded within the curriculum. Two examples of an implementation strategy are presented here. The first is adapted from Leeds Beckett University and focuses mostly on the process of developing a framework and embedding it within curricula (Smith and Thomson, n.d.):

1 All academic units (Schools/Departments/Colleges/Faculties etc.) within an institution should understand and recognise the institutional definition of Digital Literacy, and how it is represented in the framework.
2 Academic units should consult with employers of graduates in their field (if known) on the range of Digital Literacy requirements required for the workplace (this should ideally be done annually, though it is more realistic to expect this to take place every few years; it should take place at least once in the cycle of programme review).
3 Academic units should also consult with professional bodies in the field (where they exist) to see what standards for practice in the field of digital literacies are stipulated by such bodies.
4 All academic units use the information from the Programme team, the employers and the professional bodies to identify which elements of the definition or the framework are therefore priorities for their subject areas.
5 All academic units review the current learning outcomes for their modules.

6   Units re-write those learning outcomes to ensure Digital Literacy appropriate to the programme of study is embedded within them.
7   Units then support others in the process of learning outcome redevelopment with embedded graduate attributes.

The second example is drawn from the implementation plan used at the University of Dundee and is possibly more pragmatic in that it recognises that Digital Literacy is less likely to be adopted wholesale as a fiat and that its success relies on a longer-term strategy with reliance on key individuals within Schools to champion the idea.

1   A draft Digital Literacies Framework should be developed by a small team of two to three individuals across Library and Academic Skills functions. It should be based on a synthesis of existing frameworks to find the one which most realistically reflects the needs and capabilities of the institution.
2   A short-life consultation/implementation team should be assembled, representative of the institutional stakeholders in Digital Literacies. This team should be constituted from School Learning and Teaching leads, or from identified 'champions' within a School if this is more appropriate. At the University of Dundee this group was cast as a Community of Practice alongside others, reporting to the University's Learning and Teaching Committee.
3   New programmes of study or programmes due for periodic quality assurance reviews or re-approvals should be identified, with the quality assurance process used to promote the inclusion of Digital Literacy standards within new or amended programmes.
4   Staff development activities should be introduced to enhance institutional understanding of Digital Literacy, including presentations at School Learning and Teaching Committees, workshops within Schools and University-wide staff development programmes.
5   Outcomes from the implementation project should be agreed, including some or all of the following:
    a   All Schools commit to incorporating Digital Literacy in their local Learning and Teaching strategies.
    b   All new or reapproved programmes of study should identify Digital Literacy as a key product of their programme, with the development of appropriate Learning Outcomes underpinned by Teaching and Assessment.
    c   Schools work more closely with employers in their field to ensure their graduates possess the requisite Digital Literacy skills to enhance their employability (Table 9.1).

Table 9.1 gives examples of learning activities and assessments which support the development of digital literacies in preparation for the workplace.

Table 9.1 Examples of learning activities and assessments which support the development of digital literacies in preparation for the workplace

1: Understand and engage in Digital practices	• Students undertake a reflective questionnaire on their use of digital tools and applications to establish their own level of digital competence and experience.
	    • Students might also look at the professional standards for Digital Literacy relating to their field of employment (if such standards exist)
	    • If professional standards do not exist, students could identify a set of baseline digital skills which they think an employer in their field might require.
	• Teacher discusses the ethical context of the use of information, bringing together the student experience in referencing and plagiarism and setting them in the legal context of the workplace.
	    • Ask students to find instances of legal cases of intellectual property disputes, data management issues and malpractice within the sector they are preparing to work in.
	    • Produce a plan for staff training to develop skills and behaviours which, if present, might have presented the legal situation arising.
	• Working in pairs, students should use Google and social media to assemble a profile of the other person, including any negative information.
	    • This should lead into an activity designed to help them clean up their web profile (if necessary).
	• Involve someone from an appropriate employer to describe the information systems which underpin the work of that organisation (means of communication internally and externally, work tools and digital business environment).
	    • Students then assess the differences between the use of their Institutional systems/network and the external network which has been described.
	    • Students then conduct a personal skills assessment to see what may be missing from their skillset.
	    • Students produce a personal learning plan to help them to upskill in the identified areas, drawing on good-quality training resources.

2: Find information	• Students research a prominent academic in their field and write a short overview of what they have published, whether they use social media, what impact their work has had outside of academia. • Without using resources available within the Library, students search for information to answer a specific subject-specific query. They carry out the same search to compare the information they can find using paid-for resources via the Library. • Provide students with a relevant topic and ask them to develop key terms to search with, and use two different search engines to locate information on their topic. • Have the students compare the results in terms of quantity, types of sources (e.g. government, educational, scholarly, commercial), order/sequence of results, and relevance. Pair students who used different search engines to search for the same topics, then compare results.

3: Critically evaluate information, online interactions and online tools	• Students reflect on the best way to choose a Utility supplier using discussion forums and internet sources to help them.

- Students reflect on the best way to choose a Utility supplier using discussion forums and internet sources to help them.
  - Students reflect on the relative value of the advice they obtained using a framework for the evaluation of web-based information, e.g. Audience, Authority, Content, Credibility, Currency.
- Students examine how information on a topical issue in their discipline is presented in newspapers, on websites and in academic journals and discuss the key differences in style, tone, content, language.
- Students select cost-comparison websites to discuss the trust value of a product – possibly one from a commercial organisation in their field, if this is appropriate.
- Ask students in a class to each find two reviews of a particular film or book that come to different conclusions. (Alternatively, these could be provided to students.) Compare the evidence reviewers cite for their opinions. Is there evidence used by reviewers to come to different conclusions?
- Using a product/service specification from an appropriate organisation, students assess the relative merits of a variety of social media applications in promoting and supporting that product/service.
  - What are the particular characteristics of each social medium which might improve promotion
  - What characteristics might risk misrepresenting the product/service or hinder its successful implementation?
- Students select a recent event or news story relevant to their discipline
  - Students then gather examples of how this event was reflected by the various media
    - Official news media – print and online
    - Twitter (to give experience in using hashtags)
    - Facebook
    - Personal or organisational Blog
    - YouTube or other sources of video content
  - Students should describe how they would analyse and evaluate the authority the author(s) of the information.
    - Are there ways to determine whether the individual was an actual witness or participant in the events?
    - Are there ways to identify whether the individual or group that developed a collection of information has a particular political bias?
    - Can they determine whether the author(s) has a particular status within the group he/she represents or is the individual reporting as an 'average citizen'?

(continued)

Table 9.1 Examples of learning activities and assessments which support the development of digital literacies in preparation for the workplace (*continued*)

4: Manage and communicate information	• Students read through a commercial or professional document from an organisation within their field.
	    • Students then draw out the key points from the document to produce a variety of summaries aimed at different audiences – colleagues within a work team, a manager or supervisor, a potential client, a lay person.
	• Ask students to create a 'citation web' using a citation analysis database, and conduct a content analysis of the linked authors by affiliation (workplace, academic preparation, geography, subject expertise).
	    • Do authors cite each other?
	    • Are there some authors who are outliers in the web? How do such connections impact information generation?

5: Collaborate and share digital content	• Students work to a brief relating to their subject to find suitable images for use in a peer/class presentation using Creative Commons content. • Students prepare a presentation using a tool other than PowerPoint (or even no tool) and reflect on the value of this approach to putting across their point. • Students are encouraged to join an appropriate social network and reflect on how this could be used in a professional capacity to support their learning e.g. using LinkedIn groups or following relevant organisations on Twitter.

Source: Adapted from the London School of Economics Digital and Information Literacy Framework (London School of Economics, 2013).

References

American Library Association (2015) *Workforce Innovation and Libraries: The Workforce Innovation and Opportunity Act: Summary of Library Provisions.* Available at: http://www.ala.org/advocacy/advleg/federallegislation/workforce. Accessed 27.07.16.

Barrie, S. (2004) A research–based approach to generic graduate attributes policy. *Higher Education Research and Development,* 23(3), 261–275.

Bath Spa University (2015) *Bath Spa's Graduate Attributes.* Available at: http://www.bathspa.ac.uk/Media/University-governance/Strategy%202020.pdf. Accessed 20.07.16.

BCS (2014) *Digital Literacy and employability.* Available at: http://www.bcs.org/category/17854. Accessed 27.07.16.

Bennett, S., Maton, K. and Kervin, L. (2008) The 'digital natives' debate: A critical review of the evidence. *British Journal of Educational Technology,* 39 (5), 775–786.

Bloomberg (2015) *These are the job skills employers want but can't find.* Available at: http://www.bloomberg.com/graphics/2015-job-skills-report. Accessed 20.07.16.

Cardiff University (n.d.) *Digidol: developing Digital Literacy.* Available at: http://digidol.cardiff.ac.uk/learning-literacies-framework/. Accessed 20.07.16.

Chartered Institute of Management Accountants (2015) *75% of UK school leavers lack essential job skills according to finance bosses.* Available at: http://www.cimaglobal.com/About-us/Press-office/Press-releases/2015/75-of-UK-school-leavers-lack-essential-job-skills-according-to-finance-bosses/. Accessed 20.07.16.

Crawford, J. and Irving, C. (2007) *A National Information Literacy Framework Scotland*. Glasgow: Glasgow Caledonian University.

Economist, The (2010) *The net generation, unplugged*. Available at: http://www.economist.com/node/15582279. Accessed 20.07.16.

Education for Scotland (2015) *Digital Strategy consultation – ICT in education – Learning and teaching*. Available at: http://www.educationscotland.gov.uk/learningandteaching/approaches/ictineducation/digitalstrategy.asp. Accessed 27.07.16.

European Commission (2013) *DIGCOMP: A framework for developing and understanding digital competence in Europe*. Available at: http://ftp.jrc.es/EURdoc/JRC83167.pdf. Accessed 27.07.16.

European Commission (2016) *New Skills Agenda for Europe – Employment, Social Affairs and Inclusion – European Commission*. Available at: http://ec.europa.eu/social/main.jsp?catId=1223andlangId=en. Accessed 26.07.16.

Farmer, A. (2013) *UK skills gap in STEM subjects*. Available at: https://yougov.co.uk/news/2013/10/11/uk-skills-gap-stem-subject/. Accessed 20.07.16.

Goldstein, S. (2016) *A graduate employability lens for the SCONUL Seven Pillars of Information Literacy*. Available at: http://www.sconul.ac.uk/sites/default/files/documents/Employability%20lens%20and%20report.pdf. Accessed 22.07.16.

Hague, C. and Payton, S. (2010) *Digital Literacy across the curriculum: a Futurelab handbook*. Available at: https://www.nfer.ac.uk/publications/FUTL06/FUTL06.pdf. Accessed 20.07.16.

House of Lords Select Committee on Digital Skills (2015a) *Make or break: the UK's digital future*. The Stationery Office. Available at: http://www.publications.parliament.uk/pa/ld201415/ldselect/lddigital/111/111.pdf. Accessed 27.07.16.

House of Lords Select Committee on Digital Skills (2015b) *Key suggestions from witnesses*. Available at: http://www.parliament.uk/documents/lords-committees/digital-skills/key-suggestions-from-witnesses.pdf. Accessed 27.07.16.

House of Lords Select Committee on Digital Skills (2015c) *Written evidence – Virgin Media*. Available at: http://data.parliament.uk/writtenevidence/committeeevidence.svc/evidencedocument/digital-skills-committee/digital-skills/written/12560.html. Accessed 27.07.16.

Inskip, C. (2014) *Information literacy is for life, not just for a good degree*. Available at: http://www.cilip.org.uk/blog/information-literacy-life-not-just-good-degree. Accessed 27.07.16.

Jisc (2015) *Developing students' Digital Literacy*. Available at: https://www.jisc.ac.uk/guides/developing-students-digital-literacy. Accessed 27.07.16.

Leeds Beckett University (2015) *The Little Book of Graduate Attributes*. Available at: https://my.leedsbeckett.ac.uk/bbcswebdav/institution/Graduate_Attributes/Flippable_Little_Book_of_Graduate_Attributes/index.html. Accessed 20.07.16.

Lloyds Bank (2014) *Benchmarking the digital maturity of small and medium-sized enterprises and charities in the UK*. Available at: http://businesshelp.lloydsbankbusiness.com/downloads/LB_UK_Business_Digital_Index_31_03_14.pdf. Accessed 28.07.16

London Metropolitan University (n.d.) *Clued Up! Digital skills for the 21st Century Student*. Available at: http://learning.londonmet.ac.uk/digital-literacies/ambassador.html. Accessed 27.07.16.

London School of Economics (2013) *Digital and Information Literacy Framework*. Available at: http://lti.lse.ac.uk/digital-and-information-literacy/. Accessed 27.07.16.

London School of Economics (2015) *Student Ambassadors for Digital Literacy: Senior Ambassadors*. Available at: http://blogs.lse.ac.uk/lsesadl/our-ambassadors/senior-ambassadors/. Accessed 27.07.16.

Martin, A. (2008) Digital Literacy and the "Digital Society". In: Lankshear, C. and Knobel, M., *Digital Literacies: concepts, policies and practices*. New York: Peter Lang.

McKinsey and Company (2011) *Internet matters: The Net's sweeping impact on growth, jobs, and prosperity*. Available at: http://www.mckinsey.com/insights/high_tech_telecoms_internet/internet_matters. Accessed 27.07.16.

McKinsey Center for Government (2014) *Education to Employment: Getting Europe's Youth into Work.* Available at: https://www.mckinsey.de/files/a4e2e_2014.pdf. Accessed 20.07.16.

Mongoose Librarian, The (2015) *UEA Digital Scholar course.* Available at: https://librariangoddess.wordpress.com/2015/07/27/uea-digital-scholar/. Accessed 27.07.16.

National Association of Colleges and Employers (2014) *The Skills/Qualities Employers Want in New College Graduate Hires.* Available at: http://www.naceweb.org/about-us/press/class-2015-skills-qualities-employers-want.aspx. Accessed 20.07.16.

New Media Consortium, The (2016) *NMC Horizon Report > 2016 Higher Education Edition.* Available at: http://www.nmc.org/publication/nmc-horizon-report-2016-higher-education-edition/. Accessed 27.07.16.

Open University (2012a) *Digital and information literacy framework.* Available at: http://www.open.ac.uk/libraryservices/pages/dilframework/dilframework_view_all.pdf. Accessed 27.07.16.

Open University (2012b) *The Open University student employability policy statement.* Available at: http://www.open.ac.uk/students/charter/sites/www.open.ac.uk.students.charter/files/files/ecms/web-content/student-employability.pdf. Accessed 28.07.16

Oxford Brookes University (2016) *Graduate attributes – Oxford Brookes University.* Available at: http://www.brookes.ac.uk/ocsld/your-development/teaching-and-learning/graduate-attributes/. Accessed 20.07.16.

Prensky, M. (2001) Digital Natives, Digital Immigrants Part 1. *On the Horizon,* 9(5), pp.1–6.

Quality Assurance Agency (n.d.) *Extra-curricular awards stimulus papers: Association of Graduate Careers Advisory Services (AGCAS) perspective.* Available at: http://www.qaa.ac.uk/en/Publications/Documents/extra-curricular-awards-AGCAS.pdf. Accessed 20.07.16.

SCONUL (2015a) *Employability toolkit.* Available at: http://www.sconul.ac.uk/page/employability#Case studies. Accessed 27.07.16.

SCONUL (2015b) *Focus 64.* Available at: http://www.sconul.ac.uk/sites/default/files/documents/Sconul%20Focus%2064.pdf. Accessed 27.07.16.

SCONUL (2015c) *University of Portsmouth: Identifying the employability skills gained from library work.* Available at: http://www.sconul.ac.uk/sites/default/files/Employability_case_Study_Portsmouth.pdf. Accessed 27.07.16.

SCONUL (2015d) *Edge Hill University: Employability Sessions and Support.* Available at: http://www.sconul.ac.uk/sites/default/files/Employability_Case_Study_EdgeHillFeb2015.pdf. Accessed 27.07.16.

SCONUL (2015e) *Employability Case Study: Manchester Metropolitan University.* Available at: http://www.sconul.ac.uk/sites/default/files/Employability_Case_Study_MMUJan2015.pdf. Accessed 27.07.16.

SCONUL (2015f) *Leeds Beckett University: Libraries and Learning Innovation.* Available at: http://www.sconul.ac.uk/sites/default/files/Employability_Case_Study_LeedsBeckettJan2015.pdf. Accessed 27.07.16.

SCONUL (2016) *The SCONUL 7 Pillars of Information Literacy through a Digital Literacy 'lens'* Available at: http://www.sconul.ac.uk/sites/default/files/documents/Digital_Lens.pdf. Accessed 22.07.16.

Sharpe, R. and Beetham, H. (2010) Understanding students' uses of technology for learning: towards creative appropriation. In: Sharpe, R., Beetham, H. and Freitas, S. (2010). *Rethinking Learning for a Digital Age.* Routledge Falmer, London, pp. 85–99.

Smith, S. and Thomson, S. (n.d.) *Embedding Digital Literacy.* Available at: http://www.eshare.edgehill.ac.uk/1766/1/Day_2_Session_5_We've_Made_an_eBook_-_text.pdf. Accessed 27.07.16.

Thaxter, H. and Koseoglu, S. (2015) *Plugged in or turned off: A critical reflection on the Digital Literacy of 21st century students in higher education.* Available at: http://edcontexts.org/pedagogy/plugged-in-or-turned-off-a-critical-reflection-on-the-digital-literacy-of-21st-century-students-in-higher-education/. Accessed 20.07.16.

UK Commission for Employment and Skills (2010) *Horizon Scanning and Scenario Building: Scenarios for Skills 2020 A report for the National Strategic Skills Audit for England 2010.* Available at: http://webarchive.nationalarchives.gov.uk/20140108090250/http://www.ukces.org.uk/assets/bispartners/ukces/docs/publications/evidence-report-17-horizon-scanning-and-scenario-building.pdf. Accessed 27.07.16.

University of British Columbia (n.d.) *Digital Tattoo.* Available at: http://digitaltattoo.ubc.ca/. Accessed 27.07.16.

University of Glasgow (2013) *Guide to Graduate Attributes.* Available at: http://www.gla.ac.uk/media/media_191877_en.pdf. Accessed 27.07.16.

University of Sydney (n.d.) *The Sydney graduate: policy framework.* Available at: http://www.itl.usyd.edu.au/graduateAttributes/policy_framework.pdf. Accessed 22.07.16.

US Congress (2014) *Text – H.R.803 – 113th Congress (2013–2014): Workforce Innovation and Opportunity Act.* Available at: https://www.congress.gov/bill/113th-congress/house-bill/803/text?overview=closed. Accessed 27.07.16.

US Digital Literacy (2015) *US Digital Literacy website.* Available at: http://digitalliteracy.us. Accessed 20.07.16.

Ward, S. (2015) *There is no skills-gap: it is employers who have not kept up with the improved skills of graduates.* Available at: http://blogs.lse.ac.uk/politicsandpolicy/what-if-we-turned-the-skills-gap-debate-around/. Accessed 20.07.16.

Williams, D., Cooper K. and Wavell, C. (2014) *Information literacy in the workplace: an annotated bibliography.* Available at: https://www.informall.org.uk/wp-content/uploads/2015/11/Workplace-IL-annotated-bibliography.pdf. Accessed 27.07.16.

Chapter 10

The Reflexive Graduate

Gaye Manwaring

Introduction: From Stomping to Dancing

Lecturers teach courses that lead their students towards the development of graduate attributes. They need to mix the specific demands of their subject discipline and any professional body requirements together with the generic attributes needed for employability and life-long learning. This chapter will explore approaches to the development of one of those attributes, *reflexivity*, through curriculum design and implementation.

Reflexivity is an important graduate attribute, and this chapter will focus on the lecturers who teach this to their students. I teach on a course on academic practice in higher education for new lecturers, so I help them to be reflexive. Biggs and Tang (2007) believe that you can encourage such reflexive thinking in your students only if you follow similar approaches yourself; many graduate attributes are also lecturer attributes.

I will discuss both how we support the new lecturers and also how we all support our undergraduate students. The course for new lecturers is generic and attracts participants from all disciplines across the university and from some external institutions. It is based largely on a virtual learning environment with some workshops. Each participant has a personal tutor who observes their teaching and gives formative feedback on all aspects of their course. As they work through their required probation programme, they realise its value both for themselves and for their students. Some lecturers who were initially reluctant to spend time away from their research move from angry stomping to enlightened dancing, as they reflect on what they have learned.

Reflection and Reflexivity

The concept of reflexivity is complex and nebulous. It is hard to find a consistent definition, but most include aspects of reflecting on what has happened, looking inwards at one's values and beliefs, analysing the context and leading to considered action. I see this as four mirrors, looking backwards, inwards, outwards and forwards, and introduce it to my students by using the metaphors of a concave mirror reflecting the past, a microscope for self-analysis, a periscope for horizon scanning, and a convex mirror beaming forward. I have represented my model of reflexivity in Figure 10.1.

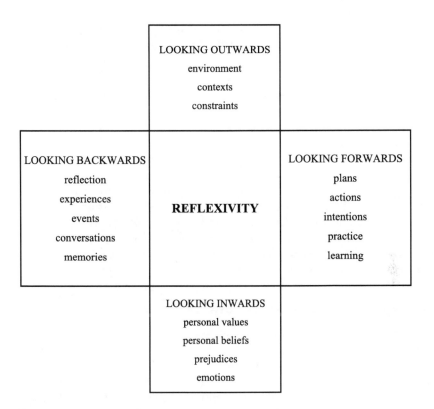

LOOKING OUTWARDS

environment

contexts

constraints

LOOKING BACKWARDS

reflection

experiences

events

conversations

memories

REFLEXIVITY

LOOKING FORWARDS

plans

actions

intentions

practice

learning

LOOKING INWARDS

personal values

personal beliefs

prejudices

emotions

Figure 10.1 Model of Reflexivity.

The terms 'reflection' or 'reflective practice' are common in the literature, but in many cases the process is broader. Light et al. (2009) refer to the 'reflective professional' that deals with complex situations and manages change. I would call this 'reflexivity' and regard the approach as both underpinning and overarching many other attributes. Reflexivity is often implicit and is a key survival skill in shaping an uncertain future.

Reflexivity goes beyond reflection. Ryan (n.d.) says it is "interactive introspection" and involves the analysis of emotions, beliefs, assumptions and contexts. Ghaye (2012: 20) says "Learning and constructing meaningful realities is then about active reflection and reflective action." Ryan (2015: 3) explains that "critical and transformative reflection ... is inseparable from reflexivity".According to Cunliffe (2004), it is not just applying theory to practice but challenging and questioning assumptions and impacts, dealing with complexity and uncertainty. It promotes an approach which is self-critical and self-conscious.This link between the personal and environmental aspects of reflexivity is explained by Archer (2012: 1) as "the regular exercise of the mental ability shared by all normal people to consider themselves in relation to their context".

Reflexivity can be seen as a metacognitive approach encompassing many attributes such as critical thinking, emotional intelligence and professionalism. Rolfe et al. (2011) discuss the simple "What? So what? Now what?" model of reflection and regard the third action-oriented level as being reflexive. They see a hierarchy in which an intervention is doing, reflection on the intervention is thinking about doing, and thinking about thinking about doing is meta-reflection or reflexivity. Reflexive analysis of a situation should lead to action planning and to greater insights so the person is better able to deal with future contexts. It moves from description through analysis to planning and action; I see it as a value-added component and as the fifth dimension. Reflexivity helps professionals deal with unpredictable situations and manage change sensitively.

Reflection is a key part of many university courses, especially those related to the caring professions. In some disciplines such as science and engineering it can seem an alien concept. When new lecturers from these areas are asked to reflect on their teaching, they initially resist it as being unscientific and too subjective. Yet when they begin to try it, they see the value of deepening their understanding to include reflexivity, so they can facilitate their students' learning better.

Reflexivity as a Graduate Attribute

Many universities have specified lists of graduate attributes and use them in various ways such as curriculum planning, marketing and providing students with evidence of employability. Some include a specific mention of self-reflection, while for most the idea of reflexivity is not explicit, but I believe it is implied if the attributes are to be useful. Hounsell (2011) refers to the ideas of Scottish universities and identifies the three main common attributes as global citizenship, communication and ethical and professional understanding. He also makes links to the learner attributes in the Curriculum for Excellence (successful learners, confident individuals, responsible citizens, effective communicators). Hughes and Barrie (2010), based on Australian universities, focus on three key overarching attributes: scholarship, global citizenship and lifelong learning. Most of these attributes should be enacted reflexively if they are authentic descriptions of abilities and attitudes involving contextual analysis and self-knowledge.

Chow et al. (2011: 155) make the case for reflexivity as a graduate attribute and for training social work students to be reflexive: "Early cultivation of reflexivity would provide them with better preparation to handle different life challenges. Reflexivity is a survival skill for the future and a significant component in the curricula of any university which aims to train future leaders." Nicol (2010), looking at Scottish higher education, states that the most important ability is for graduates to be able to evaluate their own work and I suggests this requires a reflexive approach. He suggests that curricula should be designed to include opportunities to develop the skills of self- and peer-assessment; I would encourage course developers to build reflexivity into other curricular aspects too.

I facilitated a discussion with some new lecturers in Dundee from the Universities of Abertay and Dundee. I asked them to identify graduate attributes and decide which they thought were most important. The strongest scores were for professional values, critical thinking, communication and time management. This is not surprising in universities with a vocational focus. The staff identified the tension they feel between teaching and research and the difficulty in managing conflicting demands on their time, so I suspect that managing time was not so much an attribute as a personal need. So while some attributes are for both graduates and lecturers, others are more important for lecturers. If people are to operate in a professional and ethical manner, communicate effectively and sensitively, and gain fully from critical thinking, they need to be self-aware, to challenge existing norms and to take transformative action. I would argue that this implies reflexivity.

The Code of Practice for lecturers as stated by the Higher Education Academy (2016) links to scholarship, lifelong learning, communication and professionalism, with the most common attribute being respect. The UK Professional Standards Framework for teaching and supporting learning in higher education (Higher Education Academy, 2011) lists requirements for lecturers who wish to become Fellows of the Academy. These aspects tend to relate more to skills than attributes but the ideas of lifelong learning, scholarship and professional values are clear expectations. Reflexive practice is required for these aspects to be implemented effectively,

The Scottish Credit and Qualifications Framework (2012: 26) which provides descriptors at each level of education, does not mention reflection specifically until level 11 (Masters). But the concept is clearly implied at level 10 (undergraduate honours) in the following phrases: "To practise in a range of professional level contexts that include a degree of unpredictability" and "Manage complex ethical and professional issues."

Recent work has moved beyond graduateness to identify the requirements of 'mastersness' and 'doctoralness'. Key aspects of mastersness include professionalism, complexity, unpredictability and autonomy (Warring, 2011), all of which require a level of reflexivity. I regard reflexivity as a crucial attribute for graduates, postgraduates, doctoral students and practitioners. Reference to the affective domain, emotional intelligence (Goleman, 1998) and multiple intelligences (Gardiner, 2006) produces a host of soft skills which are valued by employers and society. They are hard to teach, difficult to assess, challenging to demonstrate but easier to recognise. In most cases, there are elements of reflexivity involved. The University of Dundee (2014) has developed a new vision, based on the importance of transformation linked to sustainability, innovation and well-being. The implementation depends on the reflexivity of all concerned.

Curriculum Design

Curricula need to be designed in a systematic way considering the needs of the students and the requirements of the course. The planning process is similar whether applied to a whole degree programme, a single module or even a small element such as a lecture or a workshop. This section will explore how lecturers can address graduate attributes and reflexivity in particular through aspects of curriculum design.

Most statements of graduate attributes include something related to learner autonomy. Thus it follows that the instructional methods must give the learners the opportunity to make decisions and choices about how, what, when and where they study. A didactic course will not empower the students. Simon Barrie, a key writer in the area of graduate attributes in Australian universities, has produced a framework for their teaching. He argues that learner-centred teaching is essential for high level learning outcomes and for transformative attributes (Barrie, 2007). He is concerned that some attributes are taught in isolation from a discipline context rather than as an integrated part of the curriculum. He discusses the mismatch between some university policy statements that embrace the value of graduate attributes and the perception of some lecturers that such qualities are unimportant and not academic.

Treleaven and Voola (2008: 169) looked at the effectiveness of teaching of graduate attributes in courses on marketing and suggest an integrated approach. They make the following four recommendations, which could prove worthwhile in many other disciplines too:

- Constructively align graduate attributes with assessment criteria.
- Embed the development of graduate attributes into course content in ways that students will encounter in … jobs.
- Explicitly develop student awareness of the value of graduate attributes …
- Ensure students have substantial opportunities to engage in critical thinking processes and critical reflection in class and online.

Macfarlane-Dick (2004) has produced a useful audit tool with questions and suggestions about curricula. In the final section she deals with metacognition including reflection, personal development planning and self-assessment.

Aims and learning outcomes

A key part of curriculum design is to specify the aims of the course, usually as learning outcomes the students are expected to achieve by the end. These are a mixture of knowledge, skills and values, some subject specific and some generic and transferable. Personal attributes relate to expectations of professional and ethical behaviour. Expected outcomes must be aligned to content, teaching methods and assessment. Course induction should explain that learning objectives have both immediate and long-term value. Learning activities and assessment protocols must be explicit.

If, for example the aims include communication then students could share ideas in various ways such as written work, oral presentations and online forums. If collaboration is an aim, then the course could include group projects in which processes are taught and assessed as well as the content. Students could be introduced to models of teamwork and required to reflect on their effectiveness, both personally and as a group.

Learning outcomes are often written in opaque language designed for quality assurance procedures rather than for communication with students. So it is essential that lecturers take time to ensure that students (and colleagues) have a common understanding of the expectations and requirements. Some examples of learning outcomes referring implicitly to reflexivity are given in the Appendix. Students also need to take responsibility and ownership of their aims. It is useful if students learn how to negotiate their intended outcomes, balancing their own needs against the demands of other stakeholders. Our new lecturers create a learning plan which covers all the required outcomes and meets the professional competences yet is related to their own interests and needs. This reflexive process increases their motivation and generates assignments that have practical value.

Teaching and assessing reflexively

Knowledge is essential, but it is not enough. Consider how important patients regard a doctor's 'bedside manner'. A good solicitor must know the law but should also have excellent communication skills and be sensitive to the emotional needs of clients. Such skills cannot be taught in lectures but approaches such as role play, video analysis of practice and case studies can help students become more self-aware. However, lecturers must explain the significance of such activities, linking them to learning outcomes and professional competences, giving detailed feedback, ensuring students reflect on and learn from the experience. Peer and group assessment including the setting of criteria can be valuable exercises (Orsmond, 2004) and can develop collaboration skills too. Mueller (2013) argues for the value of authentic assessment and has a toolbox that provides an array of examples which give motivating assessment applied to the real world.

Reflexivity is not easy, and lecturers need to persuade students to accept some counter-intuitive ideas:

- The process and impact of a project are as important as the product and outcomes.
- Challenges lead to better understanding and greater learning than easy options.
- In problem-solving, the solving is more important than the problems.
- Reflection needs experiences, and the staff can provide or orchestrate appropriate situations.

Ashwin et al. (2015) discuss the characteristics of reflective teaching and some of these are just as relevant to reflective learning. Lecturers need to ensure that students understand the importance and complexity of reflexivity. Dissatisfaction and frustration can lead to a helpful if uncomfortable questioning of normal assumptions. Appreciating the emotional dimensions of a situation allows for deeper reflection. The context is a key part of the event and should be considered so that relevant learning can be transferred to another context. Dialogue and discussion enhance reflexive practice as they allow greater understanding of what has happened and the reasons behind behaviour and the role of the learner.

Knight and Page (2007) have discussed the assessment of 'wicked' competences, and their list of these soft skills is close to many statements of graduate attributes. They refer to qualities that cannot be precisely defined, vary in different contexts and keep on developing. The authors believe the problems associated with the assessment of wicked competences are so complex that they are not accepted or are poorly understood by many academics. They propose that the teaching and assessing of such competences should be planned across a whole programme and that attribute development should be measured incrementally and progressively. Following the work of Boud and Falchikov (2006), they argue that students should be fully involved in all aspects of the assessment process and should develop the skills of reflexivity. After each assignment tutors ask students to reflect on what they have learned and to identify their transferable skills and map them against their portfolio of learning needs.

New lecturers on our programme are required to write a final reflexive commentary as part of their formal assessment, and the following extracts illustrate how powerful the process can be:

> Through reflection, I have challenged my practice resulting in changes that have improved my performance. I have used both 'reflection-in-action' and 'reflection-on-action' which has assisted to deepen my understanding and promote growth and change in my professional practice which can be referred to as reflection for action.
>
> Overall this module has been instrumental in positively changing my practice, which is evident from the evaluations and feedback from students, colleagues and peers within the activities undertaken. I have gained confidence in my teaching ability by undertaking this module and feel much more equipped to take on new responsibilities which I hope will enhance both my career and the learning experience of all the students whom I encounter.

Formative assessment is perhaps the most significant help a lecturer can give to a student. This allows students to learn from mistakes and sharpen their criticality. The use of learning conversations can be very valuable as they encourage learners to reflect on their learning. Conversational learning models refer explicitly to reflection, yet this is really closer to reflexivity, given the focus on adaptation and interaction (Laurillard, 2002) and on new insights and impact in the model of deep learning in online communities (Chapman et al., 2005).

Another approach that encourages students to develop their reflexivity is action research (McNiff and Whitehead, 2011). This is research in which the practitioner is part of the problem and part of the solution and it involves analysis, intervention, evaluation and reflection. It examines the links between theory and practice in both directions, and considers personal learning and future development needs and that makes it a highly reflexive process. These ideas are explored further by McIntosh (2010). Typically a work-based student will undertake a small investigation into their own professional context, trying out something to improve some aspect. They will evaluate the intervention using a variety of methods to collect data from different stakeholders, including their own reflection. The use of participatory evaluation methods can be especially powerful (Zukoski and Luluquisen, 2002). The module assessment is a write up which must include the results of the investigation and also what they have learned about such as aspects as ethical practice, data collection, designing questionnaires and sensitive interviewing.

Another highly reflexive process is the appreciative inquiry approach (Cooperrider et al., 2008), which is the cornerstone of a postgraduate work-based module on collaborative inquiry. The students analyse their own preconceptions, the beliefs and values of the stakeholders, and the complexities of the situations and contexts. The assignment focusses on the challenges of the process as much as on the agreed innovative approach.

In an on-campus course, students give a presentation to their peers and tutors about a project in progress. Members of the audience ask questions and provide written feedback to the presenters. When the students write up their project report they must include a section responding to the comments from their peers and tutors, which forces them to think reflexively, justify their decisions and deepen their understanding.

Teaching reflexivity

When I introduce reflexive practice, I relate to the general and generalisable aspects as well as the specific points from a particular situation. I developed my conjunction framework (see Table 10.1), so named because it illustrates the conjunctions between actions and future impacts, and because the key words are grammatical conjunctions.

It encourages a learner to examine a situation in detail, plan how to make specific improvements, consider broader applications to future contexts and evaluate if this impacts on policy. I introduce the framework to work-based students in an online module. They email in a completed example of reflexivity using the framework (see Appendix), and the tutor gives formative feedback. Follow-up workshop activity includes peer discussions about their examples, which deepen their reflection and clarify their understanding of their own values and assumptions. Summative assessment requires them to demonstrate reflexivity using any model of their choice, and many students prefer to use the conjunction framework. They say that, as they have both a personal and a managerial role, this helps them look at their own growth as well as team learning and organisational development. I have used this model with students on several courses and also with the new lecturers, and it has received positive evaluative comments as a useful tool that provokes deep thinking and leads to improved practice.

Table 10.1 Conjunction Framework for Reflexivity

WHAT: description
What happened? Who was involved?

WHY: analysis
Why did you behave as you did? How did you feel? Why do you think others behaved as they did? What contextual factors were under your control? What could have been different?

SO: specific plan	**ALSO: generalised plan**
What will you do next? Why? What outcome do you expect?	What could you have done differently? What preparation would help in future?
BUT: other considerations	**BUT: other considerations**
Do you have all the information you need? Are there other possible actions? Will it affect anyone else?	Do you need a range of strategies for different contexts?

THEN: policy
Are there bigger issues here? Who should you discuss it with?

We use video clips of teaching sessions as the focus for detailed analysis aiming to identify and improve effective practice. The excerpts allow people to remember what happened, what they did, how they felt at the time and what motivated their behaviour, and to analyse and plan in a reflexive manner. The purpose is to look back in order to move forward. The types of questions might include the following:

> Why did you behave in this manner?
> Did you notice what happened when you did that?
> Did you see how well your students responded when …?
> Have you ever tried …?

Reflective conversations can be a valuable addition to private reflection. The interrogator may be a tutor, peer learner, mentor, colleague or any other person who has the courage and time to listen and ask probing questions. Such discussions look back and forward and can enlighten and empower the learner (Ghaye, 2011). I encourage the new lecturers to use Brookfield's (1995) four lenses to reflect on their teaching. These are: autobiographical self-reflection (which is reflexivity), students' views, colleagues' opinions, and theoretical literature. I use a peer discussion reflexivity tool (see Appendix) with both new lecturers and work-based undergraduates: they complete a framework of prompts, and then share their notes with a partner who asks challenging questions to deepen their reflection.

Taylor (2010) encourages reflective practice for healthcare professionals using a wide range of strategies including drawing, dancing, composing music, singing, painting and poetry as well as the more traditional talking and writing. She also discusses the value of archiving stories from practice that can be revisited. A curriculum for psychiatric nurses include mini lectures with reflective exercises, case studies, clinical vignettes, structured assignments (Horton-Deutsch et al., 2012: 348): "Our reflection-centred curriculum structures the entire educational experience ... allowing them to emerge with stronger intrapersonal and interpersonal skills and excellent clinical reasoning skills." The whole curriculum is designed and modified based on student evaluation and reflection by the staff.

Reflexivity can have different meanings as investigated by D'Cruz et al. (2007). They found that social workers identified six themes in relation to reflexivity in their practice and it would be interesting to see if other disciplines agreed with these findings:

- Self-reflection
- Combining objectivity and subjectivity
- Critical appraisal of action
- An introspective tool
- A learning tool
- Critical reflection on policy.

Chow et al. (2011) developed a programme to promote reflexivity in first-year social work students. They used the three aspects of intra-, inter- and trans-views and designed learning activities to facilitate self-reflection, group interaction and critical reflection of social issues in the group. These included journal writing, group discussions, meditation, video triggers, experiential exercises, presentations and projects. The students showed increased levels of reflexivity, greater openness to knowledge and a wider appreciation of the importance of insight. Chow et al. (2011: 143) say that having a "better understanding of oneself is the foundation for reflexivity."

Glass (2015) taught reflexivity to social studies students on a field course using journals, blogs and group projects. He recommended that reflexivity theory should be introduced gradually to help students become more comfortable with honest self-critique and that the curriculum must allow enough space and freedom for the students to develop their curiosity.

Critical reflexivity is regarded as a core competency for social workers, and Trevelyan et al. (2014: 23) have taught it using arts-based installations comprising videos, printed guides and objects. The installations act as a catalyst that confronts students with professional dilemmas and emotional challenges. Trevelyan et al. argue that such disjuncture is necessary for transformative learning and talk of an "optimal level of anxiety or discomfort that initiates and supports meaningful forms of reflexive engagement". They suggest that arts-based media can promote transformative, critically reflexive processes in their learners.

Many modules involve project work allowing students the choice of topics and methods. In one course, participants upload their project proposals online and post comments on each other's work for a week. Then the participants revise their plans and submit the improved proposal to their tutor. Some students have been reluctant to spend time reading and giving feedback on their peers' work, so we explained that this process had a dual purpose. The students developed their own critical skills as well as persuading the participants to revisit their ideas.

Reflexive writing

Many courses involve reflective writing – in a diary or blog, or as part of an assignment. One of the activities I use is to ask participants to write about an incident or to bring a section from their reflective journal they are happy to share. Then they interrogate each other in pairs, aiming to deepen the reflection. They ask questions such as following:

> Why did you do it that way?
> How did you feel when …?
> What would have happened if …?
> What would you do in a similar situation?

This dialogue turns the reflective writing into reflexive thinking and encourages generic learning from a specific situation.

Ryan (2014: 73) has used reflexive prompts for self-assessment in writing, and, although her work was with school pupils, I believe the approach would transfer well to higher education. She suggests, "New and changing conditions require a meta-reflexive approach to writing development … reflexive self-assessment strategies…encourage students to draw on … personal resources to find a sustaining and effective way to perform as writers in different contexts".

Since reflection or reflective writing is mentioned in many learning outcomes, it must be assessed and I have included examples of assessment criteria in the Appendix. This can be problematic as staff feel it is hard to make judgements on such personal aspects. Kember et al. (2008) have specified a four-tier approach to the assessment of reflective writing. The highest level (critical reflection) shows reflection leading to a transformation of perspective – that is, reflexivity. Our new lecturers have to discuss the development of their learning through the programme, and many are pleasantly surprised, as the following quotes show:

> I was somewhat apprehensive when I discovered it was a compulsory requirement for probationary lecturers. However, having completed the course, I understand its importance and relevance to me as a lecturer and feel that my participation has been beneficial. I now feel more integrated into the academic community. Although I am aware of my lack of self-confidence, I now feel enabled to improve my performance.
>
> The last six months have been a shock to the system in terms of my comfort zone. It has been eye opening. It has meant I have got much more out of this

than I could possibly hope for. It has not been easy but I have learned a great deal about myself and have increased my number of core skills. I now know a great deal more about the education and teaching side of working in a University.

Students may censor their reflections, so that what is shared is a diluted version. We appreciate this and provide electronic journals or e-portfolio frameworks which have a private and a shared area for reflection. Students select what they share with their peers or their tutors and choose extracts to feed into assignments. I suspect that the public document may demonstrate reflection, while the private journal goes deeper and allows reflexivity.

All students have access to an electronic tool for personal development planning which they use throughout their university course. It provides frameworks to help students formalise their goals, identify their strengths and areas for development, plan relevant activities, reflect on and evaluate their performance and record evidence of their abilities. This powerful tool encourages autonomous learning, increases motivation and builds confidence. It encourages students to become aware of how they learn and to explore different learning styles. It also allows the student to create a map of their competences which can be used when applying for jobs. This portfolio is separate from individual modules but can incorporate module activities and assessments as well as extracurricular experiences. Repeated cycles of reflection develop self-knowledge and empowerment. Detailed advice for lecturers and institutions on the implementation of electronic portfolios is available in the toolkit from Miller et al. (2011).

Student support and mentoring

Students need an extensive support network including academic staff, support staff, peers, friends and family. Developing the skill to choose which member of the support team to use for which problem is a high level ability. One of the most important of the supporters is a mentor. The crux of an effective mentoring relationship is that it provides both support and challenge (Connor and Pokora, 2007) and encourages reflexive practice. It is developmental and progressive.

I have run mentoring training programmes for staff and students. The agenda for mentoring meetings is led by the mentee and is focussed on their needs. By careful discussion, the mentor can lead the mentee to new insights about their own assumptions, patterns of behaviour and strategies for improving performance. The mentor helps the mentee revisit events, analyse the complexities and evaluate possible actions and their impact. The mentoring record (see Appendix) that I use encourages participants to reflect on the process and the relationship regularly. I encourage professional mentoring using one of the basic models in common use. The GROW model (Whitmore, 2009) covers the following four aspects: Goal, Reality, Options and Way forward. It helps mentees analyse contextual factors and appreciate their own assumptions and prejudices before deciding on a justified action. Effective mentoring can lead to reflexive thought at each stage.

Programme Structure and Reflexivity

Modules

Most programmes are based around modules, even though the chunks of learning are not necessarily all of the same size. The advantages of modularisation relate to standardisation of levels and to administrative convenience. But there are key dangers if students regard them as separate learning objects to be completed and filed away. It is essential that students identify the transferable learning within a module and make explicit links between different modules and beyond graduation.

Lecturers can aid this process by taking time to explore the relationships between modules and by including evidence of application within assessment. Ideally, students can become aware of their generic learning and collect evidence of their transferable skills. The assessment can include both products and processes so a report could be accompanied by a discussion of how it was compiled including reflexive comments on any difficult or contentious areas. In some courses, students can personalise the modules by choosing content, study methods or assessment mode. This gives freedom and responsibility to the learners and requires careful support and moderation from the tutors.

Open learning and work-based learning

Open learning approaches encompass two philosophical aspects, related to practical delivery and to a power shift in decision making. Distance learning and online programmes enable participants to study at a time and place that suits them and fits in with other commitments. This provides practical freedoms but does not necessarily give curricular liberty to the learners. Allowing students to choose their own aims, content, ways of learning and modes of assessment will make their lifelong learning much more effective. Many programmes begin with an induction into being an effective learner including a range of tools to encourage reflection and self-assessment. Students use diagnostic tests to identify preferred effective learning approaches and regularly evaluate how they learn as well as what they learn.

Work-based learning and placement learning provide a realistic context for students to practise and develop key competences and attributes. Clear communication about learning outcomes, appropriate activities and assessment is essential between lecturers, students and workplace supervisors (Ball and Manwaring, 2010). Students can maximise their opportunities if they have a structured approach such as professional development planning based on a reflexive portfolio (Miller et al., 2011). Jackson (2006) discusses the value of work placements in providing a real context to allow the development of professional attributes. Evidence of learning from such real situated experience can be a powerful convincer for future employers.

Business education students were given social enterprise placements and required to write a reflexive evaluation of their experience. They found it valuable and said it increased their self-efficacy and self-confidence and gave them a broader outlook (Atfield and Kemp, 2013).

Accreditation of prior experiential learning

Accreditation of prior experiential learning can be used for advanced entry into a programme or to gain modular credit. It allows a student to use their experience to claim credit but only if it is linked to learning. This can include work experience and extra-curricular activities. Typically the student is asked to produce a portfolio of evidence plus a reflective account demonstrating how their experience equates to learning at a particular level or against specific learning outcomes. The accompanying account is in effect a reflexive narrative detailing what happened and why and explaining the key generic learning points that led to subsequent changes and developments. The best examples talk about personal insights, improved practice and the impact on procedures and policies.

In one course, highly experienced professionals can claim credit for recognition of prior learning mapped against core capabilities. These include the following:

- To communicate effectively to a range of audiences
- To plan and organise systematically and responsively
- To analyse and evaluate challenging situations
- To behave in a professional and ethical way

They must consider their past practices in a reflexive manner and write about them in a detailed and honest fashion, linked to documentary evidence. The formative discussions with their tutor show them just how well they have performed. Reflexivity turns experience into experiential learning.

Lecturers and Reflexivity

Inclusion

Inclusion is not expressed explicitly in many lists of graduate attributes yet it is a legal and moral requirement to make anticipatory plans to meet a wide range of student needs. This includes a raft of provisions from prayer rooms and accessible furniture to curricular changes to support those with disabilities. The increase in internationalisation and global education means that lecturers and students need to become culturally aware of the needs of others and of their own values. If lecturers are to provide appropriate support in a thorough, professional and sensitive manner, they need a reflexive approach. DART, the Disabilities: Academic Resource Tool (University of Loughborough, 2008), gives ideas and case studies for dealing with many problems, but the consequences can be challenging. It is common to allow dyslexic students extra time in formal examinations, but some students who have not been diagnosed in this way may feel this is unfair. One solution is to challenge the need for a time limit for anyone. I remember observing a class test when a signer was employed, as there were hearing-impaired students in the class. Other students complained, as they thought the signer was giving the answers as well as the questions. It took all the skill of the lecturer to defuse this situation and to rebuild the supportive dynamic within the class.

UK Professional Standards Framework

While helping their students develop the graduate attributes, new lecturers are also enhancing their own skills and need to match them to the UK Professional Standards Framework for teaching and supporting learning in higher education (Higher Education Academy, 2011). Some attributes are common to lecturers and graduates. Reflexivity is an essential key to help lecturers in any discipline adopt a scholarly approach to teaching and learning in higher education. Bryan (2015) suggests that reflective practice can lead to the construction of new knowledge as well as deeper understanding.

Graduate attributes are not pegged at one level on the Scottish Credit and Qualifications Agency (2012) and are just as relevant beyond graduation for lifelong learning. Norman Jackson and others have developed this into a broader concept of lifewide learning dealing with ongoing development in a complex world (Lifewide Education, 2014), which chimes with reflexivity. These attributes are essential for a successful lecturer too, especially if they are to help their students develop their full potential.

Personal philosophies

An important aspect of reflexivity is an understanding of one's own values, beliefs and frames of reference. At the start of our programme the new lecturers are asked to begin to write their own philosophy of teaching, to suggest how they will implement it, and to identify possible problems. They revisit their philosophy throughout their studies, reflecting and adapting it as necessary. Although it is a private document, they often choose to refer to it in their assignments. The following quotes indicate the impact this has had in some cases:

> I have become my own personal philosophy which I was able to explore through the teaching observations and this is something I can expand on throughout my career.
> Reflection on teaching forced the development of my teaching philosophy.
> It helped me explore my value base. As I reflected on this I also appreciated how it influenced how I teach or facilitate learning.
> My personal philosophy of teaching was awakened by the programme.

Conclusion

Reflexivity offers multiple perspectives which allow a practitioner to make informed judgements, undertake appropriate actions and learn experientially. Academics need to behave reflexively in all aspects of their professional practice including curriculum design and delivery. They should encourage their students to develop reflexive approaches in their studies that can transfer to their future roles in the workplace.

I believe that the most significant role a lecturer can play is to facilitate the development of reflexive thinking, collaboration and self-assessment in their students and in themselves. I like to think of myself, the new lecturers I teach and all our students as reflexive practitioners. Reflexivity is reflection with street cred. The city of Dundee was famous for 3Js: Jam, Jute and Journalism. Dundee's reflexive graduates can now demonstrate the 3 Es: Empowerment, Engagement and Enlightenment.

References

Archer, M. (2012) *The Reflexive Imperative in Late Modernity*. Cambridge: Cambridge University Press.

Ashwin, P., Boud, D., Coate, K., Hallett. F., Keane, E., Krause, K., Leibowitz, B., MacLaren, I., McArthur, J., McCune, V. and Tooher, M. (2015) *Reflective Teaching in Higher Education*. London: Bloomsbury.

Atfield, R. and Kemp, P. (Eds) (2013) *Enhancing Education for Sustainable Development in Business and Management, Hospitality, Leisure, Marketing, Tourism*. Higher Education Academy. https://www.heacademy.ac.uk/resources/detail/sustainability/ESD_Summary_final. Accessed 23/05/16.

Ball, W. I. and Manwaring, G. (2010) *Making It Work: A Guidebook on Work-based Learning*. Glasgow: The Quality Assurance Agency for Higher Education http://www.qaa .ac.uk/Publications/InformationAndGuidance/Pages/Making-it-work-a-guidebook-exploring-work-based-learning.aspx. Accessed 23/05/16.

Barrie, S. (2007) A conceptual framework for the teaching and learning of generic graduate attributes. *Studies in Higher Education*, 32 (4) 439–458.

Biggs, J. and Tang, C. (2007) *Teaching for Quality Learning at University*. (3rd ed). Buckingham: SRHE and Open University Press.

Boud, D. and Falchikov, N. (2006) Aligning assessment with longterm learning. *Assessment and Evaluation in Higher Education*, 31 (4) 399–413.

Brookfield, S. (1995) *Becoming a Critically Reflective Teacher*. San Francisco: Jossey-Bass.

Bryan, C. (2015) Enhancing student learning. In J. Lea (Ed) *Enhancing Learning and Teaching in Higher Education*. Maidenhead: Open University Press.

Chapman, C., Ramondt, L. and Smiley, G. (2005) Strong community, deep learning: exploring the link. *Innovations in Education and Teaching International*, 42 (3) 217–230.

Chow, A. Y. M., Lam, B. O. B., Leung, G. S. M., Wong, D. F. K. and Chan, B. F. P. (2011) Promoting reflexivity among social work students: The development and evaluation of a programme. *Social Work Education*, 30 (2) 141–156.

Connor, M. and Pokora, J. (2007) *Coaching and Mentoring at Work*. Maidenhead: Open University Press.

Cooperrider, D. L., Whitney, D. and Stavros, J.M. (2008) *Appreciative Inquiry Handbook* (2nd ed.) Brunswick, OH: Crown Custom Publishing.

Cunliffe, A. L. (2004) On becoming a critically reflexive practitioner. *Journal of Management Education*, 28 (4) 407–426.

D'Cruz, H., Gillingham, P. and Melendez, S. (2007) Reflexivity: A concept and its meaning for practitioners working with children and families. *Critical Social Work*, 8 (1).

Gardiner, H. (2006) *Multiple Intelligences: New Horizons*. (2nd ed). New York: Basic Books

Ghaye, T. (2011) *Teaching and Learning Through Reflective Practice*. (2nd ed). London: Routledge.

Ghaye, T. (2012) Empowerment through reflection: Is this a case of the emperor's new clothes? In T. Ghaye and S. Lillyman (Eds) *Empowerment Through Reflection* (2nd ed). London: Quay Books.

Glass, M. R. (2015) Teaching critical reflexivity in short-term international field courses: Practice and problems. *Journal of Geography in Higher Education*, 39 (4) 554–567.

Goleman, D. (1998) *Working with Emotional Intelligence*. London: Bloomsbury.

Higher Education Academy (2011) *The UK Professional Standards Framework for teaching and supporting learning in higher education*. http://www.heacademy.ac.uk/assets/documents/ukpsf/ukpsf.pdf. Accessed 23/05/16.

Higher Education Academy (2016) *Fellowship of the Higher Education Academy Code of Practice*. https://www.heacademy.ac.uk/system/files/downloads/code_of_practice_28.06.pdf. Accessed 23/05/16.

Horton-Deutsch, S., McNelis, A. M. and O'Haver Day, P. (2012) Developing a reflection-centred curriculum for graduate psychiatric nursing education. *Archives of Psychiatric Nursing*, 26 (5) 341–349.

Hounsell, D. (2011)*Graduates for the 21st Century*. Quality Assurance Agency. http://www.enhancementthemes.ac.uk/docs/publications/graduates-for-the-21st-century-institutional-activities.PDF. Accessed 23/05/16.

Hughes, C. and Barrie, S. (2010) Influences on the assessment of graduate attributes in higher education. *Assessment and Evaluation in Higher Education*, 35 (3) 325–334.

Jackson, N. (2006) *Work Placements and Placement Learning:Views of work placement tutorsand colleagues involved placement management*. Guildford: Surrey Centre for Excellence inProfessionalTraining and Education. http://learningtobeprofessional.pbworks.com/f/PLACEMENT+LEARNI NG+WORKING+PAPER+VERSION+1+JULY+FINAL.pdf. Accessed 23/05/16.

Kember, D., McKay, J., Sinclair, K., and Wong, F. K. Y. (2008). A four-category scheme for coding and assessing the level of reflection in written work. *Assessment & Evaluation in Higher Education*, 33 (4) 363–379.

Knight, P. and Page, A. (2007) *The assessment of `wicked' competences*. http://www.open.ac.uk/opencetl/sites/www.open.ac.uk.opencetl/files/files/ecms/web-content/knight-and-page-(2007)-The-assessment-of-wicked-competences.pdf. Accessed 23/05/16.

Laurillard, D. (2002) *Rethinking University Teaching*. (2nd ed). Routledge: London.

Lifewide Education (2014) http://lifewideeducation.co.uk/. Accessed 23/05/16.

Light, G., Cox, R. and Calkin, S. (2009) *Learning and Teaching in Higher Education: The Reflective Professional*. London: Sage.

Macfarland-Dick, D. (2004) *Teaching for employability audit tool*. Higher Education Academy. http://www.heacademy.ac.uk/resources/detail/employability/employability458. Accessed 23/05/16.

McIntosh, P. (2010) *Action Research and Reflective Practice*. London: Routledge.

McNiff, J. and Whitehead, J. (2011) *All You Need to Know about Action Research*. (2nd ed). London: Sage.

Miller, K., Weyers, J., Cross, S., Walsh, L., Monaghan, E., Manwaring, G. and Ball, I. (2011) *A Toolkit for Enhancing Personal Development Planning Strategy, Policy And Practice in Higher Education Institutions*. (2nd ed). Glasgow: The Quality Assurance Agency for Higher Education. http://www.qaa.ac.uk/Publications/InformationAndGuidance/Pages/PDP-toolkit-second-ed.aspx. Accessed 23/05/16.

Mueller, J. (2013) *Authentic Assessment Toolbox*. http://jfmueller.faculty.noctrl.edu/toolbox/. Accessed 23/05/16.

Nicol, D. (2010) *TheFoundation for Graduate Attributes: Developing Self-Regulation Through Self and Peer-Assessment*. http://www.enhancementthemes.ac.uk/pages/docdetail/docs/publications/the-foundation-for-graduate-attributes-developing-self-regulation-through-self-assessment. Accessed 23/05/16.

Orsmond, P. (2004) *Self- and Peer-Assessment* http://www.bioscience.heacademy.ac.uk/ftp/TeachingGuides/fulltext.pdf. Accessed 23/05/16.

Rolfe, G., Jasper, M. and Freshwater, D. (2011) *Critical Reflection in Practice*. (2nd ed). Basingstoke: Palgrave Macmillan.

Ryan, M. (2014) Reflexive writers: Rethinking writing development and assessment in schools. *Assessing Writing*, 22: 60–74.

Ryan, M. (2015) Introduction: Reflective and Reflexive Approaches in Higher Education: A Warrant for Lifelong Learning. In M. Ryan (Ed) *Teaching Reflective Learning in Higher Education*. Cham, Switzerland: Springer.

Ryan, T. (n.d.) *When You Reflect Are You Also Being Reflexive?* http://oar.nipissingu.ca/PDFS/V812E.pdf. Accessed 23/05/16

Scottish Credit and Qualifications Agency (2012) *Level Descriptors.* http://www.sqa.org.uk/files_ccc/23SCQFRevisedLevelDescriptorsAug2012.pdf. Accessed 23/05/16.

Taylor, B. J. (2010) *Reflective Practice for Healthcare Professionals.* (3rd ed). Maidenhead: Open University Press

Treleaven, I. and Voola, R. (2008) Integrating the development of graduate attributes through constructive alignment. *Journal of Marketing Education,* 30: 160–173.

University of Dundee (2014) *Transformation.* http://www.dundee.ac.uk/transform/. Accessed 23/05/16.

University of Loughborough (2008) *Disabilities: Academic Resource Tool.* http://dart.lboro.ac.uk/tool/. Accessed 23/05/16.

Warring, S. (2011) An analysis of learning levels within and between a degree and a diploma: New Zealand case study. *Quality Assurance in Education,* 19 (4) 441–450.

Whitmore, J. (2009) *Coaching for Performance: GROWing Human Potential and Purpose* (4th ed). London: Nicholas Brealey.

Zukoski, A. and Luluquisen, M. (2002) *Participatory Evaluation.* http://depts.washington.edu/ccph/pdf_files/Evaluation.pdf. Accessed 23/05/16.

Appendix 10.1: Practitioner Guide and Resources

1. Conjunction framework for reflexivity: an example of a reflexive analysis

Table 10.2 shows an example of the model.

Table 10.2 Example of a Reflexive Analysis

WHAT: description
I introduced some small tasks (paired discussion) in my lecture. Students did not respond to the activities, but seem confused. I told them I thought they were being lazy.

WHY: analysis
Perhaps they did not understand why I asked questions rather than telling them things. Some did talk to their neighbour but were reluctant to call out their views. The lecture was from 11 until 1 so they were tired and hungry. I felt angry and embarrassed.

SO: specific plan	ALSO: generalised plan
Tell them if they respond they can have a 10 minute break. Ask them to write comments on Post-its or use a snowball approach.	Tell them at the start of the session they are expected to be active in lectures and explain the value of this.
BUT: other considerations	**BUT: other considerations**
Will they come back? Will the activities take too much time?	How will this affect other classes and other staff?

THEN: policy
Raise it at a team meeting so we can plan for more active involvement next session and include it as a learning outcome. Evaluate a range of different interactive approaches.

---

2. Extracts from course documents relating to reflexivity

Personal Philosophy and Reflexivity

A key aspect of the Associate Module is to support your critical engagement with the concept of reflective practice. As a resource for your reflection, you will need to make explicit your personal philosophy of teaching. We will start with reflection and the tools you might need to develop it. Then we will look at your personal philosophy and how it might take shape during the course of your study in the module.

Reflection and reflective practice are ways of learning and contributing to your professional development through challenge, questioning and the creation of new learning. Reflection encourages us to have critical conversations about our work. Dealing with challenges and dilemmas can be an emotional experience. Your practice can be further enhanced by adopting a reflexive approach to your learning.

Reflexivity is

- reflecting not only on what changes you make as a result of your learning but what has influenced those changes; and
- reflecting on the impact of those changes you have made.

Programme Handbooks

The modules encourage participants to apply and reflect upon their learning in relation to theory and their own practice within the workplace setting. By engaging actively with the module content, participants are encouraged to challenge the values and assumptions that inform their professional practice and make a difference to the quality of the service offered.

The main purpose of this module is to enable you to show that you are a reflective practitioner, who can evaluate your prior experience and learning to enable the award of credit. The assessment is a reflective account on the specific topics that follow.

Examples of Learning Outcomes in Various Module Specifications

- Discuss the theory and application of reflective practice.
- Present a reflective analysis of research design processes in relation to personal professional and organisational development.
- Reflect on personal and professional issues associated with mentoring.
- Reflect and critically analyse the role and rationale of training and development in your organisation.
- Demonstrate critical reflection related to your practice.
- Reflect on and evaluate the process and methodologies you have used.
- Reflect critically on flexible and innovative pedagogies.
- Reflect critically on your assessment and feedback practice.

- Reflect upon the way in which the support systems help the child and family in the promotion of positive behaviour.
- Reflect on how reading and research enabled you to interrogate your own views and understandings.
- Reflect on how an individual's personal attitudes and values can impact the quality of inter-professional relationships
- Present a reflective analysis of the processes of research design and literature review in relation to personal, professional and organisational development.

Assessment Criteria from Various Modules

- There is an excellent reflection of the process of the literature review given, with detailed consideration of personal, professional and organisational development. Reference is made to an extensive range of appropriate literature on writing a literature review.
- Ability to reflect critically on professional practice, which is evidenced by appropriate extracts, for example, portfolios and research journals.
- Discuss personal and professional dilemmas associated with evaluation.
- Analyse reflectively an understanding of how an individual's personal attitudes, values and understanding can impact the quality of inter-professional collaboration at a local level.
- Critique and reflect on theories of learning, teaching and assessing and their applications within the higher education context.
- Analyse, reflect and evaluate on ethical issues and professional practices.
- Reflect critically on contemporary issues and innovative practice in higher education.

3. Reflexivity tool

Based on Brookfield, S. (1995) *Becoming a Critically Reflective Teacher*. San Francisco: Jossey-Bass.

Instructions

- Focus on aspects of your professional life.
- Write notes on your own reflections on each tool.
- Share them with a partner who will ask you probing questions to deepen your reflection. You do not have to disclose everything to your partner.
- Consider whether talking to a partner helped clarify your thoughts and deepen your reflection.
- Complete the tools again at a later date and discuss the changes.

A. WEEKLY LOG

Focus on the events of one specific week in your role as a professional practitioner that have made a real impression on you. Look for patterns.

- What made you feel the most satisfied?
- What made you feel the most dissatisfied?
- What took you most by surprise?
- What would you do differently in terms of your practice?

B. LEARNING AUDIT

Think back and complete the following sentences in the context of your professional practice. Compared to this time last year

- I now know that ...,
- I am now able to ...,
- the most important thing I've learned about my colleagues/clients is, and
- the most important thing I've learned about my practice is....

C. ROLE MODEL PROFILE

Think about the colleagues you admire and the characteristics you like about them.

- Which of their actions most typifies what you admire?
- Which of their abilities would you like to make part of your own practice?
- How would you try to develop these qualities in yourself?

D. SURVIVAL ADVICE

Imagine that today is your last day in your current role. You have five minutes to help your replacement cope.

- What does he or she need to know to survive?
- What should he or she avoid doing?
- What do you now know that you wish you had known at the start?
- What advice could transfer to any new situation?

4. Mentoring Record

Mentee: Mentor: Date:
   Follow-up on previous action plan:
   What is going well?
   What is not going well?
   Options
   Action Plan
   Reflection on mentoring process
   Date for next meeting

Conclusion

Graduate Attributes for a 'Multi-Stage' Life

The concept of graduate attributes is not a new one. Its widespread acceptance by the sector followed seminal research by Simon Barrie in Australia, which went on to impact work across the sector, and most notably in Scotland under the auspices of the QAAS Enhancement Themes. It can also be argued, however, that its pedigree is a much longer one that reaches back to original ideas around the development of 'transferable skills' and in some respects has always been around in relation to the requirements of particular disciplines, for example, in developing a positive ethical stance in Law and the healthcare professions. There has been an element of mission creep for the transferable skills agenda over the years, as the focus on employability has shifted from school leavers to encompass college students, adult education returners, and subsequently all areas of higher education. Nonetheless, it is perhaps inevitable that universities have taken the concept of transferable skills and re-packaged it for the higher education sector as graduate attributes. This approach distinguishes the tertiary level experience and differentiates it from that of further education and more general vocational opportunities.

The incorporation of this agenda within the higher education sector of adult and professional learning has also seen an increase in its complexity and changes in ownership of the concept. Drawing on the work of Darkenwald and Merriam (1982), Smith (1999), writing in infed.org, identifies adult education as "work *with* adults, to *promote* learning *for* adulthood".

> Adult education is concerned not with preparing people for life, but rather with helping people to live more successfully. Thus if there is to be an over-arching function of the adult education enterprise, it is to assist adults to increase competence, or negotiate transitions, in their social roles (worker, parent, retiree etc.), to help them gain greater fulfilment in their personal lives, and to assist them in solving personal and community problems.
>
> (Darkenwald and Merriam, 1982: 9, cited in Smith, 1999)

This description associates the outcomes of successful adult education with personal and individual development, enhanced ability to successfully negotiate personal societal roles, and in use of learning to positively address issues within an individual's local sphere of influence. Although Darkenwald and Merriam do not specifically refer here to the benefits of adult education within a workplace setting, the close interplay between study, life, work and value in twenty-first-century society makes this connection inevitable. Employers and the economy have now become acknowledged beneficiaries of adult education and universities are seen as the purveyors of such benefits in an increasingly crowded marketplace of suppliers. Everyone is now a stakeholder in the continuing development of graduate attributes. This development is perhaps a reflection of the democratisation of learning and a better understanding of the roles that all stakeholders have to play in the educational process; however, it is also useful to reflect on where the real ownership of graduate attributes should lie: a theme that we return to at the end of this chapter.

The continuing development and re-interpretation of graduate attributes is perhaps inevitable in light of the ever-changing nature of 'the graduate'. The widening access agenda and a greater emphasis on inclusion for individuals who may previously have been marginalised in terms of higher education has, quite literally, changed the face of our university graduates and in addition to greater diversity we now also have greater numbers. The development of the sector into one whose walls have become increasingly permeable, if not yet universally scalable, is a benefit to society in many ways. Yet, this proliferation of graduates into the marketplace raises a new question, where a degree has become commonplace and employers sift through ever larger piles of CVs with first class honours; what is the value of a degree? Further differentiation amongst graduates is demanded in response to this dilemma and universities have responded with skills awards schemes, placement and internship opportunities, extra-curricular training courses and career planning modules in order to provide learners with opportunities to add extra value to their degree studies. With the marketplace continuing to demand increasingly refined workplace skills at a much earlier stage – essentially, pre-employment – and attributes such as emotional intelligence, creativity, enterprise and entrepreneurship becoming more highly valued, the identification of specific sets of attributes provides a further route to differentiation. As a result of this, graduate attributes continue to flex and morph at the institutional level and to re-emerge as a skills and values set that identifies their particular graduates with the value-added stamp that employers demand.

It can feel as if graduate attributes are set on a treadmill of inevitable change for change's sake in response to external demands and that the individual is becoming lost within this market-driven noise and clamour. It can also feel that it is time for the individual to re-assert their personal agency and ownership over their graduate attributes in the same way that in recent years, students have re-claimed their own learning through an increasingly student-centred approach to education. In a constantly changing world, where uncertainty and transience are all our new watchwords, graduates need not just the skills and attributes that will help them to secure employment but the approaches, attitudes and understanding needed to equip them for twenty-first-century living and life-wide learning. Consequently, graduate attributes need to be re-positioned as a way for individuals to navigate the super-complexity (Barnett, 1999) of their own world and to both anticipate and deal with the changed expectations and different ways of living and working that lie ahead. In their discussion on the *The 100-Year Life: Living and working in an age of longevity*, Gratton and Scott (2016), writing in *The Observer*, make the following challenge; and pose a response in the idea of the 'multi-stage life' (our emphasis).

> How can you maintain and build productive assets when most education takes place in your 20s? How can what you have learned remain relevant over the next 60 years against a backdrop of technological upheaval and industrial transformation? … A way around this is a multi-stage life – with transitions and breaks in between … *These multi-stage lives require a proficiency in managing transitions and reflexivity – imagining possible selves, thinking about the future, reskilling and building new and diverse networks.*

We anticipate that our graduates will need to draw on all of the attributes, and more, that we have discussed throughout this book, at some stage in their careers and social lives. Living a good and successful life in the twenty-first century will become increasingly reliant on individuals' development of appropriate attitudes and values, as well as skills. An approach that is both ethical and empathic will enhance our graduates' professionalism; and skills in areas such as digital literacy will need to work in tandem with approaches that are adaptable and agile. When change is the only constant, resilience and reflexivity become essential to success and well-being. Individual self-awareness becomes the way forward for individuals to identify the personal attributes that they will need to continue to develop in order to thrive and prosper, both economically and socially; but overall, our graduates must continue to be learners. Where next, then, for graduate attributes? Working with our learners to help them to identify and take ownership of the personal attributes that they need for the life and career stage at which they find themselves will be key to the continuing value of graduate attributes as an asset to individuals, the workplace and wider society.

References

Barnett, R. (1999) *Realizing the University in an Age of Supercomplexity*. Buckingham: SRHE/OUP.

Darkenwald, G. G. and Merriam, S. B. (1982) Adult education. Foundations of practice. In M.K. Smith (1999) *What Is Adult Education?* New York: Harper and Row. http://infed .org/mobi/what-is-adult-education/. Accessed 12/09/16.

Gratton, L. and Scott, A. (2016) Our life in three stages – school, work, retirement – will not survive much longer. Opinion Piece. *The Observer* (online) Accessed 04/09/16.

Smith, M.K. (1999) *What is adult education?* http://infed.org/mobi/what-is-adult-education/. Accessed 12/09/16.

Index